A Refuge in Thunder

BLACKS IN THE DIASPORA

Darlene Clark Hine, John McCluskey, Jr., and David Barry Gaspar

General Editors

A Refuge in Thunder

Candomblé and Alternative Spaces of Blackness

Rachel E. Harding

INDIANA UNIVERSITY PRESS
Bloomington and Indianapolis

This book is a publication of

Indiana University Press

601 North Morton Street

Bloomington, IN 47404-3797 USA

http://www.indiana.edu/~iupress

Telephone orders   800-842-6796

Fax orders   812-855-7931

Orders by e-mail   iuporder@indiana.edu

The paper used in this publication meets the minimum requirements of American National Standard for Information Sciences—Permanence of Paper for Printed Library Materials, ANSI Z39.48-1984.

Manufactured in the United States of America

Library of Congress Cataloging-in-Publication Data

Harding, Rachel E., date
   A refuge in thunder : Candomblé and alternative spaces of blackness / Rachel E. Harding.
      p.   cm. — (Blacks in the diaspora)
   Includes bibliographical references and index.
   ISBN 0-253-33705-4 (cl : alk. paper)
   1. Candomblé (Cult)—History—19th century. 2. Blacks—Brazil—Bahia (State)—Race identity—History—19th century.   I. Title.   II. Series.

BL2592.C35 H37 2000
299'.673'09814209034—dc21

                                                                            99-054087

1   2   3   4   5   05   04   03   02   01   00

For Charles Dock Freeney Jr. and for George Houston Bass

In memoriam

Contents

Acknowledgments

I am profoundly indebted to a great many people for the experiences and insights that accompanied the development of this book. Indeed, to list them all would be to make an account of the past ten or twelve years of my life. There are some, however, whose efforts on my behalf or whose inspiration and example were especially critical to the completion of this work. I want to acknowledge them.

Anani Dzidzienyo, my professor at Brown, introduced me to Brazil and to Bahia. His wisdom and sensitivity have helped steer me through the challenges of interpreting the variations of black experience in the Americas. The writings of João Reis and Mary Karasch have been essential impetuses to my interest in Afro-Brazilian history for many years. Reis's collegiality and generosity during my year of research in Salvador (1994–1995) greatly facilitated the identification and collection of documents for this text.

Within the community of the *povo-do-santo* in Bahia, I hold a great obligation to several individuals and *terreiros* whose fellowship was as instructive as it was instrumental to my experience and interpretation of Afro-Brazilian religious orientation. Valnizia de Xangô Airá, Iyalorixá of the Terreiro do Cobre, and the members of that Candomblé community cannot be thanked deeply enough for the kindness, the welcome, and the kinship they shared with me. Valdina Oliveira Pinto, Makota Zimewaanga of Tanuri Junçara, has for many years inspired me through her example and encouragement. It is my great pleasure and privilege to feel myself her sister. I especially thank too the leadership and *afiliados* of Casa Branca, Jitolú, Axé Opô Afonjá, Bate Folha, and Gantois for their unfailing cordiality.

Júlio Braga provided important encouragement to return to Brazil and conduct my research as an associate of the Centro de Estudos Afro-Orientais (CEAO) of the Universidade Federal da Bahia. I thank him particularly for his wise counsel on appropriate research methodology and for his interest in my spiritual as well as my academic work. Lourdes Siqueira assisted me in making several critical contacts. I am thankful to her for her gracious hospitality and for her knowledgeable and interested conversation about my work. Ana Célia da Silva opened her home and her heart to me and shared with me the tremendous richnesses and resources of her experience and network of friends. I remain grateful for her many efforts on my behalf. I also thank her family, whose warmth and welcome made me feel that I was never a stranger.

Like most scholars, I am especially indebted to a variety of archivists and librarians. In Bahia, Ana Amélia Vieira Nascimento, Dona Edir, Joel and the other members of the staff of the Arquivo Público do Estado da Bahia receive my particular thanks. Also, I acknowledge the invaluable help of the interlibrary loan departments of the Norlin Library at the University of Colorado at Boulder, Penrose Library at the University of Denver, and Taylor Library at the Iliff School of Theology.

During my period of research in Bahia I depended greatly on the support of Isabel Cristina Ferreira dos Reis. Her assistance with the archival work for this book was excellent, generous, and indispensable. I dearly treasure her collegiality and her friendship. I am also thankful to Vera Virgens who helped me tremendously—especially in the early months of my stay as I was trying to find my way around the archives, the subject matter, and the life of the city. In the same period, several other scholars kindly spent time with me sharing insights from their own research and discussing various aspects of my work. Muniz Sodré, Renato da Silveira, Ubiratan Castro, Juana Elbein dos Santos, and Maria Inês Cortês de Oliveira come most readily to mind. I am grateful, in large and small ways, to all of them. I also thank Alexandra Brown and Jocélio Teles for sharing documentary resources with me.

Among my greatest joys during the research period in Brazil was the opportunity to cultivate friendships which yet sustain me in important ways. Daniel and Marcia Minter, Ajanae Edwards, Bauer Sá, Charles Rowell, and Don Webster helped make my time in Salvador especially meaningful and enjoyable—as did Lindi, Maia, Luciene, Suka, Eliane, Tom, Kutu, Gleide, Lindinalva, Saraí, Cosme, Gildália, Deborah, and all of my other brothers and sisters, *mães, ebomis, ekedis,* and *ogãs* from Cobre. A very special thanks is due to Arnaldo Barros for his assistance, forbearance, and wonderful companionship.

I am singularly grateful to my dissertation committee members Robert Ferry, Evelyn Hu-DeHart, Charles Long, Donna Goldstein, Thomas Skidmore, and Virginia Anderson. Each of them, in individual and collective ways, gave significant support to this project—often going considerably out of their way to encourage me and help locate financial, documentary, and interpretive resources for my work. The pre-doctoral and doctoral fellowships program of the Ford Foundation, the Chancellor's Fellowship and the Bean Fund of the Department of History greatly facilitated my study at the University of Colorado and my research in Brazil. I am also especially thankful to Mary Lowe in the Graduate School Fellowship Office and to Diane Johnson, the Graduate Secretary in the History Department, for their responsiveness, concern, and support. And I thank my fellow staff members of the Gandhi Hamer King Center at the Iliff School of Theology for allowing me the flexibility I needed to complete the revisions of this text.

David Carrasco and, especially, Charles Long helped me develop the interpretive tools to approach a meaningful engagement of Afro-Brazilian religious history. This book would not have been possible without their wonderful counsel and guidance. I thank Michael Harper, Orlando Bagwell, Manning Marable, Hazel Marable, and Ndugu T'Ofori Atta for the encouragement they provided to this project. The comments and critiques of the anonymous readers who reviewed my original text have also helped enrich the work considerably.

I extend my greatest appreciation to my mother, my father, and my brother; to my cousin Charles for the "dancing clothes"; and to the rest of my family for their continued love and support. Obviously, none of these people is in any way culpable for whatever mistakes and misinterpretations I may have made in this book. They all, however, share responsibility for its *axé*.

RACHEL E. HARDING
Denver, Colorado
April 1999

Introduction

A velha preta, the old black woman, is a colloquial term by which the city of Salvador is sometimes known. For nineteenth-century visitors, especially those from outside the Portuguese and Brazilian empires, the city's populace and physical aspect must have borne a striking, if metaphorical, resemblance to the image. The overwhelming presence of Africans and their Brazilian descendants; the worn streets and deteriorating façades of once-grandiose colonial and ecclesiastical structures; the constant laborings of black and brown bodies in a slavery so tenacious and ubiquitous that it was the last to be abolished in the western hemisphere (in 1888) were all among her resonances. And for those who knew her well, *a velha preta* was also sacred ground, a place made holy in trauma, a territory of suffering and resistance in whose body was inscribed the meaning slaves and their descendants wrestled out of the disjunctions of their experience.

One aspect of that "wrestling" process is the subject of this book—an Afro-Brazilian religion known as "Candomblé," which developed in Salvador and the Recôncavo[1] under the specific conditions of nineteenth-century slavery in that capital entrepôt and its environs. Candomblé is a rich, poetic complex of ritual action, cosmology, and meaning with deep and obvious roots in several religious traditions of West and West Central Africa—especially Yoruba, Aja-Fon, and Bantu. It is a (re)creation of these traditions, and others, from within the matrix of slavery, colonialism, and mercantilism which characterized Brazil and the other new societies of the western hemisphere from the sixteenth through the nineteenth centuries.

Like many other African American[2] religious traditions developed within that period (such as Santeria in Cuba, Winti in Surinam, Vodou in Haiti and the Black Protestant Christianity of the southern United States), Candomblé took its shape and meaning from the experience of African people and their descendants in slave-based societies as they tried to make sense of themselves, their condition, their relation to the structures of temporal power, and their relation to the structures of Being. For African American people, these religions served as important groundings from which they negotiated space for the expression of identities (personal and collective) that served to oppose those identities which had been signified upon them by the dominant sectors of the society.

The coastal regions of the land that would become Brazil, the largest single nation in the continent of South America, were "discovered" by Portuguese navigators around 1500. It is estimated that the Native American population in Brazil in the early sixteenth century was about 2.5 million.[3] At the time, the Portuguese crown was more concerned about its network of Asian and African trading posts and thus paid little immediate attention to settlement of the newfound territory; it sent criminals from Lisbon's prisons to be the area's first Portuguese inhabitants. Only after several attempts by the French to occupy the land did the Portuguese put more concerted effort into peopling Brazil and establishing military defenses there. But the territory eventually claimed by Portugal (in disregard of the Tordesillas treaty boundaries) was so vast that throughout the colonial and imperial periods it was never more than sparsely populated. The early establishment of large agricultural and cattle estates and the almost complete absence of industry during the colonial period (because of mercantilist restrictions) ensured that Brazil's population remained largely rural and that the capital cities held only about 10 percent of the nation's inhabitants through the end of the nineteenth century.[4]

The lifeways of Brazil's backlands in many ways set the tone for the country's character and development in the first 400 years of settlement. Religion had a strikingly lay, popular, and mystical character. Most people were not literate. Even during the empire (1822–1889) the number of people who did not read and write was never below 85 percent of the population. Brazil's early economy centered around plantation agriculture (especially sugar, tobacco, cotton, and, later, coffee), mining, subsistence farming, and ranching. And black slave labor was the linchpin of production in most areas of the nation's economic life. The relative paucity of Portuguese women among the settlers, and the license of Portuguese men who often had African and Indian women under their economic and political control, contributed to the early establishment of a substantial mixed population—which would eventually come to represent the majority of Brazil's people.

Port cities such as Rio, Salvador, Recife, Santos, and the inland town of São Paulo (which grew in the eighteenth century as a direct result of its contacts with the mining regions) were exceptions to the general rule of rural life in colonial and imperial Brazil. As important entrepôts, Rio and Salvador especially were places of considerable commerce and trade as well as the headquarters of large colonial/imperial bureaucratic, ecclesiastical, and military apparatuses.[5] In these cities, in addition to Europeans from a variety of nations; Portuguese and Brazilian whites; and a large population of free and freed people of mixed European, African, and Indian descent there were thousands and thousands of slaves. These captives performed the widest imaginable variety of work. Many were African born and most depended heavily on their relations with other blacks (free and slave) for the re-creation of their identities within the Brazilian social space.

While African religious traditions were maintained and re-articulated in many parts of Brazil, the cities often provided a level of physical mobility and relative residential and economic autonomy which enabled Africans of the same or related ethnic groups to more easily gather and re-member together aspects of their cultural and religious life. Whether in the mud houses or rented rooms of freed Africans, in the streets at fountains or plazas, or in suburban and forested areas which afforded more privacy and protection, these gatherings were among the means used to (re)create spaces where blacks were no longer "slave" or "subaltern," but where they in fact called into being prior and new meanings of themselves and reshaped these to help survive the jeopardous situations of the New World.

In 1822, in the whole of the newly independent nation there were close to four million inhabitants. About half that number were enslaved people—*crioulo* (Brazilian-born black) and African.[6] The ratio of African to *crioulo* slaves varied in different epochs and from place to place, but overall more slaves were needed in plantation and extractive labor than in urban activities, and more blacks were present in the rural *fazendas* (farms), *engenhos* (sugar mills; plantations), and mines than in the cities. However, in the early nineteenth century, with the relocation of the Portuguese court to Rio de Janeiro and the reinvigoration of the sugar industry in Bahia, the port cities of Salvador and Rio saw increased numbers of African-born slaves in their populations. João Reis has estimated that by 1835 in Salvador, for example, African slaves represented 26.5 percent and *crioulo* slaves represented 15.5 percent of a total population of 65,000. Freed Africans accounted for 7.1 percent and free and freed people of color accounted for 22.7 percent of the population of that city.[7]

Thus, the Africans who constituted fully a third of the city's inhabitants shared the emotional and physical disjunctions of capture, the Middle Passage, and adjustment to the labor requirements, humiliations, and legal-social status of slaves everywhere in the Americas. For these people and for many of their descendants, Candomblé was an important means for the engagement of trauma. It represented an inte-grative process—pulling together and (re)organizing that which had been rendered asunder: family, identity, and psyche. Where families were separated by the slave trade—mothers sold from daughters, nephews sold from uncles, whole genealogies lost—Candomblé reestablished connections of kin by means of ethnic alliance and shared devotion to the deities. Where the identities of Africans, *crioulos,* and *pardos* were largely restricted by Brazilian social organization to that of "slaves," "plebeians," "low-class folk," "riffraff" and "scum,"[8] Candomblé pro-vided a means of re-membering and (re)creating an identity of value and connectedness—to Spirit, to a pre-slavery past, to ancestors, to commu-nity. It also provided, through its emphasis on the cultivation of African deities and the use of African material and cultural elements in its rituals, an alternate meaning of Africanness, an alternate identity of blackness. And where the myriad ignominies of life in Brazil created crises in psychic integrity, Candomblé offered transformative music and dance, community, and magico-pharmacopoeic healing. In the mutual embrace of humanity and spirit in Candomblé emerged intimations of whole-ness—representations of the reciprocity of devotion and responsibility, the sharing of burdens and joys.

My usage of the term *space* in the title of this book refers to physical, socio-political, cultural, psychic, and ritual-religious locations within Afro-Brazilian experience. In one sense it is perhaps an overly encom-passing reference—covering a variety of aspects of the *situation,* the *location* of blacks in nineteenth-century Bahia. At the same time, it is a particularly appropriate term because the idea of space, of location, contains the implication of both boundary and movement. That is to say, positionality in space suggests other unarticulated locational possi-bilities. This was certainly the case for blacks in colonial and imperial Brazil. While relegated to degraded space by the dominant ideology, Africans and their descendants were constantly engaged in the process of creating alternative orientations which redefined their identities. The spaces assigned (or signified) to black being by Brazilian society were the lowest possible in terms of social location. Blacks were either slaves or were associated with the stigma of slavery by the pigment of their skins, the fact of their ancestry; they were overwhelmingly among the poor-est and most disenfranchised of the colony and the nation's inhabitants. In terms of physical location, the spaces reserved for blacks were most often the least honorable, the least desirable. The "street," recognized in the nineteenth century as a place of disorder (in contrast to the "house"), was a space ceded to blacks and to the lower classes of Brazilian society generally.[9] Slaves often lived in the most humble surroundings, wattle-and-daub *senzalas* (plantation slave quarters) or the drafty hallways and stifling basements of the urban townhouses of their masters. In the mind of Brazilian elites, blackness and Afro-Brazilian culture represented the antithesis of "civilization" and, especially in the nineteenth century, many of the efforts to destroy *candomblés* and other black religio-cultural manifestations were articulated in terms of their supposed nefarious effects on public morale and their inappropriateness for a modernizing society. What I am suggesting is that blacks in Brazil were involved in a continual process of transformational engagement with the assigned spaces, the signified identities imputed upon them by the dominant slavocratic and racist society. Through a variety of means—ritual, communal, familial, aesthetic, etc.—Africans and their descendants created alternative spaces, alternative definitions of themselves and of the meaning of their presence in the New World.

This book is not primarily a description of Candomblé ritual and practice. Nor does it include a detailed discussion of the African cosmologies and mythologies central to the oral traditions of the religion. There are a number of important works written on these issues, and while I include some of their insights in this study, my principal task is different.[10] This book is an examination of the development of Candomblé in terms of the elements, experiences, and meanings which lie at its foundations in nineteenth-century Bahia. In other words, I am looking at the nature and experience of slavery in Brazil (and particularly in the northeastern captaincy/province of Bahia); the specific conjunction of Africans and Brazilian-born blacks in Salvador and the Bahian Recôncavo; the role of freedpeople in the leadership and development of the religion; networks of support and repression; the complex of magico-pharmacopoeic, ludic, divinational, and relational elements which came to comprise Candomblé; and especially, the role of the religion in the development of alternate meanings of human community and black identity within the matrix of slavery.[11]

My primary research draws heavily on a series of police documents housed in the Arquivo Público do Estado da Bahia (hereafter referred to as APEB) in Salvador, consisting of correspondence among various officers of the military and police corps, local magistrates, individual complainants and litigators, and the vice-president and president of the captaincy/province. I analyze documentation spanning the years 1800 to 1888. Although it was impossible to examine every *maço* (bundle—the papers are kept in stacks enclosed in brown wrapping paper and tied in string) for the entire chronological period, I was able to carefully consult a representative sample and I collected over 150 documents relating to Candomblé and other Afro-Brazilian religio-cultural manifestations in Bahia. It is from these documents (and supplementary published sources) that I outline the constituent elements of Candomblé and offer an interpretation of the religion's development and meaning in the nineteenth-century context.

The first of two introductory chapters focuses on issues of plantation slavery, the marginal position of African freedpeople in Bahia, and nineteenth-century ideological concerns about the relationship of black presence to national identity in Brazil. The discussion then moves to a more specific examination of the contours of urban life and work in the city of Salvador, Bahia—where, due to the significant presence of African-born slaves and freedpeople, Candomblé developed strong roots. This second chapter explores the social organization of Bahian society, particularly the significance of categories of race, ethnicity, and legal status. The third chapter begins an examination of Afro-Brazilian religious orientations and focuses on two religious forms, *calundu* and the *bolsa de mandinga*, which preceded the emergence of Candomblé in colonial Brazil. The idea of fetish/*feitiço* is introduced here as a tool in the interpretation of layers of meaning in Afro-Brazilian religion. In the fourth chapter I attempt to further locate Candomblé within the continuum of Afro-Brazilian religious and historical experience. Here I include an examination of various pan-African and New World influences on the religion's development as well as a reflection on the role that "Nagô-centric" academic observers have played in the interpretation of Candomblé. Chapter 5 outlines trends in the religion's development over the course of the nineteenth century, grounded in a basic quantitative analysis of data collected from the police correspondence. A religious leadership that was largely African born, a participant base that had a majority of females, and the increasingly "pan-black" character of ritual communities are some of the central features of nineteenth-century Candomblé reflected in the documentary analysis. Several freed African healers/religious leaders are profiled in Chapter 6. The profiles examine the lifestyles and commitments of these originators of Candomblé; the connections between healing and cultivation of *axé* (life force) in their activities; and the nature of the ritual communities which developed around them. A variety of networks in nineteenth-century Bahia served as social-structural foundations for Afro-Bahian life and culture. *Cantos, quilombos, irmandades,* the *ganho* labor system and the peculiarities of urban slavery all aided the development and maintenance of physical and ritual space for Candomblé in Bahia. These networks of support and countervailing forces of repression are the subjects of the seventh chapter. Chapter 8 is an interpretive essay based in the idea of Candomblé as *feitiço,* a means to the transformative engagement of the experience of blackness in Brazil from an experience of signified subalterity to an alternative construction of personal and collective identity. A final chapter returns to more general nineteenth-century political and ideological developments with a discussion of the context of the abolition of slavery and the continuing role of Candomblé as a space for alternative black being in the late empire and early republic.

A glossary of pertinent Portuguese and African language terms appears at the close of the text. There is also an appendix of documents selected from among those located in the APEB police correspondence related to Candomblé. One final note: No general agreement exists among scholars or practitioners about capitalization of the term "Candomblé." I have elected to capitalize when referring to the religion as a practice; individual ritual communities (*terreiros*) are *candomblés,* in lowercase letters.

1

Slavery, *Africanos Libertos,* and the Question of Black Presence in Nineteenth-Century Brazil

Slavery was one of the defining characteristics of Brazilian society and economy throughout the colonial era and most of the nineteenth century. The nation organized itself around an almost complete reliance upon black slave labor in all aspects of its productive life. Even after political independence from Portugal in 1822, the conservation of traditional social and economic structures ensured slavery's continuance. According to historian Emilia Viotti da Costa, there was hardly any segment of the Brazilian economy which did not depend more or less heavily on the forced labor of blacks for its survival and prosperity. In Brazil, slaves were everywhere: planting and chopping cane, turning cane into molasses and sugar, weeding between the rows of cotton, harvesting cacao, piling coffee beans into baskets, loading bales of tobacco onto ships, feeding the masters' children their own babies' milk, or carrying the well-to-do in palanquin chairs through the steep hills and narrow streets of port cities. In the countryside and in the city, Africans and their descendants "were the principal instruments of labor."[1]

An appreciation of the nature of Brazilian slavery is essential to an understanding of Candomblé because it was within the context of response to enslavement and resistance to dehumanization that the religion emerged among blacks in Bahia. Candomblé became a collectivizing force through which subjugated peoples organized an alternative meaning of their lives and identities that countered the disaggregation and the imposed subalterity to which they were subjected by the dominant social structure. The tradition of slavery in Brazil was long and deeply entrenched. Its roots extended back to the forced labor of Indians in the sixteenth-century donatory captaincies[2] of the new colony, which stretched along the Atlantic from São Vicente in the south to Pernambuco in the north. After brief attempts to create an extractive economy of dyewoods and other forest products through the coerced labor of Native Americans, Portuguese colonists turned their attention to the recent successes of the sugar production complex operating in the Atlantic islands off of Africa's northwest coast. They hastily attempted to grow and process sugar cane all along the coastal regions of Brazil, although the majority of these efforts failed—often due to inappropriate environmental conditions, but also because the Indians who were forced into working the first plantations resisted continuously (and often violently), had low rates of productivity, and were susceptible to the diseases of Europeans to which they had no immunity.

Those colonists based in northeastern Brazil, however, enjoyed almost immediate success with the new crop, due in large part to an ideal geography. The dark-red, mineral-rich, clayey soil of the Bahian Recôncavo (called *massapé*), and the freshwater underground springs which fed it, encouraged the swift development of a profitable sugar economy in the region. Within a matter of a few years, and "with tragic ease," the fully developed system of sugar production was transported from the Madeiras and São Tomé to the captaincies of Pernambuco and Bahia.[3] Before long, this transference included a heavy reliance on imported African slave labor and massacres of the Tupinambá peoples who lived in the Recôncavo and who resisted the usurpation of their ancestral lands. In the *engenhos*[4] of the Brazilian northeast captaincies, a model of sugar production and plantation agriculture was established and perfected that by the mid seventeenth century would be adopted throughout the colonial island economies of the Caribbean, at great human cost to Africa and great financial reward to Europe.[5] This was an essential element in the colonial enterprise in the Americas. Within the colonial mercantile Atlantic system, the raw materials and agricultural products for European commercial and industrial development were provided by the colonies of Portuguese and Spanish America, the islands of the West Indies, and the southern states of North America. Portuguese colonial administration focused all of Brazil's attention on the development of exports. This emphasis and the monopolistic economic structure were designed to favor the European metropole and limit the development of independent political, industrial, and commercial activities.

Most Brazilians in the seventeenth, eighteenth, and nineteenth centuries were engaged in agricultural, mining, or cattle-raising work. There was no manufacturing base in the backland towns because of royal restrictions. What industry existed was limited to the cities and to a few essential enterprises like shipbuilding. Large rural estates used slaves and other craftsmen for the manufacture and repair of whatever was needed. Anything that could not be supplied "in house" was imported from Europe. Because so much of the development of Brazil's society and economy was based on the plantations of the rural backlands, owners of large sugar, tobacco, cotton, and coffee estates held great power and influence, both in their respective regions and as a group in colonial/ imperial politics. The structures of dependency, patronage, and patri- archalism they established in their dominions became the paradigms by which Brazilian society functioned throughout the colonial and imperial period and, some would argue, well into the present day.

Within the Brazilian plantation system, the labor of slaves occupied a position of central importance. Most of the agricultural, and many of the extractive, economies of the colonial Americas depended substan- tially on the work of enslaved black people. Brazil, however, over the more than three hundred years of slavery in that country, maintained the dubious distinction of consuming the labor and lives of the largest number of Africans of any of the New World societies. Over the course of the four centuries of this nefarious enterprise, an estimated fifteen-and- a-half million Africans were transported from ports all along the Atlan- tic and even the lower Indian Ocean coasts of Africa to the Americas.[6] By the conservative estimates of Philip Curtin, close to 4 million Africans arrived in the slave markets of Brazil from the mid sixteenth through the mid-nineteenth centuries. Of that number, almost one-and-a-half million landed at Bahia.[7] Most of these individuals were men. In gen- eral, slavers purchased twice as many males as females for the American trade. This ratio was, for the most part, maintained on the plantations of Bahia throughout the colonial period.[8] Most were also young—predomi- nantly between the ages of sixteen and thirty. And most did not live to be old. A nineteenth-century Bahian planter once explained to a foreign visitor that the average duration of a slave's life after leaving Africa was a scant six years. It was unusual for a person to last more than ten years under the arduous conditions of plantation labor.[9]

The work days lasted twelve to fifteen hours with more duties at night. Henry Koster, an English visitor to Bahia in the early nineteenth century, described the exhaustion of slaves working on the *engenhos* during the six-to-eight month *safra* (harvest): They worked up to the very brink of their physical capacities such that they would fall asleep anywhere they could lay their heads.[10] Female slaves performed largely the same tasks as men, especially on the sugar plantations.[11] Housing was often drafty and damp: wattle-and-daub huts or long barracks with little or no privacy. Clothing was insufficient and often ragged. The beans, manioc flour, and occasional jerked or salted beef (which were the staples of most slaves' diets) provided insufficient nutrition, and slaves were often ill from parasites, fevers, tuberculosis, and syphilis. During the nineteenth century, Bahia endured recurrent epidemics of cholera and yellow fever—during which slaves often suffered disproportionately due to the precarious conditions under which they lived. Physical mistreatment from masters was another element of slave life in Brazil—punishments using stocks, whips, and a wooden paddle called the *palmatória* were the most common. But manacles, neck shackles, and other more idiosyncratic and bizarre inflictions were used as well. As historian Robert Conrad concludes, most enslaved people in Brazil were literally worked to death.[12]

Newly arrived slaves tended to die fastest, succumbing to disease, the tortures of the "seasoning process," and, at times, to a "fatal homesickness" called *o banzo*. Newly arrived Africans, or *boçais*, also tended to attempt escape and suicide more frequently than slaves who had lived in Brazil's harshnesses for longer periods. And as in most plantation areas of Latin America and the Caribbean, Brazil's northeast suffered from natural decrease in the slave population—that is to say, the numbers of deaths always exceeded the number of births. Several reasons have been offered for this by contemporary observers and scholars over the years: the unequal ratio of male to female slaves; the dire conditions of life and labor, especially on plantations; the notorious lack of adequate health provisions in colonial and imperial Brazil; suicides and brutal punishments; and the reluctance of some slave-owners to provide adequately for children not yet old enough to be productive workers. It has also been suggested that women practiced natural methods of birth control as well as abortion and possibly infanticide, simply refusing to bring children into the life they lived.[13]

Slave-owners in Brazil had little or no incentive to improve the conditions of their slaves or to encourage a higher birthrate (at least until the third decade of the nineteenth century and the final move toward abolition of the slave trade in 1850), because the purchase price of a slave could be recouped in two to three years of labor. Within six years, an owner's investment would have doubled. Thus it was easier and more profitable to work a slave to death in seven years or so and buy another than to properly feed and provide for the worker. And in general this was the way it was done.[14] A slave in Brazil, whether Brazilian or African born, was looked upon primarily as "an expendable instrument of production, a tool to be acquired, maintained and replaced at the least possible expense."[15]

In light of the conditions in which slaves lived and worked in Brazil it seems remarkable that revolts were not more frequent. In Bahia, in the period preceding and following the independence struggles (1807–1835), a number of African-led slave uprisings shook the province and unnerved local elites already concerned about the effects of the Haitian Revolution on their own society. According to Dale Graden, for about fifty years after the Santo Domingo revolt, Bahia's ruling classes spoke of the possibility of slaves and free blacks creating "another Haiti" by means of violent rebellion.[16] Further evidence of this concern was seen in the many restrictive measures taken against Africans—especially freed-people—from the 1830s until abolition. These African *libertos* were seen as an especially dangerous element of the population and efforts were made to limit their mobility, restrict their capacity to earn a living, and even tax their very presence in Brazil; all were attempts to prod them to return to Africa.[17]

The most spectacular of the nineteenth-century black rebellions in Bahia was the "Revolta dos Malês," which occurred in January 1835 and was organized by Yoruba and Hausa Muslims. The uprising involved hundreds of local black slaves and freedpeople.[18] After the Malê rebellion Africans in Bahia were subjected to tremendous repression and brutality—some of it quite random and much of it at the hands of the soldiers of the city's police force, most of whom were mulattos. Measures were introduced by Chief of Police Gonçalves Martins and the municipal council to limit the mobility and rights of slaves and African-born freedpeople. Africans were required to annually register themselves in the district where they lived, obey a curfew, pay a head tax, suffer restrictions on their economic activities, and prepare to be deported. The houses of many Africans were searched for evidence of conspiracy and African religious practices. Speaking of the *libertos,* Chief of Police Martins declared: "None of them has the rights of a citizen, nor the privileges of a foreigner." This language blatantly contradicted that of standard manumission documents which bestowed a freedom "as if from a free womb born." However, the police chief's words were more representative of the nation's reality. As Reis notes, in nineteenth-century Salvador, Africans had no rights at all. They were simply inhabitants.[19]

In this anti-African atmosphere, the need for alternative spaces of black identity and black community was particularly acute. The emphasis on ethnic identification among African-born blacks was one means of securing a personal and collective sense of self beyond the subaltern status imposed from outside. Within the physical and ritual space of Candomblé ceremony the sense of African ethnic identity was both heightened and reconfigured toward a more pan-African meaning of black being in Brazil. Yorubas, Jejes, Bantus, and others congregated with fellows of the same ethnicity to celebrate collective ancestors and national deities. More significantly perhaps, the experience of shared oppression in the New World also served to bring Africans of various ethnic groups together with Brazilian-born blacks into an experience of the communal redefinition of the meaning of their lives and the nature of their solidarities and tensions. The discomfort that Bahian police, politico-economic elites, and others expressed regarding Africans may have been especially fierce in the post–Malê Revolt atmosphere of Salvador and the Recôncavo, but it was by no means an isolated phenomenon. In fact, questions about the nature of African participation in Brazilian society (and black participation more generally) were increasingly raised in the years after independence as the new nation began to wrestle with its sense of identity and direction.

The nineteenth-century literary tradition in Brazil made liberal use of an idealized image of the Indian as representative of the nation's identity. Beginning in the years that followed independence and continuing into the second half of the century, writers such as Domingos José Gonçalves de Magalhães, Antônio Gonçalves Dias, and José de Alencar reflected and contributed to an attempt to define the new country and its imagined best qualities (courage, uncorruptedness, noble character, strength) in terms of a romantic vision of the land's first inhabitants. Sociologist Muniz Sodré writes that in the post-independence ideologies of romantic indianism, Brazil's ruling classes sought a symbolic alliance with the indigenous people as a means to legitimate the domination of the Brazilian nation by plantation owners and urban businessmen—to the manifest exclusion of people of African origin.[20] This tendency to look to the New World lands and their original inhabitants for a meaningful sense of collective and national selfhood was common, to greater or lesser extents, in all of the newly independent Latin American nations. Of course, it involved some terrible ironies. One was that official policies toward most actual (as opposed to imagined) Indians in the hemisphere in the early nineteenth century bore little resemblance to the poetic and mythologized notions promulgated in the literature. Another irony—especially significant for Brazil—was that the attempt to idealize the conception of a nation born of the encounter between a noble and uncorrupted native and an adventurous, progressive (if sometimes raffish) European ignored the history and meaning of a tremendous African presence. Manuela Carneiro da Cunha sees a corollary in the political writings of the era, wherein a restricted definition of nationhood and citizenship (flagrantly contrary to liberal-democratic ideas of equality) sought to "tacitly maintain the relations of power without having to explicitly enunciate them." Thus the Brazilian Constitutional Charter of 1824 could define freedom and equality as inalienable rights while millions continued to be enslaved.[21]

In a variety of forms throughout the nineteenth century, via discourse, doctrine, and opinions, as well as through military/police force and discriminatory laws, Brazil's elites looked for ways to exclude blacks from participation in citizenship. Increasingly, in the second half of the century, Brazilian ruling classes—already accustomed to a paradigm that privileged whiteness and much concerned for a means to manage the progress of the nation toward a European ideal of the nation-state— were influenced by popular European and North American theories of scientific racism, social Darwinism, and especially Comte's positivism. Yet even as elite concepts of the Brazilian polity sought to ignore, destroy, deport, or "whiten" the African element, blacks in Brazil were involved in the work of consolidating an identity of their own.

2

Salvador: The Urban Environment

To those approaching from the sea, Salvador was a city upon a hill. Visitors entering the Bay of All Saints in the nineteenth century often remarked at its uncommon beauty, the blueness of its sparkling waters, the striking appearance of tiers perched in the rocks overlooking the shoreline. This was their introduction to the capital of the province of Bahia, which shared the bay with sugar mills, tobacco plantations, manioc farms, and other small-scale subsistence agriculture, and especially, vast extensions of canefields planted in the *massapé*.

By the end of the eighteenth century, the black slave laborers on the plantations of the Recôncavo had enabled the port of Salvador to become a major commercial center in the Portuguese Atlantic. Agricultural exports from around the region were warehoused and shipped from the city's docks to European markets. Manufactures from Europe and Asia; slaves, oils, and spices from Africa; earthenware pottery, foodstuffs, and tanned hides from the province's interior; and products from Rio and São Paulo as well were gathered in Salvador's markets. These would be sold in the city for redistribution to the hinterlands and to Minas Gerais.[1]

Until well into the nineteenth century, Salvador had no industry to speak of. It was a commercial port and regional administrative center and all of its inhabitants—from the wealthiest merchants to the masses of slaves and free poor—were connected to the web of commerce and trade which gave the city its identity. In the mid-nineteenth century, largely as a result of monies newly available for investment following the abolition of the slave traffic, Salvador began to develop a small base of manufacturing. Early factories in the city included textile mills, metallurgic enterprises catering to the repair needs of *engenhos* and sea-going vessels, cigar-makers, and other small works that produced paper, hats, shoes, soap, oils, coal, candles, and matches. Most of these businesses employed a combination of slave and free labor.[2] The small-scale enterprises did not, however, change the basic fact of the absence of industrial development in Bahia. Even at the end of the century, when Rio and São Paulo were rapidly expanding their industrial bases, Salvador maintained its colonial and imperial role as an intermediary city.

Founded in 1549 as the first seat of Portuguese colonial government in Brazil, Salvador was formed of two major divisions created by a geological fault: the upper city (*cidade alta*) and the lower city (*cidade baixa*). The upper city was the principal site of administrative and ecclesiastical governance. The governor's palace and residences of the chief civil and church officials were located here. The lower city was the commercial heart of Bahia, and until 1870, that activity—in all its multifariousness—centered on and around a single avenue running between the Conceição Basilica and the Church of Nossa Senhora de Pilar. Everything was there: the customs building, the public granary, the marine arsenal, and the *bolsa de mercadorias*.[3] Also along this stretch were the various warehouses that held tobacco, cotton, and sugar awaiting export and the items which had arrived from overseas for distribution in the province and beyond.

The commercial district held an abundance of bazaars, shops, and markets offering all manner of merchandise for sale; as Katia Mattoso notes, everything "from fresh vegetables to slaves." Clothes, jewelry, cloth, shoes, food, drinks, caged birds, pharmacopoeic remedies, and more were displayed in the stores and stands of vendors large and small. In addition, all kinds of services and trades were available to the city's residents and to the sailors, merchants, diplomatic functionaries, and other visitors who passed through. Locksmiths, snuff and chewing tobacco manufacturers, and barbers set up shop on the sidewalks and plazas. And there were the slaves. Men and boys, women and girls in groups of up to several hundred waited on the floors of large warehouses or were exhibited individually in the doorways of shops to attract the attention of interested passersby.[4] Many of the ambulatory vendors were themselves slaves, as readily evidenced by their bare feet; slaves in Brazil were by custom forbidden to wear shoes. Mary Karasch notes that in nineteenth-century Rio de Janeiro, anyone fortunate enough to amass the funds for manumission and be sold his or her freedom considered shoes the symbol of status as a freedperson.[5]

James Wetherell, British vice-consul in Bahia, remarked in 1845 at the absence of modern modes of transportation in the city. He described the atmosphere of Salvador's streets as one of an odd quiet. Unlike other foreign observers and even Bahians themselves, who regularly commented on the variety of sounds in the city—calls of hawkers selling food and other items along the city's streets, work songs of the black slaves and freedpeople who carried burdensome loads to and from the docks, the barking of the mangy *cães de costa*[6] and squeals of pigs being raised, against ordinances, within the city limits—Wetherell was struck by a certain strange silence. To be sure, he was speaking specifically about the absence of vehicles in the provincial capital. In comparison to mid-century England, Salvador's lack of horses and wheeled conveyances surprised him. Virtually all transportation, of human beings as well as merchandise of every description, was carried on the shoulders, backs, or heads of black workers. The British visitor described the sound of the city as that of "the nearly noiseless tread of the unshoed black population."[7]

Wetherell's "unshoed population" accounted for 42 percent of the city's 65,500 inhabitants in 1835; in 1872, slaves constituted 11.5 percent of a total population of 108,138 in the city.[8] In Bahia, until the second half of the nineteenth century, slave ownership was a widespread phenomenon. In spite of the fact that most of Salvador's free population lived, in Mattoso's words, "at the margins of poverty," many owned slaves.[9] People of quite modest means strove to purchase at least one or two slaves who would be set to the domestic tasks of the household, or, oftentimes, sent into the streets *de ganho*[10] to earn the owner's living. Owning slaves was both a symbol of status and a livelihood and only the poorest freedpeople in Bahia were without captive laborers.[11] Maria Graham, an Englishwoman traveling through Pernambuco in the early nineteenth century commented on the ubiquity of slave ownership in Brazil: "Many, of all colours, when they can afford to purchase a negro, sit down exempt from further care. They make the negro work for them, or beg for them, and so as they may eat their bread in quiet, care little how it is obtained."[12] Later in the century, Wetherell, writing from Bahia, would make a similar comment emphasizing more strongly the degradation of physical work and the connection between status and the use of slave labor. In his observations, Wetherell noted that Brazilians, on the whole, "are exceedingly lazy and indifferent to labour or its results." The state of affairs was fed by the overwhelming presence of slavery in the country, and the use of slaves "in every way that servants or workmen are required." Like Graham, Wetherell noted that slaves provided the subsistence of many Brazilians who lived off the labor of the people they possessed—whether two or two hundred. And, Wetherell wrote scornfully, it was the idleness of the owners of slaves which gave them the right to think of themselves as "gentlemen."[13]

Slave ownership in Brazil did not follow easily delimited class or even race lines. Reis writes, "Slaves were not owned just by people one could rightly call 'the ruling class', namely wealthy planters and urban merchants. People in very different social and economic circumstances owned slaves. There were even cases of slaves owning slaves."[14] The ubiquity of slave ownership and the centrality of slavery in Brazil's society and economy for so many hundred years meant that by the nineteenth century in Bahia, the master-slave relationship was well established as the "structural matrix" or basic paradigm of social organization.[15] This paradigm was visible in patterns of deference, structures of paternalism/patronage, and especially in hierarchies of race and color.

Africans and their descendants in the larger port metropoles, like Salvador and Rio de Janeiro, were an inescapable and marked presence. Robert Avé-Lallemant, visiting Brazil from Lübeck, Germany, in the late 1850s, described the scene of his disembarkation in Salvador in these terms: "Everything looks black. Blacks on the beach, blacks in the city, blacks in the lower part, blacks in the upper neighborhoods. Everything that runs, shouts, works, everything that moves and carries is black."[16] Avé-Lallemant's description may have exaggerated slightly, but in characterizing the streets of Salvador as an essentially black social and labor environment he was not far off the mark. B. J. Barickman has suggested that in 1780 the entire captaincy of Bahia had approximately 220,000 inhabitants. Although scholars differ on late colonial population figures, most agree that from one-third to one-half of the captaincy's people were enslaved and about two-thirds to three-fourths were people of color, free and slave. In the early nineteenth century (1816–1817) there were approximately 90,000 slaves in the Recôncavo. Only a small minority of the people living in the Recôncavo were white—perhaps less than one-fifth. Indians by this time were also few. The vast majority were Africans and Brazilian-born blacks, and Bahians of mixed European and African descent.[17]

Estimates for the population of the city of Salvador during the nineteenth century vary widely and scholars warn of the inexactitude of figures until the first nationally conducted census in 1872. Several European travelers in the city offered approximations of the city's populace. Alcide D'Orbigny, a French visitor to Salvador in 1831, numbered the city's inhabitants at 120,000, two-thirds of these being *negros*. D'Orbigny's reckoning made no distinction between slave and free or freed blacks. Robert Avé-Lallemant, writing in 1859, opined that the city held 180,000 souls, one-half of whom were *negro*, one-quarter *mestiço*, and one quarter *branco*. In 1860, Maximiliano de Habsburgo suggested that there were 120,000 people living in Salvador—80,000 *negros* and 20,000 *brancos*.[18] Modern historians of the period have suggested somewhat more modest numbers. João José Reis and Paulo César Souza estimate the population in the mid-1830s at 65,500. Ana Amélia Vieira Nascimento suggests a gradual increase in the city's population throughout the nineteenth century from 41,154 in 1800 to 108,138 in 1872 at the time of the national census. Katia Mattoso's estimates follow a similar trajectory.[19] Reis's calculations indicate that an overwhelming majority of the city's population, slave and free, were people of African descent: 71.8 percent were blacks and mulattos. There were 27,500 slaves (42 percent of the population) and 19,500 free and manumitted people of color (29.8 percent of the population).[20] And even in 1872, at the time of the first national census, slaves in Salvador and the Recôncavo townships numbered over 70,000.[21] In Salvador itself, in 1872, slaves were 11.5 percent of the population. The ethnic breakdown, which included slaves and free people, was "43.7% mulatto, 30.9% white, 23.5% *negros* and 2% *caboclos*."[22] These statistics are in agreement with the fundamental trend in nineteenth-century Brazilian demography—that people of color were the fastest-growing segment of the nation's population.[23] Whatever the discrepancies among the calculations, it is certainly clear, as Reis writes, that by the 1830s, "Bahia was a heavily black province, and Salvador a black city."[24] Slaves and freedpeople, Africans and *crioulos*, shared work and life in the streets of Salvador.

Bahia's was a society highly conscious of social status and its markers. Although the vast majority of people were of African descent and lived uncomfortably close to destitution, there were nonetheless important distinctions around race/color, ethnicity/origin, and legal status. A primary distinction between segments of the populace was that of legal status: the difference between slave and free. Simultaneously, however, as evidenced in the situation of African freedpeople, there were elements mitigating that basic distinction. One of these was race/color. In Salvador and the Recôncavo, the elite or ruling class was composed of Brazilian-born and European whites. They were the large plantation and mill owners in the rural areas and the wealthy merchants and highest-ranking state, church, and military officials in the cities. These people were often aspirants to titles of nobility—a fact which reflects the sense in which race, in Brazil, created an alternate system of estates analogous to that of the European society of orders. In place of royalty, nobility, clergy, and commoners, or, more broadly, simply nobility and commoners, there were in Brazil whites and a hierarchy of non-whites.[25] Whites were also significant in the Bahian middle class, which they shared with some mulattos and a very small number of Brazilian-born blacks.

Between whites and blacks were the intermediate categories of *pardos* (meaning "browns," this term indicated a skin tone between black and white; also called "mulattos") and *cabras* (literally "goats"; darker-skinned people of mixed African and European descent, basically a *pardo* and black mixture). The people described by both of these terms were Brazilians and could be slave, freed, or free. Indians were a very small percentage of the population in Salvador and the Recôncavo by the nineteenth century. According to their mixture with whites or blacks they might be included in the category of *pardos* or identified as *indios* or *caboclos*.

People who were identified as "black" in Bahia were generally either slaves or *libertos* (freedpeople). If they had been born in Africa, they were called *Africanos* or *pretos*. If they were natives of Brazil they were called *crioulos*. The term *negros* was occasionally used to indicate all dark-skinned people of African descent. However, in the nineteenth century, due in large part to the massive importations of African slaves (and to the wave of slave revolts which swept the region in the first forty years of the century), language in Bahia was moving toward more precise differentiations between the supposedly trustworthy *crioulos* and the rebellious Africans.[26] While *negro* suggested a generalized category of dark-skinned people, as in a race, *preto* was used exclusively in reference to Africans and denoted the *color* black more specifically than it did a general racial category. The term for Brazilian-born blacks, *crioulo* (creole), made no explicit reference to color at all; rather it indicated New World nativity. Within the highly color-conscious structure of Bahian social relations, there thus existed a linguistic-ideological tendency to associate explicit *blackness* with Africa and Africans while Brazilian-born blacks were offered a mitigated nomenclature which did not expressly refer to their skin color.

Henry Koster, an early nineteenth-century visitor to Salvador from Britain, observed the attitudes of Bahians about race and color. His statements help us to understand some of the political purposes of the distinction between *crioulos* and *Africanos* and their basis in Brazilian anti-black ideology:

> The mulattos, and all other persons of mixed blood, wish to lean toward the whites, if they can possibly lay any claim to relationship. Even the mestizo tries to pass for mulatto and to persuade himself, and others, that his veins contain some portion of white blood, although that with which they are filled proceeds from Indian and negro sources.[27]

Koster noted that blacks who had no obvious mixture with other races saw themselves as sharing an affinity with others of similar circumstance:

Those only who can have no pretensions to a mixture of blood, call themselves negroes, which renders the individuals who do pass under this denomination much attached to each other, from the impossibility of being mistaken
for members of any other [caste].[28]

This issue carries particular significance for an examination of ways
in which alternative orientations served to inform and create collective
identity among Africans and Brazilians of African descent. Essentially,
what occurred in the development of Candomblé was an embrace of
"things African" and of *blackness* which at many levels challenged the
hegemonic assumptions about the relative value and desirability of European versus African identification. A central thesis of my discussion is
that the alternative spaces of blackness in nineteenth-century Bahia
were not limited to those individuals identified as *preto* (that is, generally,
African). The documentation suggests that many *crioulos* and some
pardos as well often participated in the collectivizing activities of Afro-
Brazilian religio-cultural manifestations—such as *batuques, quilombos,
candomblés,* and the private spaces of black family interaction. Afro-
Bahians of a variety of colors, origins, and social statuses (as well as some
whites) were involved in the creation of alternative meanings of blackness. Unless otherwise noted, the term *black* in this text will denote
Africans and Brazilians of African descent in general. I use the more
specific terms "Africano," "Africana," "African" (and individual ethnic
denominations), "crioulo," "crioula," "pardo," "parda," and "cabra" when
making distinctions among members of the large, multifaceted black
Bahian population.

In addition to race and color, another factor in the organization of
Bahia's nineteenth-century social structure was ethnicity or national
origin. Brazilians, Europeans, and Africans were the three major groups.
European whites were of several nationalities, predominantly Portuguese, but also Spanish, Italian, French, German, Swiss, and British.
Africans were identified by their ethnic or language groups or more
broadly by the ports from which they were purchased and shipped. In the
nineteenth century, in Salvador and the Recôncavo, the majority of
Africans were of so-called Sudanese ethnic and language groups. These
included Yorubas, Hausas, Tapas (Nupes), Ewes, and Aja-Fon peoples.
Although Bantu-speaking Africans (especially Cabindas and Benguelas)
predominated among those imported to Brazil in the seventeenth century, these peoples made up only about a third of Bahia's African population in the early 1800s.

There were three possible legal conditions: free, slave, and freed. An
African or person of African descent might belong to one of these cate-

gories, but those who were former slaves possessed a "freedom" which, in Bahia, "did not mean absolute equality with the free."[29] Whites, on the other hand, were never enslaved. Maria Inês C. de Oliveira, in her study of freed Africans living in Bahia, suggests that race served to negatively diminish their juridical status. The social stratification of Bahian society was strongly tied to a racial stigma which superseded legal station. *Libertos*, in spite of being legally free men and women, continued to suffer a social and occupational segregation which essentially disallowed full integration into Brazilian society and served to emphasize their foreignness as well as their former condition of servitude.[30]

Katia Mattoso and F. W. O. Morton have elaborated schematas of Bahian socio-economic organization in the nineteenth century. Mattoso's analysis features four categories and emphasizes economic and political prestige as more salient characteristics than color. For Mattoso, planters, large-scale merchants, the highest-ranking state and church officials, and military officers constituted the top level of Bahian society. These were the powerful and the wealthy. Her second category includes middle-level government and church officials, professionals, officers in the military, merchants, wealthy master artisans, "and a sizable contingent of Bahians" whose income derived from renting slaves and buildings or from usury. A third level was comprised of lower-level civil servants, soldiers, less prestigious professional groups, innkeepers, artisans, and street vendors. At the bottom were slaves, beggars, and vagabonds, considered "the dangerous classes of the time."[31]

Morton's analysis is simpler than Mattoso's; it has three levels instead of four. In contrast to Mattoso, Morton seems to suggest that color in nineteenth-century Bahia played a major role in determining class position. For Morton, the upper class was all white and divided between a relatively small group of Brazilians and Portuguese; Brazilians were the more numerous group. The middle class was divided among mulattos, whites, and a few *crioulos*. Most of the whites, Brazilian and Portuguese, fell into this segment of the population. For Morton, the lower class held the majority of the city's mulattos and a few poorer whites. A sub-bottom level in this model, considered more an appendage than truly an element of the schema, encompassed the slaves—African, *crioulo,* and mulatto.[32]

While these analyses differ in their emphases, both suggest the possibility of a certain mobility within Bahian society—especially in Salvador—but almost exclusively for the white minority. Education, family ties, patronage, and money were all determining factors within the structure of social organization. For most Bahians, access to these resources was limited. The quest for higher status was considerably more anguished for blacks than for others. Some mulattos, even, might train and practice as lawyers or physicians, but Africans and *crioulos* were impeded from such opportunities. And for slaves in urban areas, while there existed the possibility of buying freedom, it could be accomplished only through tremendous personal (and sometimes collective) effort. Even in situations where manumission was achieved and a modicum of prosperity attained, the structures and limitations of the larger system (racist and slaveholding) created serious restrictions for freedpeople.[33]

One of the most obvious elements of such limitation was the association between Africanness and slave status, between blackness and labor. But, inasmuch as the dominant ideology restricted economic, social, and political opportunities for *libertos,* it also served to enhance the development of collective identity among blacks. Slaves and freedpeople generally shared the same occupations in the Bahian capital. And in many cases they worked together in organized groups (*cantos*). They also lived in close proximity to each other, often in the same dwelling. This was one of the most important characteristics of slavery in Salvador and it facilitated the development of alliances and shared experiences among various elements of the community of blacks.

The *ganho* or "earning" system was the major form of black labor in the city. It involved relatively unsupervised labor and payment for wares sold or tasks completed. If the *ganho* worker was a slave, he or she worked away from the owner's house, often as a street vendor or transporter of people or merchandise, and was obliged to return a daily or weekly percentage of earnings to the master or mistress. The amount remaining was the slave's to keep. From this sum, the slave was often required to provide for his or her own upkeep and perhaps, by means of great sacrifice and extraordinary labor, save enough to eventually buy freedom. Freedpeople who did similar kinds of work were called *negros de ganho,* or *ganhadores* (terms which could include slave workers as well). Among the occupations fulfilled by *ganho* laborers were: chair-carriers, stevedores, cargo-carriers, water-carriers, and wood-carriers; in ambulatory commerce they sold fruit, fish, cloth, shoes, bread, and sweets. *Negros de ganho* were also tailors, barbers, shoemakers, washers, starchers, lacemakers, seamstresses, and embroiderers. Many of the blacks who worked as street vendors were women—*negras ganhadeiras.* They specialized in the sale of foodstuffs—produce, fish, and prepared dishes. Women were also used in heavy manual labor in Salvador. Until 1850, female slaves did construction work. Women were also water-carriers who balanced full buckets and heavy barrels on their heads and backs as they supplied the homes and businesses of their owners or sold portions to customers in the street.[34]

Many blacks were domestic workers; slaves—especially women—predominated in these occupations. Domestic slaves in Bahia did all kinds of work related to the maintenance of the owner's house and household. They were cooks, butlers, wet nurses, washerwomen, starchers, personal attendants, and footmen.[35] House slaves were also responsible for disposing of the family's bodily wastes and bathing water each day. Domestic slaves generally had greater restrictions on their movement than did *escravos de ganho*. They also had little or no access to money and were more dependent on relations with their owners. But the categories between the groups were permeable and a domestic slave might be sent to work in the streets or rented to another person when not engaged in the owner's house. The other form of slave labor common in Brazil was that of *aluguel* (rental). Carpenters, ironworkers, stonemasons, personal servants, street vendors, cooks, agricultural workers, tailors, and goldsmiths were among the occupations held by slaves whose labor was leased for a specified period. The practice of renting slaves seems to have been lucrative for some masters—especially for those whose slaves were trained in domestic and artisanal work.[36]

Not all slaves in Salvador lived with their owners. In fact, many of the *escravos de ganho* were able (oftentimes even required) to find space in some other location and accept full responsibility for housing, feeding, and clothing themselves from their portion of earnings. Slaves who lived with their owners were generally housed in poorly ventilated basements or ground floors of *sobrados* (townhouses of several stories)—sometimes also in tiny cubicles on upper levels. Their habitations were often damp and dark and had very minimal furnishings. A straw mat or wooden board might serve as a makeshift bed. More often though, slaves slept on bare dirt or cement floors. Sometimes they shared space in an owner's house with warehoused merchandise or even animals. In other cases, when they could, city slaves would rent a corner in the room of a freed friend where personal items and savings might be kept in a box or chest away from owners and where the slave might go for a few moments during the workday or on Sunday to rest. Other *escravos de ganho* were fully responsible for their own upkeep and would find lodgings with fellow slaves or in the houses or rooms of freed acquaintances. Not uncommonly, African slaves of a particular ethnicity would rent a small space from others of the same ethnic group. Many *escravos de ganho* lived alone, however, in areas of the city with large free poor and *liberto* populations.[37] The rooms and houses of most of Salvador's blacks—

slave, free, or freed—were of modest size, extremely sparsely furnished and often of precarious construction or in a dilapidated state. But regardless of proportion or condition, the living spaces blacks were able to maintain away from masters and bosses were important factors in their ability to create a certain place of autonomy. Homes of freed Africans, for example, were especially significant. They were often places where slaves, *libertos,* and free people of color gathered to share each other's food, celebrate their deities, look for guidance in divination, find healing from physical ailments, seek the aid of a priest or priestess in achieving freedom, or simply make a temporary refuge from slavery.

It was Africans such as these—spiritual leaders and healers, at whose residences and in whose presence many in Bahia sought healing, community, and intimacy with the gods—who gave Candomblé in Bahia its structure and meaning.

3

The *Bolsa de Mandinga* and *Calundu:* Afro-Brazilian Religion as Fetish and *Feitiçaria*

African Cosmology and African American Religious Orientation

Throughout the Americas, wherever Africans encountered indigenous peoples and Europeans, there arose modes of religious expression which varied to some extent in their external symbols, but which often shared an essential worldview or orientation. Whether the enslaved men and women were of central, western, southern, or eastern African origin, they often held in common certain fundamental elements of understanding about the nature of human existence and human relation to the universe.[1] This shared orientation, this cosmology, explains the basic functioning of the universe; and gives meaning and order to social relations, societal institutions, and the state (or process) of being human. It is a relational, ontological concept more than a historical one; a way of perceiving connections and influences among all presences (material and immaterial) in the cosmos. It provides certain keys for understanding historical circumstances, fortunes, and misfortunes, as well as the day-to-day experiences and sentiments of people. It also establishes the parameters of human response to the situations in which individuals and groups find themselves.

Historians and anthropologists of African religions have consistently noted the flexibility of these traditions—their ability to incorporate new symbols, rites, and myths and reorganize older ones in an effort to respond to the immediate needs and situations of their adherents. At the same time, African religions or orientations have maintained a stability and traditional grounding over many centuries.[2] This plasticity within constancy is one of the central elements shared by traditional African cultures across the continent. For Brazilian sociologist Muniz Sodré, the permanent and stabilizing factor within African religious institutions is "a basic cosmovision which places the force of the universe, the power of realization and transformation, at the center of the natural order of things." This cosmic or universal force is known by many names. For Bantus it is *Muntu*, for the Yorubas it is *Àse*, among the Congos it is *Ngolo*, and the Nyanga call it *Karamo*.[3]

Another of the central aspects of traditional African religion is the overwhelming concern with human beings, their proper relation to each other and to the world, and their earthly, physical, present-life well-being. Historian of religions Charles H. Long suggests a definition of religion as "orientation in the ultimate sense, that is, how one comes to terms with the ultimate significance of one's place in the world."[4] This is especially useful as we consider the meaning of African religiosity and the New World traditions created by enslaved Africans and their descendants. This meaning of religion perforce includes a central consideration of materiality—the orientation of the body. Such a perspective assumes that the spiritual or the religious is contained not only in systems of belief and institutions of faith, but within the physicality of experience, within the material of life. Religion becomes a question of how human beings orient themselves (physically, psychically, individually, and collectively) in relation to an ultimate reality. And the question of orientation then leads us to a consideration of space.

Theoretician of religion Jonathan Z. Smith writes: "It is the relationship to the human body, and our experience of it that orients us in space, that confers meaning to place. Human beings are not places, they bring place into being."[5] As we consider the role of religion in the creation of alternative "black" spaces in colonial-imperial Brazil, we are reminded of the constant tension between the imposed or assigned place of blacks, of blackness, of Africans, within Brazilian society and the creation of alternative identities by blacks themselves. In Brazil and other New World slave-based societies, religion was present not only in ritual ceremonies but also, for example, in the organization and rhythms of work, in verbal culture, and in the ludic sensibility which permeated many of the "secular" gatherings of slaves and freedpeople. All of these actions involved the effort to continually recreate a meaning of humanity fragmented and disoriented by the experience of slavery.

Recognizing orientation or religion within physical action is crucial to the task of exploring Afro–Latin American culture, life, philosophy, and resistance in the colonial period. Most enslaved people did not read and write[6]—that is to say, they were not literate in the European alphabets and systems of writing. Because modern western history has been greatly dependent on records kept in those systems of writing, it has, perforce, limited the "voices" of slaves and others to whom written language was unavailable. However, in large measure, Africans in the

Americas "read" the meanings of their liturgical rhythms and dances and they "wrote" the physical symbols of their religion and "re-wrote" Catholic and Protestant symbols to serve African American purposes. They also "read" the limitations imposed upon them by slavery and the developing culture of white supremacy; but at the same time they "wrote" forms of negotiation, resistance, and transformation.

João Reis and Eduardo Silva have discussed the need for historians to be willing to identify the ideas, points of view, and values of enslaved Africans by means of the actions of those men, women, and children. In spite of the fact that we have precious few of their own words, we do have many accounts of what slaves *did*. According to Reis and Silva, if we are perceptive and open enough (and adequately prepared), those actions can suggest their meanings to us.[7] If we look for orientation and meaning within the actions of slaves themselves, we may discover that the earliest generations of African Americans left us an invaluable historical resource. Furthermore, we may also come to see that their view of who they were and how they were related to the rest of the universe transcends many of our limited notions of what it meant to be a slave in the New World. The movements of enslaved people—in labor, in celebration and worship, in family relationship, in collective organization, in quotidian attempts to negotiate safety and refuge, and in violent rebellion—can aid us in understanding how traditional African orientations toward the cosmos influenced the ways in which black people responded to and resisted the many attempts at their dehumanization.

Speaking primarily of indigenous South American peoples, but expressing an idea that applies equally well to the Africans enslaved in the Americas, historian of religion Lawrence Sullivan states: "South Americans offer original appraisals of the experience of being human. Nowhere is this more evident than in their religious life, which is the foundation of South American cultures."[8] The religious life of people of African descent, their way of understanding and being in the world, was not stripped from them by the holocaust of enslavement. However, in engagement with the particular psychic and material circumstances of New World colonialism and slavery, the ultimate orientation of African Americans developed new exigencies. It is there, in the religion of enslaved people—at the center of individual and collective experience, at the heart of their efforts to "mash out a new meaning" of what it was to be black and to be human in the Americas—that we must first turn in any examination of how those women and men perceived themselves and their situation.[9]

Whether they found themselves in Cuba, Brazil, Venezuela, the

United States, or any of the other continental or Caribbean nations of the Americas, Africans fashioned responses to their circumstances which deeply reflected the values they brought to those places. As we have established, at the heart of those values were the generally compatible religious sensibilities of traditional African cultures. These included: the importance of communal worship; the cultivation and expectation of intense, pragmatic, physical communion with representations of the forces of the universe (many deities or one supreme deity); the special role of drama, music, and dance in religious culture and expression; the perception that New World enslavement represented a fundamental imbalance of cosmic energy, or sin; rites of healing and purification; and the belief that natural forces can be manipulated by certain individuals to effect a variety of ends.

The *Bolsa de Mandinga*

These elements, as we will see, form the core of many of the Afro-Brazilian religio-cultural manifestations which developed over the almost five hundred years of that country's existence. This chapter examines two of the predecessors of Candomblé in Afro-Brazilian religiosity —the *bolsa de mandinga* and *calundu*. The *bolsa de mandinga* (mandinga pouch) is a more individual, person-centered manifestation, related in ways to William Pietz's idea of the fetish.[10] *Calundu,* a more collective experience, is in some apparent ways, an earlier (sixteenth- through eighteenth-century) form of the orientation that also engendered Candomblé—sharing many of the most central components. The *bolsa de mandinga* and *calundu* were both understood as expressions of *feitiçaria* (witchcraft; sorcery) in the colonial Luso-Brazilian milieu. Those people who used them as resources for the negotiation of life as enslaved and subordinated peoples were accused of evildoing and devil worship.

The *bolsa de mandinga, calundu,* and Candomblé can all be seen as "crossroads" orientations in that they developed in the opposition between the experience of colonialism/slavery and the effort to maintain an alternative understanding of one's place in the universe. They also developed out of the need to speak to, and in some measure redress, the nature and tensions of colonialism—particularly the arbitrariness, violence, and inequality of master-slave relations.

"Calundu," "Batuque," "Zangu," "Tambor de Mina," "Xangô," "Tabaque," and "Candomblé" were among the terms used to denote black religio-cultural manifestations at various points and places in colonial and imperial Brazil. Although there was sometimes an ambiguity in the minds of authorities about whether these manifestations were religious or purely secular diversions, all shared the centrality of collective music and dance as a core element. And it was the fact of that core, and the accompaniment of an intensity of expression and, at times, radically altered states of being, which contributed in large part to the perception that black religion was "witchcraft pure and simple."[11] Roger Bastide, eminent scholar of Afro-Brazilian religions, indicated that the "frenetic dancing and especially the episodes of possession" central to rituals of Afro-Brazilian religion were interpreted by church and civic authorities as having a demonic quality.[12]

As historian Laura de Mello e Souza has ably demonstrated, uncovering *feitiçaria* and pacts with the devil were substantial preoccupations of the Holy Inquisition which visited areas of Brazil in the colonial era. In the sixteenth century, to the metropolitan Portuguese, Brazil represented an unstable and uncivilized location where an edenic geography was spoiled by the influence of Indians—seen as savage, barbaric, and even monstrous in their otherness.[13] From the idea of the land's original inhabitants as the essential locus of evil in the New World, the demonization of colonial inhabitants had clearly spread by the eighteenth century to also encompass first African slaves and then all Brazilians as a group.[14] In the Portuguese imagination, from the sixteenth to the eighteenth centuries, Brazil was a land of purgatory (if not a form of hell itself) and it continued to be a place where convicted criminals (*degregados*) from the metropole were sent to atone for their sins.[15] From at least the seventeenth century, civic and religious authorities in Brazil associated blacks with witchcraft and devil worship because of the intense dances and episodes of possession associated with their ceremonies and the use of so-called diabolical arts by slaves attempting to avoid the castigations to which they were often submitted.[16] It appears that in the context of Portuguese colonialism, the association between blacks and sorcery developed largely as a result of the attempt of slaves to alter the nature of colonial relations—especially the tension between masters and captives. Slave-owners feared ritual gatherings of blacks as possible precursors to insurrection, and apprehensions about poisonings and supernatural retribution were also common.

One of the earliest-noted aspects of Afro-Brazilian magico-religious response to slavery was the *bolsa de mandinga*. These small pouches of leather or cloth enclosed a variety of ritual elements and were worn about the body. According to Souza, they were "the most typically colonial form of feitiçaria in Brazil."[17] Which is to say that from a grounding in the experiences and necessities of slaves (and used primarily among those people), *bolsas de mandinga*, or just *mandingas* or *patuás*, were also used by others of Brazil's colonial inhabitants. Souza suggests that part of the popularity of the *mandingas* was their syncretic "resolution of European, African and indigenous cultural habits."[18] During the colonial period in Latin America, amulets, talismans, charms, and other portable magico-religious objects were a common feature among many of the European, Indian, and African peoples brought together in the territories. Thus the concept of *mandingas* was received with relative ease by many of Brazil's colonial inhabitants. However, it was not simply the familiarity and generalized use of *mandingas* which made them significant. The specific uses to which these objects were put and the substances which formed them—that is, their materiality—allow them to serve as a means to a fuller understanding of the colonial context. They also suggest an appreciation of the ways slaves and freedpeople, in particular, manipulated materials and negotiated living and working spaces for fuller expressions of their humanity.

"Bolsa de mandinga" itself is an illuminating term. The Mandinga people (also known as Mandingos or Malinkes) from the Senegambia region of West Africa were among the earliest black captives in Brazil. Some in their number were Muslims and had developed the tradition in Africa of carrying verses of the Koran or other prayers in pouches or similar small containers close to their bodies. Mandingos were respected in Brazil, as well as in other parts of Latin America, for their especially strong abilities as sorcerers. In fact, the widespread use in South America of the term *mandinga* to indicate "sorcery" is an indication of the influence of these peoples on the development of Afro–Latin American magico-religious practices.[19] The *bolsas de mandinga* were also the most consistent magico-religious manifestation of master-slave tensions in the Portuguese colonial empire. There are examples of the use of *mandingas* from widely divergent geographical areas—Minas Gerais, Bahia, Rio, and various cities in Portugal itself.[20] In both the metropole and the Brazilian cities those accused of carrying *mandingas* were often Africans. In Bahia for example, in 1853, a search by police of rooms rented to Africans turned up several of the small packets containing words in a script illegible to authorities.[21]

Documentation further suggests that one of the major uses of *patuás/mandingas* was for protection against harm. In an eighteenth-century example cited by Souza, Manuel da Piedade, a slave in Lisbon who had been born in Bahia, was tried by the Inquisition for being a *feiticeiro* (witch doctor, sorcerer). He admitted to carrying in his pocket a prayer "do Justo Juiz," given to him in Bahia, to protect himself from the dangers of the sea and against beatings. These prayers, its seems, were in common use in Brazil. Piedade was also accused of selling ingredients needed to make *bolsas de mandinga*, which he was said to have prepared in the countryside "with the help of the devil."[22] One element in the *mandingas* was such a prayer, which, in order to be effective, had to be placed on a *pedra d'ara* (a specially consecrated stone used by Catholic priests for communion), over which should be said three masses.[23] In another case from Lisbon, in 1731, José Francisco Pereira, a slave born in the Mina Coast of Africa was accused of being a *feiticeiro* who made *feitiços* (spells; magic objects; fetishes, "made things") for the obtaining of freedom and *mandingas* for protection. In his testimony, Pereira explained that as soon as he arrived in Portugal from Brazil—where he had lived for a time—he was approached by many blacks who wanted him to provide them with *mandingas*. They assumed that having recently arrived from Brazil he must have brought *mandingas* with him. Blacks in Lisbon beseeched Pereira to prepare the objects for them, into which it was said he commonly placed a strong-smelling root which would prevent the users from being beaten.[24]

Pereira had an assistant, José Francisco Pedroso, who was also a slave, had also been born on the Mina Coast and, like Pereira, had spent time in captivity in Brazil. Pedroso reported in his testimony that while living in Rio (where he was baptized) he heard talk of *mandingas* for the first time. It was in that city that he learned they were good protection against lacerations.[25] The *mandingas* made by the two José Franciscos in Lisbon and presented to the Inquisition were of cloth, generally white. These were designed primarily to protect their wearers from knife wounds and gunshots and contained the following items: *pedra de corisco* (literally, "lightning stone"; perhaps a meteorite), *olho de gato* (literally, "cat's eye"; probably a leguminous seed), sulfur, explosive powder, a lead shot, a silver coin, a bone, and prayers written in blood and placed on the *pedra d'ara* for consecration. The prayers were written in the blood of a white (or sometimes black) chicken or sometimes with that of Pereira's own left arm. Copied out by someone known to Pereira—as the slave was himself illiterate—the prayers were rhymed supplications to Saint Marcus, Jesus, Saint Manso, God the Father, God the Son, the Holy Spirit, and Lucifer for protection against harm and enemies. When ready, the *mandinga* would be smoke-cured with incense. Sometimes the contents were buried at midnight and then dug up and packed together. On the night of the Feast of Saint John, the *feiticeiro* would put the *mandingas* over a bonfire to increase their effectiveness.[26]

Another description comes from Henry Koster, who, while traveling in Pernambuco in the early nineteenth century, encountered a *feitiço* called a *mandinga*. This one was a ball of leaves about the size of an apple, tied with vine. According to Koster, "the ball of mandinga was formed of five or six kinds of leaves of trees, among which was the pomegranate leaf. There were likewise two or three bits of rag, earth of a peculiar kind, ashes which were the bones of some animal." Koster acknowledged that the *mandinga* might contain other elements but that the ones listed were all he recognized. Finally he suggested that the *mandinga* was probably made by an elderly sorcerer (*mandingueiro*) for a woman who confessed that she wanted to entice a man to prefer her over someone else.[27] Koster's example gives us a sense of the variety of uses to which "made things" of African origin were put in colonial-imperial Brazil.

The Inquisition records gathered by Souza, however, return us to the magico-material means by which slaves sought to mitigate the violence against them and the power of masters over them. Slaves from Minas Gerais reported that the root of the wheat plant which grew in marshy areas had the power to protect them from the brutalities of their owners. Other slaves from Bahia and Rio confessed that they scraped the dust from the bottom of their masters' shoes so that they would not be beaten. Marcelina Maria was a slave in Lisbon who had been born and raised in Rio; she had come to Portugal while still a young girl. Marcelina was discovered to have the scrapings of the soles of her mistress's shoes wrapped in two small papers. According to the documents of her trial, when the moon rose, Marcelina would make three signs of the cross and then put the paper packets in the folds of her skirt, after which she placed them between her legs as she slept.[28]

Reporting to the Inquisitors that she changed masters with some frequency, Marcelina emphasized that she hated captivity and being mistreated. It seems that for many of the men who owned her, Marcelina served as an object of sexual desire; their wives were often jealous.[29] In fact, the contents and placement of Marcelina's packets may have been designed to protect against the vengeance of such a mistress. Historian Sonia Maria Giacomini indicates that particularly in instances of sexual jealousy, Brazilian mistresses would beat their female slaves on the most sensually appealing parts of their bodies—hands, faces, breasts, and thighs.[30] Marcelina's masters would themselves become envious of boyfriends she might arrange on her own. The records of her trial report that one of Marcelina's owners, João Eufrásio, in such a situation, sadistically humiliated her in front of "six or seven men," including the owner's eldest son.[31]

For black slaves in colonial Portugal and Brazil, *mandingas*, the scraped dust of shoes, plant roots, and other magico-material resources were essential elements in the effort to negotiate a path through the humiliations and uncertainties of their subaltern position. References to the use of *mandingas* and other protective substances repeatedly surface as responses to the dangers associated with slave status and colonial life. What we see in José Francisco Pereira's *bolsa de mandinga* and Marcelina Maria's packets of shoe dirt are the means by which colonial struggles and tensions were given material representation in attempts to address and redress the inequalities of power and the arbitrariness of violence.

The Fetish

The above examples illustrate the ritual organization of materials and their meanings in the context of both traditional African orientations and a Pietzian understanding of "fetishism." In his classic book *African Traditional Religion,* Geoffrey Parrinder (who was writing against the backdrop of the 1950s), understandably cautioned against the use of the word "fetish" as a descriptor of African traditional religious practices. He saw the term as disadvantageous because it tended to exoticize and deprecate a concept as exclusively African (and therefore "primitive," etc.) when in fact, most other cultures around the world have and use "magical objects" as well. Parrinder recommended that more appropriate and universal terms such as "amulets," "talismans," "medicines," "medallions," and "charms" be used instead.[32] Granted that Parrinder's concerns are well taken in the atmosphere of condescension and racism which has characterized western approaches to African religious sensibility in the modern era, it nevertheless seems to me appropriate to examine more closely the original context and meaning of the term "fetish." Doing so may help us better understand the significance of materia-magica like the *bolsas de mandinga.*

Pietz, an interdisciplinary scholar, has made a careful elaboration of the idea of the fetish as it developed in the context of trade relations between Europeans and Africans along the west coast of Africa in the sixteenth and seventeenth centuries. His essays, published between 1985 and 1988 in the anthropological journal *Res,* suggest a model for understanding the problem/idea of the fetish in terms of four principal themes: a) materiality, b) historical context, c) social value, and d) relation to the body. In his examination of the history of the usage of the term "fetish" Pietz found the above four themes to be constant elements in its meaning across a wide variety of disciplines, chronological periods, and historical situations. Pietz acknowledges that the "discourse of the fetish has always been a critical discourse about the false objective values of a culture from which the speaker is personally distanced."[33] He indicates that an examination of the roots and nature of that discourse in the historical situation of European mercantile expansion in Africa (and the concomitant implication of the colonial project in the New World lands) may be suggestive of deeper understandings encased within the concept itself. Pietz's deconstruction of the idea of the fetish seems especially relevant to a discussion of the meaning of Afro-Brazilian religion in colonial context. The Pietzian model enables us to recognize—in the development of the concept of the fetish, as well as in the objects themselves—structures of colonial relation and re-formulated meaning.

It is important to note that the Pietzian concept of the fetish is not synonymous with African religiosity. For Pietz, "fetish" is a European term used to explain as well as to obscure developing commercialization and the denial of rights. At the same time, his deconstruction of the Euro-mercantile ideation of the fetish refers to sixteenth- and seventeenth-century European travelers who recognized that West African orientation was informed by an order of value radically distinct from that accepted by whites. The Dutch merchant Willem Bosman, for example, complained that African religious and cultural values blocked a recognition of rational self-interest and social order by anthropomorphizing nature—attributing characters and meanings to objects, animals, and other non-human life forms—which in the European Enlightenment perspective was simply a perversion of reality.[34] My analysis of Afro-Brazilian religious orientation in terms of the concept of *feitiço* attempts to hold in tension the Pietzian idea of fetish and the idea of African religiosity as embodying a fundamentally different order of value than that recognized by the European colonial-mercantile project. In this sense the most important elements of the idea of the fetish will be: a) its meaning as an interstitial negotiating tool, and b) its representation of an alternative understanding of the world.

The English word "fetish" is itself suggestive of roots in Iberian colonial-mercantile experience. It originated in the pidgin term *fetisso* which developed in the language of trade and commerce along the West African littoral—especially the Mina Coast—where there existed a triangulation of Christian feudal, African lineage, and merchant capitalist social systems. *Fetisso* was a middleman's term which served to gather a variety of African objects and practices into a single category—thus enabling people from "bewilderingly different cultures" to form a basis for commercial relations. The word derived from the Portuguese *feitiço* which in the late Middle Ages meant "magical practices" or "witchcraft."

The etymological roots of *feitiço* are in the Latin *facticius,* which originally meant "manufactured," a made thing. Pietz suggests that the term "fetish" may be alternately understood as a failed translation of West African meanings, or, as he prefers, it can be seen as something in itself, "a novel word responsive to an unprecedented type of situation."[35] For Pietz, "fetish" originated from, and as a term remains specific to, the problem of the constructed social value of material objects "as revealed in situations formed by the encounter of radically heterogeneous social systems."[36] The discussion below examines each of the four major aspects of the Pietzian idea of the "fetish" and then provides two examples from the originating African context. Subsequently, it considers the possible applications of a Pietzian meaning of the fetish to the *bolsa de mandinga* as an Afro-Luso-Brazilian hermeneutical space in which central elements of the black experience in Portuguese colonial context have been fixed.

Elements of the Pietzian Model, Examples, and Applications

A) *Materiality.* The fetish is characterized by an "irreducible materiality." That is to say that for the fetish, the locus of "religious activity or psychic investment" is in matter, in the material object itself. The fetish is not an iconic representation of something else, it is a material embodiment itself. (In this sense, Peitz asserts, the fetish is clearly distinguished from the "idol"—which is a representation of a transcendent reality.)[37]

B) *Historicization.* Central to the idea of the fetish is historical specificity and fixation. The fetish has its origin in a singular historical conjunction of "radically heterogeneous elements," whose ordering is capable of being repeated, or "fixed."[38] Thus a particular historical context of the encounter of very different ways of being, of different orientations to the world, becomes the grounding for the emergence of the fetish. This element can be seen not only in terms of the differing value systems of Europe and Africa, but also in the nature of colonialism and the way that colonial structures establish oppositional categories of relationship: master/slave, colony/metropole, etc.

C) *Reification.* This is what Peitz terms the constructedness or nonuniversality of social value. The meaning of the fetish is related to a specific social construction of reality. The fetish depends for its meaning and value on a particular order of social relations, which it in turn reinforces. European traders, for example, constantly remarked at the "trinkets and trifles" which they traded with Africans for objects of "real value."

D) *Personalization.* The fetish has meaning in active relation to the human body. It is worn on or about the body and is designed to achieve tangible effects (such as healing or protection) "upon or in service of the user."[39]

To demonstrate the way that social and economic interactions between Europeans and Africans along the West African coast gave rise to the idea of the fetish as defined in the above elements, Peitz suggests a number of historical examples of fetish from the transatlantic African context. Two of these are Akan brass gold weights and Portuguese *padrões.* The gold weights are small brass figures used as counterweights in the measuring of gold dust. They were created in "a direct cultural response to the impact of gold-seeking European (and Arab) traders and to the 'quasimonetarization' of the domestic Akan economy through the circulation of gold-dust as a measure and store of value." The weights served to connect completely unrelated social values. On one hand, they represented traditional proverbs or were used as personal amulets for healing. On the other hand, they expressed the market values introduced by foreign traders.[40] The *padrões* were monumental stone markers transported on ships and set up on the banks of rivers and capes "both as claims of possession and as navigational landmarks."[41] These stone structures bore the coat of arms of the Portuguese crown and were inscribed with the name of the "discoverer" and the date of erection at a certain place. They served to territorialize the codes of Christianity and Portuguese feudalism into the African landscape, thereby reifying the space in terms of those value codes and by means of the "discoverer's" founding.[42]

The *bolsa de mandinga* may be interpreted at various levels in terms of Pietz's categories of the fetish. At perhaps the most obvious, the *bolsa de mandinga,* although it followed the model of existing magico-religious objects in traditional African societies, took on a form, usage, and meaning particular to the experience of colonial Portuguese and New World slavery. One might say that the *bolsa de mandinga,* like the original concept of the fetish, is a "crossroads" object with a meaning that encases and expresses the tensions and values of its interstitial location.

Construction of the cloth *mandingas* involved a gathering of material elements representative of specific dangers and tensions in the colonial experience and a fixation of constituent factors into what could perhaps be seen as a kind of prophylactic magico-pharmacopoeic homeopathy. The *mandinga* thus became an intermediary object enabling the negotiation of hazard while pointing to, and perhaps even invoking in some measure, the sources of hazard. Small amounts of sulfur, gunpowder, and lead shot, for instance, might serve as inoculations against serious harm from those elements. Or the silver coin, a representation of value in the Portuguese colonial economy, might similarly evoke worth and effectiveness in the *mandinga*. Prayers said over Christian-consecrated stone and written in sacrificial blood suggest a combination of efficacies arising out of the colonial encounter. Blood is an important element in many traditional African cultures for the imbuing and revitalization of life force or "the power to make things happen." And the inclusion of Lucifer among those to whom appeal is made for safety recalls anthropologist Michael Taussig's description of the "Devil in the Mines" and the problem of how to negotiate a terrorized life.

In his book *The Devil and Commodity Fetishism in South America*, Taussig discusses the arbitrariness of capitalist power and violence as a central feature in the lives of proletarianized Indians in Colombia and Bolivia in the twentieth century. His observations about the relationship between terror and power and about the way that relationship is ritualized and adapted by exploited workers in their attempts to mediate their vulnerability and explain the ideology of exploitation suggest the possibility of similar readings of the actions of black slaves in the Portuguese colonial empire.[43]

A comparison to the Pietzian model suggests that the *bolsa de mandinga* may be understood as a kind of fetish—an object embodying and addressing the interstices of radically different social orders—at each level of definition. At the level of materiality, the meaning of the *mandinga* is contained in the object itself. It is not a representation of a transcendent reality; rather, its value, function, and meaning are present in its construction from elements which speak to the perils of slave life and attempt to provide magico-religious efficacy in negotiating freedom, or at least a form of refuge or defense.

In terms of historicization, the *bolsa de mandinga* takes its meaning from the specific colonial experience of master-slave relations in Portugal and Brazil. Colonialism/Slavery is the specific historical event fixing together otherwise heterogeneous elements of geography, economy, cultural orientations, racial identifications, etc. In this sense, the meaning of the *mandinga* (as an attempt to negotiate space and protection within the colonial situation) is clearly created in the historical context of unequal, exploitative relations.

On the issue of repetition/fixation, recall that many slaves in Lisbon requested that *mandingas* be made for them, which Pereira and Pedroso (and others) did repeatedly. Antonio, a Hausa slave fisherman in the

Recôncavo town of Itapagipe, regularly made "amulets to heal spiritual ills and ward off bodily danger" which he sold to fellow Africans in Bahia in the 1830s.[44] In these examples, we are able to see the creation and use of the *bolsa de mandinga* as part of the continuing effort to re-order a world fractured by slavery. That is to say, that just as the experience of uncertainty and the arbitrariness of violence were ongoing realities for blacks (and others) in the colonial situation, the *bolsa de mandinga* was not a thing done once, to last. In fact its meaning is perhaps most fully appreciated upon considering the thousands and perhaps millions which must have been made to address a vast array of situations in an attempt (along with other elements of religion and culture) to repeatedly and constantly reshape the reality of disjunction into some semblance of wholeness.

As for the constructedness of social value, *mandingas*—and Afro-Brazilian magico-religious manifestations in general—took their significance from the order of colonial-imperial social relations, and in that sense, they reinforced that order. Simultaneously, they were a means of interrogating the constructed order. Inasmuch as the very presence, the necessity and form of the *mandingas* (their ingredients, their use), acknowledged the dominant social order, they were also an effort in the direction of adjusting the balance of power, of moderating the caprice of the dominant order. In this sense, the *bolsas* and other *feitiços* represented a counterforce.

Finally, at the level of personalization, the *mandingas*, designed to be worn or kept against the body, follow Peitz's model of the fetish in terms of their corporeal use in the attainment of "tangible effects." Many elements of the uncertainty, ambiguity, arbitrariness, and violence of the colonial situation were situated in the *mandingas*—ritually put there so that the *mandinga* became both a representation of colonial reality and an essential part of that reality—a necessary element in negotiating one's way through, and transforming, life within the colonial context. The *mandingas* were material embodiments and representations of power in colonial relations as well as attempts to address and redress that power.

In addition to the *mandingas*, Afro-Brazilian slaves and freedpeople created other, more collective forms of resistance based in African religious values and New World exigencies. In gatherings for community and communion, physical and psychic healing, and refuge and release from slavery, blacks in Brazil created ways of altering their relation to the constructed order by emphasizing the primacy of an alternative mode of experiencing the colonial-imperial moment. These gatherings took various forms. Some were maroon communities, such as the celebrated seventeenth century *quilombo* called Palmares in the northeastern state of Alagoas. Others were more temporary and furtive quests for a respite from the physical and psychological demands of slave status: Short-lived fugitive communities often arose in the woods surrounding Brazilian cities and plantations. Slaves, occasionally joined by army deserters, vagabonds, and other people who lived at the margins of colonial and imperial Brazilian life, would risk certain punishment for the chance to create and experience the space of an alternative community even if for just a few days.

Calundu

Among the most common forms of collective resistance to the dehumanizations of slavery were Afro-Brazilian religions. Documentation of Afro-Brazilian religion in the colonial-imperial period is, however, sketchy and is scattered in accounts of many kinds. Inquisition records, as we have already seen, are an important and rich source, as are travelers' accounts, newspaper notices, and police records. In these cases, however, description and discussion of Afro-Brazilian religion was generally organized and conducted by elites and other individuals who shared the interests of elites, most of whom were only mindful of the black traditions insofar as they represented exoticisms, nuisances, or threats.

The difficulty of trying to locate and interpret historical materials on black religion in Brazil is significant. Many practices were forced into clandestinity by repression and by the inherently private nature of some rituals, thus making their registry in the historical record problematic. Descriptions and meanings were often distorted and misconceived on the one hand, or absent on the other. As with other aspects of the history of popular sectors of Brazilian society, Afro-Brazilian religions in the colonial and imperial era existed, in Reis's words, "almost absolutely at the margin of written culture."[45] The work of historians such as Reis, Souza, and others has been, nonetheless, instrumental in taking documents on Afro-Brazilian religion written from the perspective of "elite" sources and opening them to possible understandings from the perspective of the non-elite historical agents who are their subjects.

One of the earliest descriptions of *calundu* as a specifically denominated phenomenon comes from the seventeenth-century travel narrative of Nuno Marques Pereira, whose account from Bahia describes the experience of being kept from sleep by the noise of a *calundu* celebrated nearby. Pereira's local host explained to his guest that: "These are festivals or divinations that the Negroes say they were accustomed to perform in their own lands. When they get together, they perform them here too in order to learn all manner of things; such as what is causing illness or to find lost objects, also to ensure success in hunting or in their gardens, and for many other purposes."[46] Pereira named a number of instruments heard in the "noise" of the gathering—drums, tambourines, *canzás* (percussion instruments whose sound is produced by stroking a stick across a striated surface; *reco-recos*), *botijas,* and castanets.[47]

A particularly thorough description of *calundu* in Minas Gerais comes again from the Inquisition documents collected by Souza. In 1742, a *preta forra* (black freedwoman) was imprisoned and taken to Lisbon to face the religious tribunal. The woman, Luzia Pinta, had been born in Angola and was living in the town of Sabará in Minas at the time of her arrest. She was accused of being a *feitiçeira* who made devils appear by means of "some dances, which are commonly called calundus." Luzia Pinta was questioned for several months and eventually tortured and exiled to the town of Castro Marim in the Algarve to serve a four-year sentence. She was described as unmarried, about fifty years old, *preta baça* (a brown-skinned black woman), tall and thickly built with a marking near the forehead and others on each cheek. The documents from Luzia's case suggest that she used dance as a from of divination and healing, wearing special ceremonial clothes and using percussion instruments (drums and cymbals) to bring on an altered state of being during which she "trembled greatly as if not herself."[48]

It appears that Luzia was able to divine even secret things. When a man named Domingos Pinto sought her aid in locating some gold *oitavas* (coins) which had been stolen from him, Luzia Pinta told him that a female slave of his had taken them. She further stated that the woman who had taken the coins was the same one with whom Domingos Pinto had slept without giving her anything in return. The letter directing Luzia Pinta to the Inquisition asserted that it was indeed true "that Domingos Pinto slept with one of the negras and didn't give her anything, and the said negras were in the house."[49]

Further descriptions of Luzia Pinta's ritual seem to contain or anticipate many elements of the organization and material structure of Candomblé. The Inquisition documentation reports that the Angolan woman held *calundures* [*sic*] "set in a small altar with its dossel and an *alfange* [a saber with a short, broad blade] in her hand, a large ribbon tied on her head—the points toward the back, dressed like an angel; and two negras also Angolas singing, and a preto playing drums which is a *tamborzinho* [a small drum], and they say that the *pretas* and the *preto* are her slaves, and they play and sing for the space of one to two hours, she being out of her right mind [*fora de seu juizo*], saying things that no one understands, and the people she cured lay on the floor, she passed over them various times, and it is on these occasions that she said she has the winds of divining [*ventos de adivinhar*]."[50] Luzia Pinta was sought by people in her village for help with quotidian problems: divinations, cures. All of her interventions were made via nocturnal ceremony—the *calundu*. She dressed in unusual clothing, what the trial record referred to as "inventions" (*invenções*). She covered her head with headwraps and danced to African instruments. She entered trance and responded to the needs of her clients from that altered state. Luzia Pinta "would sit in a high chair, like a throne, and jump over people who had gone there in search of cures and who, in that moment, lay themselves face down on the floor." Sometimes she prescribed medicinal leaves for those who were ill. She would smell the heads of people to determine if they were suffering from the effects of magic spells. She administered concoctions to induce vomiting. Some witnesses said she carried *cascaveis* (probably the stuffed skins of rattlesnakes) on her arms and legs and that she claimed the "winds of divining" entered through her ears.[51]

Luzia Pinto's ceremonies, and others brought before the Inquisition and local tribunals, evidence a conjunction of practices which, in whole or in part, were understood as *calundu*. As witnessed in the descriptions, a central element of these ritual activities was healing and divination by means of African-based traditions of drumming, dance, and trance. In the physical and ritual space of the *calundu*, Luzia Pinto and those who participated with her in ceremonies created responses to the physical ailments and relational disjunctions they suffered in the colonial context. The collective gatherings; ritual possession; evocation of and offerings to spirits; divining; curing; and percussive music, song, and dance— all present in descriptions of *calundu*—were similarly conjoined as elements of nineteenth-century Candomblé.

Reis has transcribed and done an engaging historical analysis of a legal inquiry into a raid on a site of Afro-Brazilian ceremonial activity in the Recôncavo town of Cachoeira in 1785. The gathering was referred to as a *calundu* by individuals interviewed during the proceedings.[52] According to the documentation, a house in which six Africans lived served as a gathering place for the celebration of *calundus* and for healing. The leader of the group, Sebastião de Guerra, was the oldest of the six and was identified by an African witness as a Dagomé—that is, a man from Dahomey. The others were a Tapa, two Mahis, and two Jejes.[53] All were freedpeople except for one woman who was a slave. It appears that the Africans were three male-female couples, each sharing a separate room in the house.

Neighbors and other witnesses who testified for the inquiry declared that it was well known that the Africans "danced calundus" in the house and that during the gatherings, songs were sung in the Jeje language. The musical instruments used were described as a "small iron item,"[54] and in place of a drum, the mouth of a pot was played. During the invasion of the house, officials came upon a scene in the bedroom of Sebastião de Guerra which led them to a more incontrovertible belief that the house was a site of *feitiçaria*. Knocking down the door to Sebastião's room, they saw in a corner a small arrow standing vertically from the floor and waggling, apparently unsupported, without falling. The arrow had two small feather plumes hanging from its points on each side and was surrounded by ritual objects—more feathers, some articles of iron, paper, coins, leaves, a jar of *aguardente* (sugarcane rum), and various small vessels with ingredients described by police as "for . . . evil-doing." Under the floor of the room were planted more items—especially small metal objects and "bolos de cera da terra cravadas de feijão, de arroz."[55]

This description is significant at many levels and helps us appreciate some of the means by which Afro-Brazilian religion was used to create a space of alternative identity, alternative being for blacks. The house in Cachoeira was not only the living space of three African couples, but was, according to the inquiry testimonies, a "public and notorious" gathering place for other blacks who came for healing and to find communion among themselves and with their deities. This *calundu* represented the beginnings of the kind of pan-African synthesis which would later be seen in more formalized ways in Candomblé. The fact that the house's inhabitants were mostly Jeje and that ritual ceremonies were described as occurring "in the Jeje language" suggests that a majority of those who participated in the *calundu* were probably Jeje peoples. But the presence of at least one Tapa man, as well as the fact that the term Jeje encompassed a variety of Aja-Fon peoples, implies that by the late eighteenth century, blacks in Bahia may have already been creating ways to recognize, reorganize, and cultivate a variety of African traditions under one roof.

That ritual items were located under the floor of Sebastião de Guerra's room is also significant. Physical implantation of ritual items under the floor of sacred spaces is an essential element in the establishment of Candomblé *terreiros*. Such an act also indicates a more or less permanent connection between the place, the spirits of the place, and the people encharged with the ritual care of both. The majority of people living in the house were *libertos;* as Bastide has suggested, the role of freed Africans was central to the development of formalized Afro-Brazilian religion. Freedpeople were able to live relatively autonomously and could amass the funds to buy, or in this case to rent, property which they felt would be sufficiently secure that they could use it as the ritual space for their gatherings.[56]

All of these elements of the 1785 *calundu*—the dance- and music-based ritual gatherings for healing and collective celebration; the presence of ritual items; the participation of members of several ethnic or sub-ethnic groups, slave and freed; and the association of African ritual practices with witchcraft—are important forerunners of nineteenth-century Candomblé. They are also evidence of the means by which Africans in Brazil were using rituals and traditions of their native lands—adapted to New World circumstances—to create spaces in which they could experience and nurture another meaning of themselves, one that emphasized their connectedness to each other, to a prior tradition, and to a space of refuge and celebration in the midst of uncertainty.

Afro-Brazilian religion in the colonial era was often perceived by non-participants as *feitiçaria*. This seems to have been due to a couple of factors: a) the nature of many of its material manifestations—drums and dances, magico-pharmacopoeia, trance states, etc., and b) the challenge it implied to the dominant social, political, and ideological order. This designation would persist into the nineteenth century as an epithet for Candomblé as Afro-Brazilians continued to embrace the spiritual traditions created in the nexus of their experience of displacement and reconstitution.

4

"Dis Continuity," Context, and Documentation: Origins and Interpretations of the Religion

A variety of co-existent and co-influential African-based religious traditions were collectively known as Candomblé in nineteenth-century Bahia. This term, of Bantu origin, was used to denote the reconfigured rituals of many South Central and West African peoples present in the slave and freed population of the province. The Gunocô cult of the Tapas, the Voduns of the Dahomean Jejes, the Inquice and ancestor traditions of the Congo-Angola Bantus, the Orixá venerations of the Yoruba, and even, evidence suggests, some aspects of the Islam of Hausas, Yorubas, and other Sudanese Muslims were collectively gathered under the denomination Candomblé. In addition, creole Catholicism and indigenous Brazilian (Indian) traditions were important elements of Bahian religiosity in the period of Candomblé's formation. According to forensic physician Raimundo Nina Rodrigues, by the late nineteenth century, Candomblé and the Malê tradition (the Islam of West African Muslims in Bahia) were the two major African-based religious orientations of the Bahian population, and Islam was clearly in decline.[1] The development of Candomblé as a formalized religion in nineteenth-century Bahia was in many ways correlative to the formation of a nuanced, multi-textured, Afro-Brazilian collectivity in the capital city and the Recôncavo.

Due in large part to the pioneering research of Rodrigues in the late nineteenth and early twentieth centuries, it has been generally accepted that Yoruba influence was predominant in the emergence of Bahian Candomblé. In Rodrigues's view, the structure of the religion, its system of myths and rituals, its hierarchy, and its language reflected a comparatively superior Yoruba-based standard to which Africans of other ethnicities (and Brazilian-born blacks) "converted" because of the numerical and cultural dominance of Nagôs in nineteenth-century Bahia and because of the inherent weakness and inferiority of other African traditions, especially those of Bantu origin. Many in succeeding generations of students and observers of Candomblé, while eschewing Rodrigues's most blatantly racist biases, continued to focus their research and interpretations on the Yoruba role in Candomblé to the neglect of other elements. This Nagô-centered perspective on Candomblé's development was fed by two principal causes. First, the influence of Nagôs in nineteenth-century Bahia was unquestionably significant. Yoruba-speaking people were, by the 1830s, the largest single group of Africans in Salvador. And because the slave trade ended in 1850 they were never replaced in numerical dominance by a new wave of slaves of different ethnicity. Second, Rodrigues's late-nineteenth-century fascination with Nagô *candomblés* (and the prestige and primacy of his research) helped make these the standard by which the authenticity of other *terreiros* was judged. Furthermore, the stamp of approval of several generations of academics and observers supported the concerns for continuity and legitimacy within the Nagô *candomblés* themselves.

Ironically, Júlio Braga suggests that Martiniano Eliseu de Bomfim (1859–1943), a son of African *libertos* and a prominent leader in Bahian Candomblé, may have been instrumental in the development of the *pureza Nagô* ideal. Seu Martiniano, as he was respectfully known among Candomblé devotees, had been sent by his parents to study in Nigeria while still a young man. During his years in Africa he studied with Yoruba priests and upon returning to Bahia was well respected among Afro-Brazilians for his erudition and skill in Candomblé tradition. He was described by a number of scholars, including Braga, Ruth Landes, and Edison Carneiro, as having been immensely concerned for the return to an uncorrupted state of African authenticity in Candomblé ritual, especially once slavery ended and opportunities increased for black Brazilians to travel back and forth to Africa. In his youth, Seu Martiniano served as an informant to Rodrigues in the latter's studies of Bahian Candomblé; and as an older man he shared his insights with scholars and artists such as Landes and Jorge Amado, effectively influencing several generations of opinion makers.[2]

Recently, the work of anthropologists such as Yeda Castro, Vivaldo Costa Lima, Renato da Silveira, Beatriz Dantas; historian João Reis; and historian-practitioner Valdina Pinto has emphasized the multi-ethnic matrix from which Candomblé emerged, often highlighting the contributions of Aja-Fon and Bantu groups.[3] Silveira has suggested, in fact, that more significant than any measure of African-Catholic "syncretism" in Candomblé were pan-African syncretic formulations arising from the interactions of peoples of a variety of African ritual traditions.[4] These interactions underscored a shared foundational cosmology with adjustable external elements, engendering the flexibility that allowed the religion to survive and develop in an often hostile environment. In general, Afro-Brazilian religion was created out of inter-ethnic commonalties—those symbolic, ritual, and philosophical meanings which were shared by Africans from a variety of points on the continent.[5]

It is my sense as well that Candomblé, while evidencing significant Yoruba participation in its formation and development, is more fully understood as a pan-African and Afro-Brazilian synthesis. And while distinct "nations" of Candomblé had developed by the late nineteenth century—Ketu, Ijexa and Ijebu (all Nagô); Congo-Angola (Bantu); and Jeje (Aja-Fon)—these increasingly represented more ritual-liturgical than strictly ethnic-genealogical designations. Specific elements varied among the constituent traditions (liturgical rhythms, language, some rituals), but the complex of practices constituting Candomblé shared an orientation directed toward experiences of communion/community, refuge/resistance, and healing/redress. This shared orientation was perhaps the most significant factor in the syncretic process by means of which a variety of African traditions (both ethnically specific and pan-African/Afro-Brazilian) existed simultaneously as "nations" of Candomblé. This chapter examines the nature and variety of influences—ethnic-ritual, contextual, and documentary—affecting Candomblé's emergence as a structured, publicly recognized tradition. I discuss the presence of ritual elements from a variety of African ethnic and Brazilian sources; the context of West African numerical and cultural predominance among the nineteenth-century Bahian slave and *liberto* population; adaptations in the New World context; and problems and perspectives of the documentation of Candomblé's development. The discussion begins, however with a reflection on Candomblé's location within the larger tradition of Afro-Brazilian religiosity.

In his classic study *The African Religions of Brazil*, Roger Bastide wrote that the circumstances of Brazilian slavery generally prohibited the development of specific, continuous religious traditions among Afro-Brazilians. Bastide argued that for most of the colonial era, there was no formal continuum of Afro-Brazilian religiosity wherein a set of practices built concretely and consciously on what came before. Rather, he suggested, various manifestations arose—in "a chaotic proliferation of cults or cult fragments"—in certain times and places, only to disappear and be replaced by new forms as historical and sociological conditions changed. Accordingly, Bastide urged that the Afro-Brazilian religious forms of the present should not be seen as survivals of more ancient sects, but as "relatively recent organizations dating back no further than the eighteenth or early nineteenth century."[6]

For Bastide, one of the major developments in Brazilian history allowing for the emergence of Candomblé as a formalized and continuous religious tradition was the growth in the number of freed Africans in Bahia during the nineteenth century.[7] The increase was facilitated by the structure of urban slavery in Salvador. Based in the *ganho* system of labor, slaves in the city were afforded relatively greater mobility and independence than their counterparts on plantations. *Escravos de ganho* often lived and worked away from the constant, direct supervision of their owners and were able to maintain and develop important cultural, religious, linguistic, and affective ties with other blacks. Also important, the *ganho* system provided a means by which some Africans could eventually buy freedom. The *ganho* system was not a nineteenth-century innovation in Bahian slavery. However, the unprecedented numbers of Africans imported to the province between the 1790s and 1850 (and reflected in the ballooning population in the capital city as well as in the Recôncavo towns and plantations) increased the pool of *libertos*. As Bastide noted, and as the archival documentation overwhelmingly attests, African freedmen and freedwomen were tremendously important to Candomblé's emergence. *Libertos* constituted the leadership of Candomblé for most of the nineteenth century.[8]

While the historical evidence certainly corroborates Bastide's assertion of the role of freed Africans in the establishment of Candomblé, it seems necessary to temper somewhat his corollary statement that Afro-Brazilian religion was essentially discontinuous prior to the end of the colonial period. We may assume an essential validity to Bastide's perspective that the inherently and profoundly disjunctive experience of the slave trade and slavery was in a sense reflected in the forms of black religion in Brazil. Nonetheless, in the totality of Afro-Brazilian religious expression (despite the discontinuity of specific manifestations), there were certain elements shared among most, if not all, of the forms. It is important to recognize historical commonalties of consciousness or orientation within Afro-Brazilian religiosity. These continuities center particularly around certain aspects of the materiality of black Brazilian religion such as the use of specific categories of physical objects (such as percussion instruments, magico-pharmacopoeic aggregations, and the human body as the site of contested identity).[9] Continuities are also clearly visible in the orientation of Afro-Brazilian religion toward experiences of refuge, community, and healing.

Perhaps a more revealing perspective on the nature and meaning of "continuity" in the Afro-Brazilian religious experience may be gained by considering the concept of "dis continuity" created by philosopher and playwright George Houston Bass. Speaking of Afro–North Americans in particular and people of African descent in New World societies more generally, Bass developed the phrase-word "dis continuity" to simultaneously denote the apparently fragmented, diverse, and discontinuous nature of black culture while at the same time indicating a continuity based in the experience of and response to disjunction. For Bass, African American culture is profoundly based in engagement with historical experiences of slavery and racism that impose limits on certain kinds of structural development, but which then necessitate the emergence of alternative structures. By means of a Black English glyph ("dis" meaning "this") Bass indicated that within the apparent (and real) fragmentation which has characterized the experience of blackness in the New World, there is also a continuity founded in and riffing on the meaning of fragmentation itself.[10] Actually, Bastide's own reflections on the mutability of African-based religion in Brazil suggest a similar recognition of the continuity within dislocation. Afro-Brazilian religion, Bastide wrote, created new structures, new communities, in which to house its spirit. "Like a living creature, it secreted its own shell, so to speak. . . . Spirit cannot live divorced from matter, and if the matter is lacking, it creates a new kind."[11] Furthermore, Long suggests that an additional layer of signification in Bass's "dis continuity" includes the contemporary meaning of "dis" as "disrespect." That is to say that the continuity of African American history and culture is a continuity simultaneously present and also denied in racist ideology. The lack of regard in the dominant paradigm for black religious consciousness and black experience is, as Long says, "an ethical fact." And yet the "dissing" of black continuity, the dishonoring and disenfranchising of black humanity and of Africa, does not destroy the essential continuity. In fact, the African American continuum gains a particular meaning in its constant, creative tension with the oppressive structures of domination.[12]

What becomes clear from an analysis of the documentation of Afro-Brazilian religion in the colonial era is that most, if not all, of the elements central to nineteenth-century Candomblé can be seen in earlier forms of collective black religiosity in Brazil. Taking the seventeenth-century Bahian *calundu* described by Nuno Marques Pereira and the eighteenth-century *calundu* of Luzia Pinta in Minas Gerais as examples, we see an extraordinary similarity to descriptions of nineteenth-century Afro-Bahian religious forms. For instance, both of the earlier *calundus* involved the use of ritual dance and music for divination and for healing. A similar tendency was seen in the 1785 *calundu* in Cachoeira described by João Reis. Also, an 1807 reference to Candomblé in the Recôncavo district of Madre de Deus emphasized the combined roles of healer and diviner as central features of the leadership of Afro-Brazilian religious gatherings.[13] Very often these activities took place in an atmosphere where ritual dance—inducing an altered state of being—was an inherent element in the curing or divination process. Percussion instruments are mentioned in practically every historical description of collective Afro-Brazilian religion. While the actual instruments varied, the emphasis remained on a rhythmic, percussive sound and its use as a means to engender and regulate communication and relationship between human beings and the divine. In the case of Nuno Marques Pereira's *calundu* we see tambourines, drums, castanets, and *reco-recos* being used for ceremonies of divination and healing. In yet another instance from 1807, this time from the town of São Francisco, the Jeje *calunduzeiro* Francisco Dosû explained that he danced to drums in order to heal people who were sick.[14] Drums and rattles (*chocalhos*) were among the items most commonly associated with raided *candomblés* and the searched homes of Africans throughout the nineteenth century.[15]

Another continuity among Afro-Brazilian religious manifestations in the colonial and imperial period was the clothing and other decorative items with specific ritual uses. Again, the particulars varied across time and geography. In the testimony against Luzia Pinta, she was described as wearing strange clothing during ceremonies: "inventions in Turkish style," "costumes not used in this country," dressed "like an angel." In several cases of the police correspondence relating to Candomblé in Bahia, "clothing of Candomblé" was listed among confiscated items. An example comes from Quintas da Barra in the district of Victoria in 1858 that lists clothes and ritual implements associated with the iconic costumes of the Afro-Brazilian deities: three tin swords; nine lace [or lace-trimmed] ladies' pants; three woolen underskirts—one yellow, two green; two *tocados;* one apron; one feathered headdress; and six white bands [of cloth]—two with red silk thread and gold tassels trimmed in cowrie shells.[16] Clothing, beads, necklaces, and other ritual accoutrements were important means to mark alternative identity and sacred space in Candomblé as well as in many of the religion's antecedents in Brazil. Percussive music, dance, ritual clothing, healing, and divination are among the clearest examples of continuities among Afro-Brazilian manifestations from the colonial period to the present day. In addition, attempts to create and re-create community among human beings, to experience communion with the natural-divine world, to find spaces of refuge from trauma, and to resist one's own dehumanization have been at the heart of the meaning of Afro-Brazilian religion throughout its history. A more detailed discussion of these questions of meaning follows later in the text, but it seemed important to at least raise them here as part of a consideration of "dis continuity" within the black religious tradition in Brazil.

Recognizing the many similarities between nineteenth-century Candomblé and its seventeenth- and eighteenth-century precursors raises the question So what makes Candomblé unique? How is it different from earlier forms? Why was it able to survive when many of the others apparently did not? In order to approach a response to these questions one must hold in tandem an appreciation of the historical circumstance of the late colonial and imperial period in Bahia as well as an understanding of the nature and role of the documentation of Candomblé. I would suggest that the differences between Candomblé and earlier Afro-Brazilian religious forms have more to do with the exigencies of specific historical contexts and with issues of documentation than with any fundamental divergence of purpose and meaning.

As I see it, several interrelated aspects of historical context affected Candomblé's nineteenth-century development: a) the diversity of African influences upon which Afro-Bahian culture was founded; b) the unprecedented concentrations of Africans from the Mono-Niger region of West Africa in Bahia—and especially in the capital city of Salvador; c) the nature of urban slavery, urban freedom, and the ability of blacks to negotiate space and identity within their contours; and d) adaptations to New World circumstances. A final issue deals with the question of documentation and its role in the history and continuity of Candomblé. This is, in a sense, a meta-historical question, bringing us into engagement with the influence of the earliest records (characterizations of and commentaries about Candomblé and its origins) on the present construction of the religion's past.

Diversity of Influences

Until the end of the transatlantic traffic in 1850, the African community in Bahia experienced a constant state of re-creation as new waves of enslaved men, women, and children were regularly imported to the province. After the mid nineteenth century, Africans and African culture in Bahia (and in other parts of Brazil as well) entered more fully into the creolization process, creating the supportive structures for a collective Afro-Brazilian identity. In the same period, Candomblé was emerging as one of the most important institutions among blacks in Bahia for the reformulation of African ethnic identities and alliances into new resources of interconnection in a New World context.

South Central African (Bantu), West African (Nagô and Jeje), and Brazilian elements can be perceived as strata of Candomblé's structure; they may also be seen as elements of the chronology of the religion's emergence. Perhaps most evocatively, they represent central aspects of the rich intercultural matrix in which Candomblé developed, sharing influences on the religion in varying intensities at different historical moments. The multi-ethnic matrix from which Candomblé emerged is evidenced in the religion in a variety of ways. At a very basic level, the name itself gives us some important clues to the nature of the formation and meaning of the tradition. *Candomblé* is a Bantu term used to describe a religious form with strong West African structural components. Bantu-speaking people constituted the first large-scale source of enslaved labor in Bahia; their importation began in the early seventeenth century. In many regions of Brazil, Central Africans constituted a majority (or at least a large proportion) of slaves until the end of the colonial era.

Linguist Yeda Castro suggests that the Bantu cultural influence in Brazil is the deepest and most widespread among the many African ethnic groups who were represented in the slave trade. Most contemporary Brazilian-Portuguese terms denoting Afro-Brazilian dance, religions, and communal forms are of Bantu origin (*samba, lundu, batuque, quilombo, mocambo, calundu,* etc.).[17] Bastide, echoing anthropologist Arthur Ramos, wrote that the term "Candomblé" early in Brazilian history signified dance and musical instruments associated with blacks. Only later did the term come to refer specifically to religious ceremony.[18] Similarly, Edison Carneiro found that the word "Candomblé" descended from "candombe," which was a name given to a dance common among slaves on coffee *fazendas.* He agreed it was also a term used for drums.[19] While the association of the word "Candomblé" with dance and percussion is clear, Castro offers a more specific etymology. She writes that "Candomblé" is derived from the Bantu "kandombile," which means "prayer, veneration [*oração, culto*]."[20] Elsewhere, Castro and collaborator Guillherme A. de Souza Santos indicate an even more detailed linguistic genealogy for Candomblé: According to their investigations, the term originates from the Bantu "ka-n-dom-id-e", itself a derivative of "ku-lomba ku-domba-a" (to pray), which in turn comes from the proto-Bantu "kò-dómb-éd-à" (to ask the intercession of).[21] Hence, from its South Central African roots the term "Candomblé" is suggestive of a devotional attitude or activity. Interestingly, Nina Rodrigues noted in the late nineteenth century that devotees of the Yoruba "nation" of Candomblé considered the term to be one imposed from outside. They seem to have preferred another designation; unfortunately Rodrigues did not indicate what it might have been.

The earliest historical documentation of the term "Candomblé" in Bahia also suggests Bantu influence on the religion. An 1807 communication from one militia officer to another refers to a ritual community established on the lands of the Boa Vista Fazenda of the Herminigildo Neto Sugar Mill in the Recôncavo district of Madre de Deus, led by a young Angolan slave named Antonio. Antonio was captured and imprisoned and was identified in the document as "the president of the terreiro of candombleis." The reporting officer noted that Antonio was the leader despite his youth, that he was accorded respect from his fellows (of whom even the eldest were obedient to him), and that on the eves of saint's days he gathered large groups of people. The report also stated that Antonio called himself a diviner and a healer.[22] Although the documentation gives us no indication of the ethnic identity of those who participated in the candomblé, we know that in the early nineteenth century many of the gatherings of slaves and freedpeople were organized along ethnic lines. Furthermore, documentation from the police files of the State Archives of Bahia indicates that prior to 1850 most (though by no means all) candomblés were organized and frequented by African-born men and women.

Bantu-speaking people of a variety of sub-ethnicities continued to be an important presence in nineteenth-century Bahia, although their proportion among the province's slave and freed population was much reduced in comparison to what it had been in the seventeenth and early eighteenth centuries. West Africans of the Aja-Fon-Ewe ethnic and language groups (collectively known as Jejes in Bahia) were the most numerous immediate predecessors to Yorubas in the province; most were imported between the 1770s and the first decades of the nineteenth century. Documents on Afro-Brazilian religion in Brazil between the late eighteenth century and 1830 evidence a strong Jeje influence and a marked presence of Jejes among African spiritual leaders.[23] Records from 1785 and 1807 also suggest that the term "calundu" was used in reference to Jeje ritual practices.[24] In fact, it seems that "calundu" as a reference to Afro-Brazilian religion was falling out of usage at just about the same time as "Candomblé" was being used to describe a similar phenomenon. In 1807, a Jeje healer and diviner called Dosû was referred to as a "powerful calunduzeiro" in the testimony of his female companion as she was interrogated by police. This was the same year in which the term "Candomblé" first appeared in written documents as a reference to Afro-Bahian religion.[25] An 1829 raid on a large Candomblé ceremony in the *freguesia* of Brotas at Accú is reported by the local justice of the peace as having involved offerings to the "Deus Vodum" (Vodum God). The letter, directed to the provincial president, does not specify whether "Deus Vodum" was a term used by the Candomblé's participants themselves or whether it was an uncorroborated reference made by the local magistrate. In either case, mention of the Dahomean term for deity or spirit suggests that Jeje influence on the Afro-Bahian religious landscape was not insignificant.

Structural elements in Candomblé also suggest considerable Jeje contributions to the formation of the religion. The major instruments of communication between deities and devotees in Candomblé carry Jeje names. The three sacred drums of the Candomblé ritual liturgy are known as the *rum, rumpi,* and *lê.* Organization and stratification of *filhas de santo* in the initiation process is also described in Jeje terms.[26] Castro suggests that other key concepts in Candomblé owe their denominations to the Jeje language: the *peji* (sanctuary, the sacred space of the deity), *runco* (retreat space for initiating devotees), and *ajuntó* (personal guardian spirit). Finally, Castro writes that the structural model for initiations in Candomblé—a lengthy, group-based retreat of strictly restricted access within the *terreiro*—follows very closely the convent-style initiation process of assistants to Dahomean high priests.[27] These elements indicate that the Jeje consecration process may have been established in Bahian Candomblé prior to, or simultaneous with, Nagô structural elements in an experience of shared ritual development.

Observers and scholars of Candomblé from Rodrigues to the present have consistently noted the apparent dominance of Yoruba-identified peoples and Yoruba tradition in the religion. While an interrogation of the meaning of this dominance constitutes a later section of this chapter, historical documentation and the analyses of several generations of historians of Bahia have indeed established the predominance of Jeje and Nagô linguistic, cultural, and religious forms among slaves and freedpeople for much of the nineteenth century in Salvador. In a statement reminiscent of Peter Wood's description of eighteenth-century Charleston, South Carolina, artist and chronicler Manoel Querino claimed that during the period of the slave trade Bahia "was a veritable African Babel"—scores of languages were spoken among its inhabitants.[28] It appears that at various points certain languages emerged as a type of lingua franca among Bahia's blacks. In the seventeenth century and early eighteenth century, a Bantu-based language likely facilitated communication among the variety of Central Africans and their descendants who comprised the bulk of the slave and freed community at the time. Later in the eighteenth century, a Jeje or Jeje-Bantu mix likely served the same function. And by the 1830s, the Nagô language had become the form of common parlance among Bahia's blacks.[29] At the end of the nineteenth century, Yoruba still served as a common language among many of the former slaves and even some Brazilian-born blacks.[30]

In the 1890s Rodrigues identified major ritual elements of Candomblé in Bahia to be of distinctly Yoruba origin. While Yoruba exclusivity cannot be convincingly determined, a model of leadership hierarchy and ritual organization which Rodrigues defines as the Nagô standard was evidenced at Ilê Oxôssi, the influential Ketu *terreiro* community he studied, popularly known as Gantois. Rodrigues wrote that his description of the Gantois community, its physical structure, social organization, and annual liturgical festival was "an exact idea of what a fetishist temple in Bahia is."[31] Gantois was located in (what was then) rural/suburban Salvador atop a high hill. Access to the *candomblé* was difficult due to the steep and circuitous path leading from the valley road up to the *terreiro*. The principal building of the *terreiro* was a large tile-roofed house known as the *barracão*, where all of the public ceremonies in honor of the *orixás* were held. The building was divided into sections—the largest single area being that where the liturgical dances were held, its floor of beaten earth. Other smaller rooms, accessible from a hallway but normally restricted to initiates, were spaces sacred to the *orixás* and areas where ritual materials were stored.

Rodrigues explained the hierarchical organization of the *candomblé*, recognizable in its construction around the spiritual and temporal leadership of a mother or father of the saint (*māe* or *pai de santo*); honorary protectors and defenders of the community (*ogās*); and initiates, daughters and sons of the saint (*filhas* and *filhos de santo*), who incorporated in their bodies the living presence of the deities. Describing the ritual process and liturgical feast dances, Rodrigues enumerated the place of sacrifice, offertory foods, and the spectacle of the dramatic arrival and participation of the deities.[32] The hierarchy of leadership within the Gantois community followed a model inherited from perhaps the oldest recognized continually operating Nagô *candomblé* in Brazil (and the *casa matriz* of Gantois): Casa Branca.[33] In Rodrigues's estimation, the Nagô model, typified by the Gantois *terreiro*, was widely adopted by other "nations" of Candomblé. Although evidence suggests that non-Yoruba elements were present within the Nagô model itself, the late-nineteenth-century prestige of Yoruba *terreiros* recommends an appreciation of Nagô strength within the Afro-Bahian cultural matrix. Yoruba dominance of Candomblé tradition at the end of the nineteenth century has continued into the present day: Now much of the public discussion of the religion occurs using Nagô terminology, such that the Jeje *voduns* and Congo-Angola *inquices* are often "translated" into the equivalent names of Nagô *orixás* outside of the ritual setting of specific Candomblé "nations."

The presence of African Muslims in nineteenth-century Bahia and the ethnic connections between them and many of the participants in the Yoruba *orixá* tradition created opportunities for Islamic influence on the emerging tradition of Candomblé. Muslim leaders in Bahia, known as *malomis,* and later, *alufás,* were widely respected for their erudition, their literacy (many read and wrote Arabic), and their spiritual powers. These priests constituted an important bridge between Yoruba Muslims and worshippers in the *orixá* tradition because they were venerated as elders by both.[34] According to Paulo Fernando de Moraes Farias, there was a tendency among some in the Nagô community to make specific distinctions between Malês and *orixá* devotees. However, he asserts that the lines between the two groups were blurred by linkages of family, lineage, and ethnic solidarity.[35] Most of Bahia's Nagô Muslims had recently converted, either in Africa or in Brazil; and because Islam in West Africa was strongly permeated with traditional beliefs, there was likely in Bahia an openness between the two religions similar to that which had existed in Africa. For example, some priests of the *orixá* tradition in West Africa identified the white ritual garments of the Muslims, their discipline, and the abstemiousness of their rites with the *orixá* Oxalá and would send to the Muslim priests persons whose problems the divination process had identified as more likely resolved by Islamic wisdom.[36] In Bahia, one of the most important emblems of Oxalá is a long white cloth, called an *alá,* which is symbolically extended over the heads of the Yoruba faithful during certain ceremonies. The ritual use of water by Muslims in Bahia may have also been associated with the Yoruba *orixá funfun,*[37] and especially with Oxalá. The most important feast day of Oxalá, the Aguas de Oxalá, is an annual ceremony during which water is collected from sacred springs to replenish the ritual containers of the sanctuary. Connections between Oxalá and Muslims are also suggested in the shared taboos which devotees of both cults are required to follow, especially that of abstention from alcohol. Reis further reflects that Friday, the Muslim day of prayer, might, in the Brazilian context, represent another possible tie between Malês and the children of Oxalá. For Candomblé devotees, Friday is the day consecrated to Oxalá. Finally, the annual celebration of the washing of the steps of the Bonfim Church in Salvador, traditionally popular among Afro-Brazilians and "with its water and white clothing" in abundance, could be a ceremony of Muslim origin.[38] Farias implies the operation of Malê influences in Candomblé in his summary of the relationship between Yorubas and Muslims in nineteenth-century Bahia. "Malê identity and Nagô identity," Farias writes, ". . . imbricated—that is, they functioned as alternative idioms of unity, each partially superimposed on the other."[39]

The effect of Brazilian customs and Brazilian-born people on Candomblé's development cannot be overlooked. Indians (known as *caboclos* in both nineteenth-century Brazil and within Candomblé) appear to have been a source of magico-pharmacopoeic knowledge for Afro-Brazilians. In 1807 an elderly Jeje slave woman named Joanna was questioned by police about the contents of a little gourd she carried with her. The small animal bone, cowrie shell, small amount of powder, and single *fava de mato* (literally, "forest bean") were, she replied, given to her by a *caboclo* of the *sertão* called Antonio. Joanna declared that the items were for medicinal use—to prevent pains and to keep snakes from biting.[40]

The use of Brazilian Catholic institutions such as *irmandades* (lay confraternities) and devotions as a base for the maintenance and cultivation of African spiritual values and traditions was very common throughout the colonial period and into the first half of the nineteenth century in Bahia. The Barroquinha *terreiro,* for example, (precursor to Casa Branca) was established by Yoruba members of lay Catholic organizations. In the town of Cachoeira, the sisterhood of Our Lady of the Good Death was organized by black women as a kind of benevolent society—through which, among other mutual aid aspects, slaves could acquire the funds to purchase their freedom. This organization counted among its membership many women in the leadership of the Recôncavo town's Candomblé *terreiros.* At present, in the late twentieth century, the annual procession of the sisters of Boa Morte is a major attraction for enthusiasts of Afro-Brazilian culture as well as for devoted Catholics and Candomblé participants.[41]

Of course one of the most commonly cited Brazilian influences on Candomblé's development is that of the association with Catholic saints. While the nature and extent of the Afro-Brazilian juxtapositions of *orixás* and saints has been widely debated, many Candomblé communities recognized some level of correspondence or relationship (whether simply symbolic or a more profound identification) between the African spiritual forces and the spiritual personages of the Catholic church. In 1862, for example, Domingos Sodré, an African *liberto* who was the leader of a Candomblé in the *freguesia* of São Pedro, was accused of enticing slaves to steal from their masters so that they could make offerings in order to obtain their freedom. When police raided his house, they made special note of its use of space. The first area they encountered was an anteroom (*sala*) in which various paintings of saints and an altar were the principal furnishings. It was in the back rooms of his house that Sodré maintained "the mixtures, clothes and emblems of his superstitious traffic." The spatial configuration of Sodré's house suggests one of the most significant means by which nineteenth-century blacks may have used Catholic symbolism and imagery. In the front of the house (the public living room), were placed the representations of religious devotion and practice which were acceptable and comprehensible within European and elite Brazilian paradigms. In the hidden spaces, in the back rooms whose access was more restricted, more private, were the materials of African religiosity; the magico-pharmacopeic cures and the belongings of the deities.[42] As Rodrigues learned in conversations with Candomblé participants in the late nineteenth century, Africans and black Brazilians raised by Africans viewed "conversion" to Catholicism as a matter of juxtaposition of exteriorities. These blacks "conceived of their saints or orixás and Catholic saints as of equal category although perfectly distinct."[43]

West African Predominance

One of the major characteristics of Candomblé is the prominence of Yoruba and Aja-Fon structural, ritual, and linguistic elements. These West African ethnic groups entered Bahia as slaves on a large scale from the 1790s through the 1830s, arriving during a period of reinvigoration of the Bahian sugar industry which followed the late eighteenth-century revolution in Santo Domingo. Historians of Brazil and the African slave trade indicate four major cycles of forced African immigration to Bahia, roughly corresponding with the four centuries in which slavery existed in the colony and empire. According to Pierre Verger, the first cycle, which began in the second half of the sixteenth century with the establishment of the sugar economy in northeast Brazil, brought a majority of slaves from the Guinea coast, the region stretching from present-day northern Senegal to Sierra Leone. The second cycle, which began in the last decades of the sixteenth century, brought slaves from the Portuguese missions and factories established along the coast of West Central Africa from Cabinda to Benguela. Bantu slaves from these regions constituted the first large-scale contingents of Africans in many areas of colonial Brazil. The third cycle, known as the Mina Coast cycle, lasted from the early seventeenth century until around 1770, during which slaves to

Bahia were shipped mostly from a series of slave castles along the shores of modern Ghana. During this period, significant numbers of Ewes began to arrive in Bahia.[44]

During the final cycle of the trade in African slaves to Bahia, (also known as the cycle of the Bight of Benin), events in Africa played a pivotal role in determining the ethnic composition of Bahia's slave population. This cycle, which lasted from around 1770 to 1850, occurred during a period of tremendous turmoil in the Mono-Niger region of West Africa. In the early nineteenth century, the Muslim wars of expansion shook the northern sections of present-day Nigeria, forcing many Hausas into captivity; in the south, by 1835, the vassal states of the Oyo empire had rebelled and destroyed that Yoruba kingdom which had once dominated much of the area between the Mono and Niger rivers. The collapse of Oyo engendered a series of internecine political conflicts which lasted well into the second half of the nineteenth century and which displaced various Yoruba subgroups—Oyo, Egba, Ketu, Ijexa, Ijebu, Ondo, etc.—due to warfare, the resultant migrations, and enslavement. The Bight of Benin cycle of the trade to Bahia was characterized by the heavy presence of Yoruba peoples. Prior to the fall of the Oyo kingdom, few Yorubas had been among those African ethnic groups captured in the transatlantic trade. However, in the nineteenth century Yorubas, Hausas, and others from the Mono-Niger nation-states represented a majority of persons transported to the remaining slave-trading societies in the Americas, particularly Cuba and Brazil.[45]

Most of the Africans arriving in Bahia in the nineteenth century, then, were from ethnic and lineage groups which predominated along the coast of the Bight of Benin and farther inland.[46] Principal among these were Jejes from old Dahomey (present-day Togo and Benin) and the eastern regions of Ghana; and Hausas, Tapas (Nupes), and especially Yorubas from what is now Nigeria and eastern Benin. The Yorubas, called Nagôs in Bahia, shared a language, a culture, and a ritual tradition linking them all to an original ancestral homeland in the kingdom of Ifè. Although some Yorubas in Bahia were Muslim, most belonged to the *orixá*-based religious tradition which served the important role in both Africa and Brazil of establishing ritual connections among the various sub-ethnic divisions within the larger group.

Urban Slavery, Urban Freedom, and African Ethnic Identity

The reconfiguration of African and Afro-Brazilian traditions into Candomblé was particularly influenced by urban slavery, urban freedom, and issues of identity and space in the Bahian context. Slavery in Salvador made possible and necessary a stronger emphasis on ethnicity as a basis for identity than would have been operative in Africa. Africans arriving in Bahia in the first half of the nineteenth century most likely would not have immediately thought of themselves in terms of a racial identity. Their ethnicity and language would have been the initial markers of self-identification and were the bases for establishing social ties and work relations among their fellows in the new environment. However, as they moved into the race- and color-conscious system of Bahian society they surely gathered a sense of the limitations imposed on them due to their blackness, their status as slaves, and their foreignness. Therefore it became all the more important to find mechanisms to assert meaningful alternative forms of personal and collective self-definition. Blacks in Bahia found various ways to do this.

In Salvador, work groups of slave and freed men and women were often organized around ethnic alliances, as were the lay Catholic confraternities which sometimes helped enslaved members purchase their freedom. African celebrations on Catholic holy days were also often organized along ethnic lines, and slaves and *libertos* of the same ethnicity commonly spoke to each other in their own languages and referred to each other as "relatives" (*parentes*). Ethnic identity was important to Africans in Bahia and played a major role in the socialization of new slaves into an already existing community of blacks. Ethnicity, nevertheless, was not the only means of alliance, and inasmuch as it emphasized distinctions among the African population, it could be problematic for a more extensive pan-African unity. But especially in the urban milieu of Salvador, there were other elements present which suggested bases for community that included, but extended beyond, ethnic identity. Religion was one such element. And African *libertos* were the primary leaders of Afro-Brazilian religious communities throughout the nineteenth century.

The role of freed Africans was central to the development and establishment of Candomblé. While *libertos* endured varying measures of surveillance and harassment by police, restrictions on their livelihood, and the suspicions of non-African neighbors, they nonetheless used whatever means were at their disposal to create a life of relative autonomy for themselves. African freedpeople used the money they earned from their trades, transport services, and petty commerce to contribute to black institutions such as *irmandades* and *juntas de alforria* (manumission clubs) and were often able to buy or build small houses or to rent rooms in which to live. They often shared living spaces with each other and with compatriots who were slaves. Ties between freedpeople and slaves in Brazil (especially among Africans) remained vital; in work, ethnic alliances, collective organizations, street culture, and religious rituals, *libertos* and slaves found ways to create community across the boundaries of legal status. Furthermore, Candomblé became one of the spaces in which other boundaries—those of color and national origin— could also begin to be negotiated toward a more encompassing identity of collective belonging within the *terreiro* community.

Many of the references to Candomblé (and to other Afro-Brazilian religio-cultural manifestations) throughout the nineteenth century indicate that gatherings were organized along ethnic lines. A particularly detailed account of this kind of ritual organization was written in 1808 in the Recôncavo town of Santo Amaro. During the Christmas holy days, distinct groups of Africans assembled from surrounding plantations to celebrate their traditional dances and feasts. According to a local observer, Hausas and Nagôs were in one location together, Angolas in another, and Jejes in a third. Although there did not appear to be any tensions among the groups, they passed the several days of religious observance in spatially distinct celebrations.[47] Due to the organization and nomenclature of ethnic identity among Africans in Bahia, these "ethnically specific" gatherings almost certainly included the participation of people from several sub-groups within a larger ethnic-linguistic-geographic designation. The Nagô group, for example, may well have included people from Oyo, Ketu, and Ijexa states. These would have been men and women whose collective identity as Yoruba-speaking peoples developed more fully in the shared circumstance of Brazilian slavery than would likely have been the case in Africa. So the beginnings of a pan-African collective identity were present even in ethnically "specific" assemblages. Furthermore, the Santo Amaro account indicates that some larger inter-ethnic conjunction was occurring as well among the Hausas and Nagôs who represented the largest grouping. This example is instructive because it represents co-existing tendencies among Bahia's nineteenth-century black populations: that of ethnically "exclusive" identifications and that of more inclusive self-identities and collective identities.

The 1785 Cachoeira *calundu* offers another instance of inter-ethnic ritual convergences which also crossed the boundaries of status.[48] The police archives include numerous others; many of which emphasize the involvement of Brazilian-born blacks (*crioulos*) in the African-based ceremonies. While the documentation is not always clear about the specific ethnicity of participants, from as early as 1829 there are records noting the existence of *candomblés* where Africans and creoles participated together in ritual ceremonies. Significantly, even earlier, in 1809, a *quilombo* of fugitive blacks was documented on the lands of the Engenho Terranova near Santo Amaro in which "six Hausas, two Angolas, two crioulos, and two pretas" and perhaps as many as eight other blacks lived.[49] Such outlying communities of Africans and Afro-Brazilians were often spaces in which African values were consciously cultivated as a respite from the ideals and restrictions of the dominant society. The 1829 *candomblé* in Accú Brotas included a substantial number of *crioulas* in addition to many African-born women (*pretas*), and a few African-born men (*pretos*). The participation of the *crioulas* in an African-identified ritual practice was particularly disturbing to the local justice of the peace who recorded the raid on the *candomblé*. He seemed to believe the *crioulas* should have known better.[50] In 1843, an instance of Brazilian and African joint participation in a *"batuque de tabaque"* (drum-dance gathering) impelled the subdelegate of the *freguesia* of Victoria to write to the chief of police and request clarification on the penalties to be suffered by "sons of the country" (Brazilians) who were involved in such "diversions." The subdelegate explained his need for clarification "inasmuch as today batuques de tabaques which were used by Africans are substituted by native sons."[51] Later, in 1874, another report from Accú in Brotas related that Africans and *"pessoas do pais"* (people of the country; Brazilians) had gathered together over several nights for drumming.[52] These examples and others illustrate Afro-Brazilian religio-cultural gatherings as a space where African and *crioulo* identity coalesced in a shared ritual community.

Within the *terreiro* communities, extraordinary respect was accorded African spiritual leaders, African deities and ritual relations, and ritual activities based in African traditions. Given the tendency in Bahia's social and economic organization to consciously distance Africans from Brazilians and to associate slave status with ethnic Africanness and dark skin, the gathering of people of African descent in Candomblé was a striking rejection of the hegemonic ideal and an embrace of a radically distinct perception. Candomblé not only brought blacks of all shades and statuses (as well as more than a few whites) into a shared experience, a shared community; it also brought Africa into the heart of the Brazilian polity—in some measure, on its own terms. It appears nonetheless that while the experience of Candomblé was often a resource for creation of community which contributed to the variability of lines of demarcation between creoles and Africans in many instances, there were also attempts to maintain separate *terreiros*. Rodrigues quotes an elderly African woman in the 1890s as saying that she belonged to a *candomblé* of

Africans whereas another *terreiro* was composed of *crioulo* participants.[53] This may have been a reflection of tendencies within the dominant social structure to emphasize and encourage distinctions between the groups. It may also have been an effort on the part of Africans to maintain a degree of ethnic distinctiveness which was central to their sense of who they were. Also, by the late nineteenth century, the changing demographics of the African presence in Bahia were affecting Candomblé's membership and leadership. Brazilian-born men and women took on greater responsibility for *terreiros* which had been founded by Africans; and in some instances Brazilian-born participants went on to found their own communities.

Over the course of the nineteenth century several types of gatherings were associated with Candomblé. Most often, rituals were held at private homes that belonged to freed Africans and usually to leaders of Candomblé communities. Other meetings were held in open spaces in the hills and woods surrounding the city. Sometimes these outdoor ceremonies functioned in conjunction with a *quilombo,* as appears to have been the case in 1826 when a *candomblé* was discovered during a police raid on an outlying fugitive community in the Urubú woods of Pirajá. At other times, the outdoor convergences were organized as celebrations of the death of important individuals, as in 1843 in Cabula when some 2,000 people gathered for the funeral of an African spiritual leader. These ritual gatherings were regularly held on the eves of holy days and saint's days, when slaves and free people were usually assured a respite from their normal work schedules. For example, in Pojavá (a rural area at the edge of the city of Salvador), a *candomblé* was investigated on Easter Sunday in 1862. According to the chief of police, a gathering of Africans occurred in the same place every year during that holiday.[54]

While Candomblé ceremonies can be identified as African and Afro-Brazilian physical and ritual spaces, they were African language spaces as well. A newspaper account cited by Pierre Verger, for example, indicates that in 1835 a group of Nagô men and women were gathered in a house in the Rua de Paço, dancing and singing in their language in a ceremony of Candomblé.[55] Also, Nina Rodrigues's account of ceremonies at the Gantois terreiro in the 1890s indicates that Yoruba was used as a liturgical language there. Africans in Bahia at the time of the Malê Revolt (1835) often called each other by their African names and sometimes were unaware of the Portuguese Christian appellations by which their fellows were known to others.[56]

The meetings for Candomblé rituals—whether in the confines of a small house, the rented rooms of freed Africans, in the sparsely populated areas on the outskirts of the capital, or in the plazas and plantations of Recôncavo towns—were (re)affirmations and (re)creations of communal ties; (re)formations of community. Participants risked imprisonment, physical punishments, and (especially in the case of freed African leaders) even deportment. In these ritual spaces, Africans and Afro-Brazilians joined to cultivate and celebrate their deities, their rites of passage, and, ultimately, their more complete and more human identities.

Adaptations

It is from the perspective of pan-African synthesis within the New World context that the character of Candomblé is perhaps most distinct from its West and South Central African origins. One of the major innovations of nineteenth-century Candomblé was the gathering of many deities, sometimes of varying ethnicities, under one roof. When we look at the West African foundations for comparison, we see that *orixás* and *voduns* were generally venerated individually according to family, lineage, or regional tradition. For example, Oxum, a water deity, was worshipped principally among the Ijexa and Ijebu peoples. She was also said to have close ties to the kings of Oshogbo, where her river has its source.[57] Oxalá-Obatala, as oldest of the *orixás*, was associated most directly with Ifè, the ancestral city of Yorubaland.[58] Oxôssi, a hunter deity, was especially venerated in Kêtu.[59] In some cases a category of workers would cultivate the patron spirit of their profession, such as the Yoruba ironworkers who venerated Ogum, god of metal, for example. In Candomblé however, it was clear by the late nineteenth century, and most likely well before, that deities from several ethnic groups (or sub-ethnic groups) were being cultivated together in a single *terreiro*. While each *orixá, vodum,* or *inquice* had his or her own ritual implements, sacred "living" space, rites, and specifically consecrated devotees within a given *candomblé*, all the divinities were ultimately the collective responsibility of the *terreiro,* and they were often jointly invoked in a single ceremony.

The observations of Rodrigues at the Gantois *terreiro* in the 1890s and the oral traditions regarding the organization of Barroquinha/Casa Branca earlier in the century suggest that the development of a community of spirits was certainly a central feature in Candomblé's emergence.[60] Given the limited time and space available to enslaved and freed Africans living and working within the structures of nineteenth-century Bahian society, the congregation of deities into a single sacred space certainly facilitated the realization of rites, the sharing of ritual knowledge, and the growth of pan-African and Afro-Brazilian collective identity among devotees. However, the historical evidence points to the possibility of a pan-African ritual synthesis in Afro-Brazilian religion in Bahia even prior to the nineteenth-century development of Candomblé. Though it is difficult to unequivocally assert when and where deities or spirits of different origin began to be cultivated in some communal form, there are signs which can at least suggest the conditions for and possible manifestations of such ritual conjunction.

In her study of late-nineteenth-century *candomblés* in Cachoeira and São Felix, historian Fayette Wimberly describes the *terreiro* of Yoruba priest Pai Anacleto Urbano de Natividade, who cultivated both Yoruba and Jeje deities in his ritual community. The central post in his *terreiro* (around which ceremonies would have been conducted) was a hog plum tree, dedicated to Iroko, a tree-deity of Dahomean origin. A sacred serpent (also a Jeje divinity) was associated with the nearby spring which Anacleto and his followers used for purifying baths. Anacleto himself was devoted to Omolu, a Jeje-Nagô deity of illness and healing.[61] At perhaps an even more basic level, a process of integration of symbolism, rites, and cosmology can be inferred from multi-ethnic participation in religio-cultural gatherings. *Calundus* like the one discovered in 1785 in Cachoeira, (where Jejes of various sub-ethnicities lived and worshipped together with at least one non-Jeje individual as well) lend themselves to such an analysis. The formation of black confraternities —whose ethnically based membership included many subgroups and, in some cases, inter-ethnic participation—also provided the interaction necessary to foster the development of pan-ethnic reformulations of specific African traditions. In fact, Silveira suggests, this is precisely what happened in the emergence of the Barroquinha Candomblé. The Bom Jesus dos Martírios confraternity and Boa Morte devotion, based in the Barroquinha chapel, are the organizations whose members are credited with founding the Barroquinha Candomblé community. These two lay Catholic associations had predominantly Yoruba membership. But even among the Yorubas there were individuals who represented several distinct regional kingdoms.[62] Other Catholic church structures also influenced the development of collective cult traditions in Candomblé. Reis suggests that some of the impetus for bringing the cultivation of many deities into one physical space may have come from African observations of Catholic veneration practices—the gathering of many Catholic saints in a single chapel or church.[63] Furthermore, both Yoruba and Catholic traditions share the paradigm of an all-powerful, albeit somewhat inaccessible Supreme Being and a kind of second tier of very approachable intercessors (saints and *orixás*) who are capable of maintaining close relationships of accompaniment, assistance, and obligation with their devotees.

Police correspondence offers further indications of multi-deity cultivation within a single ritual community. Ritual clothing and sacred implements in a variety of colors, materials, and configurations discovered within a single house or *terreiro* point to the veneration of a collectivity of spirits. Each deity is traditionally associated with a specific color or pattern in dress and with particular ceremonial accessories constructed of distinct materials. The discovery of several specific styles of ceremonial costume in a single ritual community could suggest that devotees of more than one deity participated jointly in the rites. The items discovered at the 1858 *candomblé* in Quintas da Barra offer an example. The tin swords may have been associated with Ogum or another warrior divinity who dances with a sword of white metal. The yellow and green underskirts may have belonged to deities associated with those colors, perhaps the *orixás* Oxum (yellow), Oxumarê (yellow and green), and Oxôssi, Ogum, or Ossain (shades of green). The feathered headdress is a common symbol of the *caboclo* spirit but may have alternately been associated with Oxôssi or another of the hunter deities.[64]

The question of collective cultivation of deities in nineteenth-century Bahian Candomblé is complicated even further by the fact that among many African peoples there occurred cultural borrowings generations prior to the slave trade. For example, because of military and social interactions in the Mono-Niger region of West Africa, some deities were shared among Yoruba and Dahomey peoples; also, specific traditions honoring ancestors were held in common among Yorubas and the neighboring Nupe (or Tapa) groups. Wimberly describes the trio of Jeje-Mahi deities—Nana Buruku, Omolu, and Oxumarê (a mother and two sons)—which had been widely adopted by Yoruba-speaking people in Africa and were venerated throughout the Mina Coast and Bight of Benin before being brought to Brazil during the slave trade by devotees. Though the names of the three deities varied from region to region, they represented an ancient mother figure (Nana Buruku), a deity of epidemic illness and healing (Omolu), and a snake god embodying continuity and male/female complimentarity (Oxumarê). This kind of pre-slavery inter-ethnic ritual connection highlights the essential compatibility of many traditional African religious orientations. Shared worldviews aided the creation of a variety of forms of pan-African synthesis within colonial and imperial Afro-Brazilian religion and culture.

In his description of the development of maroon societies in the Americas, anthropologist Richard Price emphasizes the relative ease with which blacks of various origins were able to formulate collective communities. Price explains that in his many years of studying black fugitive communities he has "always been struck by the earliness and completeness of the 'functional integration,'" especially given the diversity of cultures from which the enslaved Africans came to the Americas. He attributes this "remarkably rapid formation . . . of whole cultures and societies" to the previous development of local slave cultures and to "a widely shared ideological commitment to things African."[65] What Price refers to generally as a commitment to "things African" seems more fully explained by the existence and maintenance of common foundational elements of an African worldview or orientation. The issue Price raises of the role of previously existing local slave culture is also important for an examination of the development of nineteenth-century Candomblé. The Bahian slave community was exceptionally dynamic because new sources of labor were captured from varying points on the African continent throughout the several cycles of the slave trade to the region. Slave culture in colonial and imperial Bahia reflected the influence of the many groups of Africans and their descendants who formed Brazil's black population. Over the centuries of slavery, those groups changed and the particular forms of Afro-Brazilian culture reflected the changes. Nevertheless, a consideration of Candomblé's development within the context of existing local traditions returns us to the influence of South Central and Mina Coast Africans (the two largest single groups of involuntary migrants to Bahia prior to the nineteenth century) and to the Brazilian-born *crioulo* community.

In its adaptations to the New World context, Candomblé gathered numerous deities into a single ritual space. Other significant readjustments from the African matrix included choices about which deities would be venerated. Some aspects of the choices had to do with the regions and kingdoms from which African slaves were brought to Brazil. The widespread cultivation of Xangô among Candomblé devotees is likely related to the importance of the Oyo empire during the final cycle of the Bahian slave trade. Many of the West Africans who arrived in Bahia from the late 1700s through the mid-1830s—when Old Oyo was finally destroyed—were either members of the Oyo kingdom or peoples who been subjects of that largest Yoruba dominion. Xangô, the fabled fourth king of the Oyo dynasty, was the patron *orixá* of the kingdom, and a priestess (Iya Nassô) charged with the ritual care of his altars is credited as one of the founders of the Barroquinha *candomblé* community in the first third of the nineteenth century.

Another example of the influence of African regional deities in the configuration of Candomblé is that of the cultivation of the *orixá* Oxôssi. Although widely worshipped in Brazil and Cuba, veneration of this deity has virtually disappeared in West Africa. A brief examination of this story may illustrate the kinds of transformations which occurred in *orixá* practice in the Americas. Oxôssi is popularly known in Bahian Candomblé as the "king of Ketu." Ketu, one of the larger Yoruba kingdoms by the end of the eighteenth century, was almost completely destroyed by Dahomean troops in the terrible fighting which accompanied the dissolution of the Oyo empire. Many of Ketu's inhabitants were captured and sold into slavery in the early nineteenth century. Because this period coincided with the rise of sugar production in Cuba and the northeast of Brazil, it was to these areas that many of the devotees of Oxôssi were destined.[66] Yorubas from Ketu were integral to the establishment of the Barroquinha *terreiro* and the co-existence of Oyo and Ketu deities (and possibly others as well) represented an important instance of pan-ethnic cultivation of African cosmic energies in Candomblé.

In addition to issues of regional origin, the changed position of Africans vis-à-vis agricultural work is reflected in the deities of Candomblé. Bastide noted that among the major divinities cultivated in Bahian Candomblé there are none specifically related to farming or agriculture, although most of the Africans who arrived in Brazil came from societies for which agriculture was a central aspect of the social and economic structure.[67] It seems that the transition from largely self-sufficient farm labor to enslaved plantation work did not invite the intercession of deities associated with the fecundity of crops—the very productivity of the land was associated with the condition of black slavery and the increased wealth of oppressors. Notwithstanding this change, cultivation of medicinal plants was maintained due to the role of African spiritual leaders as healers, Candomblé communities as spaces of healing, and the use of magico-pharmacopoeia in ceremonies for physical and spiritual curing.

Bastide further remarks that among the most commonly cultivated spirits of Candomblé are the energies associated with justice (Xangô); militancy and protection (Xangô and Ogum); and order, arbitrariness, and communication (Exú).[68] This observation is all the more significant considering the repression Candomblé suffered throughout the nineteenth century (and well into the twentieth) and the manner in which the dominant society associated Afro-Brazilian religion with noxiousness and marginality. Candomblé's membership drew largely from the most vulnerable and most scorned segments of the society (slaves and *libertos*, Africans, *crioulos*, and some *pardos*). Participants were frequently described as uncivilized, ignorant, or criminal in their nature.[69] Deliberations of local town councils, edicts from provincial presidents, and orders from chiefs of police to their subordinates show a pattern of repression of African and Afro-Brazilian religio-cultural gatherings in Bahia during the nineteenth century. *Calundus, candomblés, batuques, sambas,* and other African meetings were all repeatedly denounced, prohibited, and punished.

The emphasis on the cultivation of protective, intercessory, and militating spiritual energies seems to have been an important adaptation in the New World context. In further commentary on Exú, Roger Bastide gives an example of changes in the roles of deities from Africa to Brazil. "Exú as god of cosmic order," Bastide writes, "was almost eclipsed by Exú the guardian of the social order, charged with averting [or, perhaps, *subverting*] the disorder of a society based on racial exploitation" (insert is mine).[70] When we reflect on Bastide's observations and recall the experience of the Indians in the Bolivian highland mines (see Chapter 3, note 43), we can perhaps interpret both the figure of the Tio (Uncle) or "Devil in the Mines" and the *orixá* Exú as acknowledgments of the arbitrary as a central aspect in the lives of exploited and enslaved people. The Devil in the Mines in one case and Exú in the other represent the principle of uncertainty. Both are ritually beseeched for aid in the manipulation of unpredictable circumstances. For the Tio, offerings are left at the entrance of the mines. For Exú, the streets and crossroads of Bahia become the sacred spaces in which slaves and others act out their apperception of the insecurity of their social position and make gestures toward the resolution of circumstances in their favor. Candomblé devotees in the nineteenth century commonly made recourse to public offerings to the deities. One case from 1854 seems by virtue of its elements to have been particularly destined for Exú. A *crioulo* named Valeriano was arrested on the evening of June 7 in the Rua da Valla carrying "a clay plate with a dead chicken and palm oil" which he intended to deposit in the street.[71] Chickens and palm oil are common ritual offerings for Exú and as a public space of transcourse the street (especially a crossroad) is the preferred location for the *ebôs* (offerings) to this divinity.[72]

In the cases of both Exú and the Tio the need to acknowledge and propitiate the element of ambiguity suggests: a) recognition of the arbitrariness of power and violence as a central feature in the lives of the oppressed, and b) attempts to negotiate a way through uncertainty and terror. The *orixá* Exú is an intermediary force associated with order as well as arbitrariness and with communication between human beings and the spiritual world. Like the other *orixás,* Exú was present in Yoruba traditional cosmology before the development of Candomblé in Brazil. The value of Bastide's insight is that it indicates that Exú's relative importance among the *orixás* may have grown in the colonial environment where the need to negotiate extraordinary uncertainty was central. The Tio, or Devil in the Mines, on the other hand, seems to be more wholly a New World product; a symbolization (or fetishization, in the Pietzian sense) of a spirit of evil which did not exist in pre-encounter Andean understandings of the cosmos. The Tio, in the words of Michael Taussig, is a representation of the contradictions "born from the structure of caste and class oppression that was created by European conquest."[73]

Another important point of connection can be seen between the Bolivian Tio, Exú in Bahia, and the inclusion of prayers to Lucifer in the construction of *mandingas* in colonial Portugal and Brazil. In all of these cases, human beings whose labor was ruthlessly commodified and exploited appealed to the representation of the arbitrary and of "evil" in their attempts to negotiate power relations with the dominant order. The proletarianized Indians of the mines and the African slaves of Bahia and Lisbon recognized in their own social location the sacrosanctity of capital for their oppressors. People whose being was objectified and signified in the most base economic-utilitarian terms came to understand and experience the primacy of capital and exploitative labor relations within the dominant paradigm. The slaves and the mine workers experienced in their own bodies the consequences of colonial and contemporary "devil worship" (worship of money, worship of capital over human life). That is to say, they recognized in very visceral and immediate ways that their oppressors were in league with some nefarious force that privileged exploitation for capital over humane relations. And in both the tin mines and the streets of the Portuguese capital and the Brazilian northeast (the sites of their exploitation), black slaves and Indian workers acted out ceremonies of recognition of the Devil's strength in modern economic, social, and political relations.

In addition to transformations in the *orixás* themselves, Candomblé communities created or adapted hierarchical functions to address their needs for protection and influence. The role of the *ogã* in Candomblé, an honorary title for certain male members who are responsible for providing the *terreiro* community with material/financial support, protecting the community from harm, and negotiating with outside authorities on the community's behalf, seems to have been created in response to the tremendous vulnerability of *candomblés* and their members. Although most of the divinities of Candomblé are of African rather than New World origin, their form, function, and meaning took on new contours in the historical and psychic space of the slave societies of the Americas. But if the *orixás, voduns,* and *inquices* were African born, they came to share the space of their spiritual communities with indigenous and creole Spirits as well. Sheila Walker indicates that one of the distinguishing characteristics of Afro-Brazilian religion is the cultivation of creole divinities, especially Indian (*caboclo*) and black slave (*pretos velhos*) entities.[74] While the incorporation of these spirits is more widely associated with Afro-Brazilian traditions of more recent origin (such as Umbanda), the acknowledgment and invocation of *caboclos* has been an important ritual element in Bahian Candomblé since at least the end of the nineteenth century.[75] And the research of Juana Elbein and Deoscóredes dos Santos demonstrates that the cultivation of ancestral energies (the *Eguns*), while ceremonially distinct from Candomblé, dates at least from the mid nineteenth century on the island of Itaparica, where it continues today.[76]

Documentation and Interpretations of Candomblé

The relationship between documentation and the interpretation and continuity of Candomblé is another issue rooted in the religion's nineteenth-century history. For most of the century, what documentation existed on the religion was in the form of police reports, trial records, ecclesiastical inquests, brief contemporary newspaper accounts, and the observations of diarists. As I noted earlier, these records were generally concerned with recording Afro-Brazilian practices as exotic (diarists), or more often as criminal, anti-religious, or subversively uncivilized behavior (police and ecclesiastic authorities). Especially in the case of police and Inquisition sources, the records document actions and policies which were disruptive of Afro-Brazilian religious traditions. The documents indicate that authorities regularly conducted raids against black religio-cultural gatherings, often breaking or burning any ritual items they discovered and jailing participants or impressing them into military service.[77] Police searched the homes (and confiscated or destroyed the belongings) of free Africans who were suspected of fomenting rebellion and encouraging "superstition" among their enslaved fellows.[78] They arrested individuals for transporting or depositing *candomblé* offerings in the streets of the city. Anyone accused of being a *feiticeiro* was singled out for special investigation and harassment;[79] and if African-born, could be subject to deportation. And, at the behest of slave-owners, police and militia forces hunted and punished runaway slaves who sought refuge in Candomblé communities.[80]

In spite of their biases, or indeed because of them, these sources are often rich in detail about many of the material aspects of the religion: the clothes people wore; the times and places in which they met; the kinds of ritual objects they used; and the ethnicity, color, and class status of participants. Also, this kind of documentation reveals valuable information about how Candomblé devotees negotiated the cultural and political structures of the society in order to create and protect the space of their religion. Thus, records that were intended to document the repression and control of Candomblé were sometimes able to suggest mechanisms which enabled the religion's continuation and development. These records, by and large, however, have not been well utilized in the reconstruction of Candomblé's development in Bahia. More commonly known, and more accessible, have been the works of twentieth-century scholars and observers who built their commentaries on a foundation laid by Raimundo Nina Rodrigues.

In the 1890s, Rodrigues published the first academic study of Candomblé.[81] Focusing on the most prestigious Nagô terreiros, he began a process of recording ritual and historical interpretations based on the experience (and his perception of the experience) of Yoruba-identified Candomblé groups. Rodrigues and the phalanx of physicians, anthropologists, sociologists, and artists who followed in his wake have been particularly influential in the documentation of Candomblé's history and in interpretations of that history. The oral traditions of the more prestigious ritual communities have often served as a basis for the interpretive work of scholar-observers. As time has passed, the written interpretations of the oral histories have become part of the histories themselves, adding not only to the status of particular Candomblé terreiros but, at a certain level, also enabling and legitimizing limited ideas of continuity and authenticity.

Anthropologist Beatriz Dantas has written extensively on what she sees as the subtly manipulative and elitist emphasis among professional scholars of Candomblé on pureza Nagô, that is, Yoruba purity.[82] This emphasis originated with Rodrigues's late-nineteenth-century studies, in which he developed a kind of hierarchy of value among the African cultures represented in Brazil. He held that the Yorubas—because they maintained a complex mythology of relations among the orixás—were more intellectually advanced than other African groups. In Rodrigues's estimation, the Nagô pantheon, with its apparent equivalencies to Catholic saints, aided in the conversion of pagan Africans to Christianity. In contrast, the "unreconstructed fetishism" of more "backward" Indian and African tribes, as well as that of some *crioulos* and *mestiços,* was indicative of their lesser mental capacities.[83]

Rodrigues's perspective viewed non-Yoruba communities as undeserving of serious scholarly attention because of their inferiority and "impurity." For example, the inferiority of Bantu *candomblés* vis-à-vis the Yoruba standard was supposedly related to the more acculturative trend within those communities, evidenced by greater inclusion of indigenous Brazilian (Indian) elements in ceremonial practice. Rodrigues's bias was carried through more or less consciously in the work of many of the most able and most prolific observers. Manoel Querino, Arthur Ramos, Edison Carneiro, and Roger Bastide were among those whose influential writings tended to privilege the Candomblé communities they viewed as most "authentically" African. This tendency has had the effect of pointing the research and documentation of Candomblé in a certain limited direction, which may, unintentionally, have created blind spots to the exploration of a more multi-sourced interpretation of the origins of the religion. It seems to me, for example, that a perspective which emphasizes the significance of slavery and its creolizing or Americanizing effect on the African body (personal and collective) will suggest analyses of Candomblé which focus more on the development of a pan-African black Brazilian tradition of alternative orientation than on a search for "uncorrupted" African origins in the religion.

Various aspects of historical circumstance and documentation have worked together as essential elements in Candomblé's continuity. The ending of the slave trade in 1850 and the abolition of slavery in 1888 meant that the Mono-Niger West Africans (and especially the Nagôs) were the last major arrivals and the culturally dominant African group in Bahia. The influence of the Yorubas and their West African neighbors was not superseded in Bahia by a new wave of blacks with distinct origins.[84] The Yoruba language was, even at the end of the nineteenth century, a kind of lingua franca among the various African ethnic groups present in Salvador and the Recôncavo. But in the years after 1850, in the absence of a constantly renewing African community, Candomblé became an increasingly creole phenomenon. Nevertheless, many Candomblé *terreiros* have tried very consciously and pointedly to hold on to a sense of their Africanness (although the meaning of that "Africanness," for participants and vis-à-vis the larger society, is not the same in 1999 as it was in 1899).

It has been the legacy of West Africans—in particular Jejes and Nagôs (coupled with the influence of academic observers who found the Nagô *terreiros* most appealing for study)—which has determined the standard by which many of the prestigious and apparently oldest Candomblé *terreiros* judge their own authenticity. Faithfulness to Yoruba and Aja-Fon traditions (or at least to conceptualizations of these traditions) is at the heart of the meaning of continuity in these *terreiros*. But although Bantu or Congo-Angola *candomblés* may have borrowed substantial elements of structure and ritual from the West Africans whose culture dominated Bahia's black communities in the nineteenth century, there is much to suggest that they also contributed significantly to the cultural matrix out of which Candomblé emerged. In the religion's nomenclature, for example, and in some of the earliest documents referring to Candomblé and to a pan-African presence in outlying fugitive communities there are distinct signs of Central African influence. Perhaps a less "Nagô-centric" bias in the scholarship of Candomblé might open our understandings of the tradition to an even wider resource base and help us appreciate the role of the religion in the development of new and complex identities of the African diaspora.

5

The Nineteenth-Century Development of Candomblé

When Nina Rodrigues began publishing his findings on Afro-Brazilian religion in the 1890s, he provided the first full descriptions of Candomblé as a practice, as a value system, as an orientation. And by the time Rodrigues was observing *terreiro* communities and interviewing informants, Candomblé had fully assumed the form and structure by which it would continue to be recognized at the end of the twentieth century. Although most earlier police documents give us only intimations and fragmentary descriptions of the ceremonies, ritual relations, worldview, and material culture of Afro-Brazilian religion, we are able to recognize many of the central elements of present-day Candomblé within the partial commentaries offered by *subdelegados* (subdelegates), *capitães mores* (rural militia leaders, often responsible for capturing fugitive slaves), *pedestres* (patrolmen), *chefes de policia* (chiefs of police), *tenentes do quartel* (barracks lieutenants), and other police and military officials charged with restricting, and often charged with destroying, Afro-Brazilian religio-cultural manifestations.

From an examination of the extant literature and from research in the police correspondence from 1800 through 1888 it appears that the term "Candomblé" was one of several used to denominate African-based religio-cultural manifestations that involved the gathering of groups of people for drumming, dancing, and other ritual activities. "Calundu,"in the seventeenth and eighteenth centuries, "batuque," "tabaque," and, beginning in the second half of the nineteenth century, "samba," were other terms used to denote drum-and-dance assemblages of Africans and Afro-Brazilians in Bahia. "Calundu" and "Candomblé," however, seem to have been used more exclusively to refer to forms of African-based cultural expression with specifically religious components.[1] Although the bulk of the archival documents reflect the language and perspective of the police authorities who created them, one is able to see in the few direct statements of observers and participants that these terms were also used by the general populace and, more important, by participants themselves.

Because of the lack of uniformity of terms in the archival documentation, I developed a set of basic criteria for ascertaining which activities and characteristics described in the records most strongly indicated a relation to Candomblé. These were: a) drums and drum-dances; b) ritual paraphernalia, such as other musical instruments (especially percussion instruments and metal bells or gongs), figurative representations of the deities, votive offerings, specially constructed clothing and accouterments of the deities, beads and cowrie shells, and magico-pharmacopoeic elements such as herbs, roots, bones, and medicinal decoctions; c) divination; d) healing; and e) seclusion—gatherings held outdoors in distant and/or wooded areas where access was difficult; also meetings held inside a house, as opposed to street gatherings. The issue of seclusion is not a straightforward one. Many ritual activities of Candomblé were purposefully conducted clandestinely both to avoid detection and repression and because of their sui generis secretive nature. However, the public space of the street was also a site of ritual action— sacrificial offerings were often left at crossroads or in the paths of persons whose behavior was to be influenced. There was a good deal of permeability between the "sacred" and the "secular" in black street gatherings in nineteenth-century Brazil. Therefore, particularly as I examined the question of location as a possible indicator of Candomblé, I tried to take into consideration as many other elements as possible to arrive at a determination.

I identified ninety-five documents from the period 1800 to 1888 which appeared to describe events related to Candomblé. Of these, sixty-five were specific enough in their characterizations that I could determine with some certainty that they described Candomblé activities. (In the analysis below, these sixty-five documents are referred to as the "positive" documents. The other thirty documents I refer to as the "probable" documents.) The analysis examines patterns in the composition of gatherings in terms of the legal status, occupation, gender, ethnicity, and race/color of participants. I also looked for patterns of locality—specific districts and sites in Salvador and the Recôncavo where gatherings were held. In addition, I was interested in knowing who were the leaders of Candomblé communities—both in terms of race/color, ethnicity, and gender, and in terms of behavioral comportment. Finally, I tried to look at all of these variables over time—choosing the periods 1800 to 1850 and 1851 to 1888 as two points of comparison in order to get a sense of changes which may have been influenced by an increasingly Brazilian-born black population in Bahia in the period after the end of the slave trade.

From the outset, it is important to note the challenges and biases of the archival materials. At one level, an anti-African and anti-Candomblé bias might be assumed in the documents because they are police records (and a few newspaper accounts largely based in police reports) related to illegal activities. While this is certainly true in a general sense, a close reading of the documents quickly indicates the complexity of comportment and perspective among police, judicial authorities, and Candomblé participants themselves vis-à-vis Candomblé ceremonies. The question of police collusion in or misinterpretation of Afro-Brazilian religion and the issue of the various means Afro-Brazilians used to negotiate religio-cultural space will be taken up further in Chapter 7 where I discuss the theme of networks. Suffice it to say, for now, that the documents themselves suggest the interracial and cross-class relations which formed an important basis for Candomblé's development and survival in the nineteenth century and beyond. It should also be remembered that evidence of Candomblé entered the police record either by means of complaints, denunciations, and accusations of wrongdoing or in response to generalized orders from the chief of police or other local authorities to periodically search the dwellings of Africans. When secrecy and discretion (or negotiation and evasion) were maintained, as appears was generally attempted, there was nothing to report. Finally, those individuals whose names appeared in records of raids on Candomblé ceremonies were those who did not evade capture and/or those who were actually arrested. In some cases, certain participants were not imprisoned—specifically whites and occasionally *crioulos, pardos,* and even some Africans.[2] Often the nature of information supplied about individuals involved in Candomblé was scant and varied from case to case. Names, legal status, gender, and origin were the most commonly repeated particulars. Even so, the majority of cases provided only a very general description of the participants (for example, "a great number of Africans" or "25 people, male and female"). Occasionally, occupation, age, and specific African ethnicity were included as descriptors; unfortunately this detail was not uniformly supplied in the records.

Nonetheless, the data available is generally sufficient (and occasionally more than sufficient) to give a sense of the activities of Candomblé communities, the nature of leadership and participation, and the areas in which ritual gatherings were held. What emerges is a picture of a community of people of various legal statuses, colors, and origins whose leadership through the end of slavery remained overwhelmingly African born and predominantly male; while the composition of those who participated—always preponderantly black—became increasingly Brazilian born over the span of the century. Women maintained a majority of between 60 and 65 percent among those involved in the religion's activities during the years of this study, and the documentation suggests that between 1850 and 1888 they came to form close to 44 percent of the leadership.[3]

Of the 65 positively identified documents, just over half (33) gave no specific indication about the origins or color of participants in ritual gatherings. Sixteen gatherings (24.5 percent of the total) were comprised of Africans—one of these was a Nagô *candomblé*, another referred to an assembly of Cabindas, and the other 14 did not specify the ethnicity of the Africans present. These 16 were all composed entirely of slaves or of a mixture of slaves and *libertos*. Another 16 (24.5 percent) were mixed *candomblés:* four involved Africans, creoles, and *pardos;* four were composed of Africans and creoles; three were described as "Africans and others"; two were composed of *pretos, pardos,* and *brancos;* and one described the participants as "various persons." The mixed gatherings usually included people of all legal statuses, although the four *candomblés* of Africans and *crioulos* involved only slaves and *libertos*.

Discounting the 33 documents which included no clear indication of origin or color of participants, the analysis suggests that 50 percent of gatherings were all African and 50 percent were comprised of Africans and Brazilians together. If the additional 30 documents that fell into the probable category are included in the tally, the percentages do not change substantially. Of the total 95 records, 49 indicated the ethnicity or color of participants. Removing the other 46 documents and enumerating only those 49 which indicated ethnicity and/or color of participants, 22 (45 percent) were composed entirely of Africans while 27 (55 percent) were composed of both Africans and Brazilians.

An analysis of the 65 positively identified documents by period suggests that participation in Candomblé communities in the nineteenth century became increasingly mixed as the importation of Africans stopped and the population of Brazilian-born blacks rose. Thirteen documents from the period 1800 to 1850 indicate specific ethnic or color identifications of participants. Of the 13, 69 percent suggest gatherings of only Africans and 31 percent suggest the joint participation of some combination of Africans, *crioulos* and *pardos*—with one case including *brancos* as well. Again, the all-African gatherings were composed of slaves or slaves and *libertos* while the mixed gatherings generally included people of all statuses (slave, freed, and free), although once more we see the pattern of African and *crioulo* assemblages including only slaves and *libertos*. For the second half of the century, 19 of the positively identified documents indicated ethnicity and/or color of participants. Of that number, 7 (37 percent) were all African while 12 (63 percent) were mixed African and Brazilian. It appears to be the case that over time association in Candomblé ceremony moved from being a largely African phenomenon to being more completely Afro-Brazilian.

In contrast to the changing ethnic and racial composition of participants in Candomblé, leaders were mostly African throughout the nineteenth century. It was only after 1850 that creole leaders began to outnumber African leaders, and then only by a slight margin. The most dramatic change in the character of leadership over the course of the century was the increased number of women. From 1800 to 1850, of the 17 people positively identified as leaders of Candomblé, 15 were men (88 percent) and 2 were women (12 percent). Eighty-eight percent of the leaders from this period were Africans—most were *libertos*, although one was a slave; the legal status of three African men was not clear. Two creoles were identified as leaders, both men. From 1851 to 1888, however, among the 24 individuals identified as leaders, 10 were women and 14 were men. Africans constituted 83 percent (20 people)—13 men and 6 women. Eleven of these were *libertos;* the legal status of the others was not mentioned in the documentation, although it may be inferred they were also freedpeople. Of the 24 leaders, in addition to the Africans, there was one *crioula,* one female slave, and two other females of unknown ethnicity, color, and status. In summation, for the period 1800 to 1888, Africans represented 85.3 percent of the leadership of Candomblé, creoles represented 7.3 percent, and another 7.3 percent was comprised of individuals whose ethnicity and color were unknown.[4] Men accounted for 68.5 percent of the leaders and women accounted for 31.5 percent. The percentage of male leaders for both pre- and post-1850 periods rises slightly when the probable documents are included in the calculations: During the period 1800 to 1888, men constituted 70.5 percent and women 29.5 percent of the leadership. This is likely due to the fact that the probable records include more street-based *batuques,* which evidence a higher participation of males because males were predominant among *ganhadores* and other street-based workers.

As I suggested earlier, the use of police documents as a resource for examination of the characteristics and development of Candomblé carries certain inherent biases. For example, Africans were considered more likely Candomblé participants and leaders than were *crioulos* and *pardos*. Candomblés, *batuques,* and *tabaques* were seen by the dominant sectors of Bahian society as African phenomena—at least until midcentury. So *crioulo* leadership may have been less noticed by police and accordingly less represented in police records. Especially after the Malê Revolt of 1835, Africans were specifically targeted for house searches and intensified surveillance. In one case in 1859, an African *liberto* healer-sorcerer held Candomblé meetings at the house of a *parda* woman—perhaps in the hope that her less suspect status would afford some protection for the gatherings. (The fact that this case is known however, is evidence that police authorities did discover the meetings. The *liberto* leader was deported to Africa.)[5] The predominance of African leadership is corroborated by late-nineteenth- and early-twentieth-century observers and in the oral traditions of present-day Candomblé communities—as well as in the historical analyses of Verger, Bastide, Reis, and others. It is in fact in the last decades of the nineteenth century and the first years of the twentieth that the Brazilian-born children and grandchildren of Africans begin to take over the direction of Candomblé *terreiros* in significant numbers.

The characterization of women in the archival documentation and suggestions as to their roles in Candomblé communities create further complexities in an analysis of leadership. In several cases, women were described in a manner which could be construed to either imply that they were auxiliaries to male *curandeiros-feiticeiros* or that they were leaders in their own right. However, in such cases the documentary record emphasized the ultimate leadership of the males. In one instance, two couples shared a living space in the attic of a house in the Sé district. Meetings of Africans were held at their home, and one of the men, a shoemaker, was identified as a *curandeiro de feitiçarias* and diviner who was "constantly sought by Africans, *crioulos*, *pardos* and even whites of both sexes." Although the two women and the second man, a sculptor, were not specifically indicated as having leadership roles, it seems conceivable that as permanent residents in the house and companions of the ritual leader they may also have had responsibilities within the religion.[6] In another case, ritual instruments and other materials were found in a house shared by a Mina *liberta* and her Nagô female slave; although when police investigated, a Cabinda man claimed that the objects (two drums—one large, one small; three small tin bells; horns painted red; and a wooden cross) belonged to him and that he used them in dance-gatherings of his fellow Cabindas on feast days, such as that of Senhor do Bomfim.[7] Because of the quality of *axé* with which ritual instruments would be imbued—if indeed these were items used in Candomblé—it seems most likely that persons of some recognized responsibility would be entrusted with their proper care. If we take such women into consideration as part of the leadership base of Candomblé, the percentages of male and female authorities for the period 1800 to 1850 become 68 and 32 percent respectively, and the final tally for the entire period of the study becomes 61 percent male and 39 percent female.

Among those persons whose names and/or genders are noted in the documentation of activities positively related to Candomblé, women represent 61.2 percent of the total number of 309 individuals over the 88-year period. Again, as in the leadership statistics, that percentage falls when the probable documents are also taken into account. Then, women account for 54 percent of those individuals listed in police records while men account for 45.5 percent. (Two children are specifically counted in one document; in other cases, they are simply mentioned without specific count.) In the period 1800 to 1850, 53 females and 29 males were specifically identified from police documents positively related to Candomblé—65 percent and 35 percent respectively. From 1851 to 1888, the numbers are 136 females, 81 males, and 2 children—59.9, 39.2, and 0.9 percent, respectively.

In the police documentation, *candomblés* were discovered in most districts of the city of Salvador as well as in several Recôncavo towns— specifically, Cachoeira, São Felix, São Francisco do Conde, and Madre de Deus.[8] The location of Candomblé gatherings in the city of Salvador corresponds particularly to areas with high concentrations of *liberto* residents and to rural areas. For most of the nineteenth century, the Bahian capital was divided into ten urban *freguesias* (parishes or districts). These were Sé, Nossa Senhora da Vitória, Nossa Senhora da Conceição da Praia, Santo Antonio alem do Carmo, São Pedro Velho, Santana do Sacramento, Santíssimo Sacramento da Rua do Passo, Nossa Senhora de Brotas, Santíssimo Sacramento do Pilar, and Nossa Senhora da Penha. (In 1871, an eleventh urban *freguesia* was created when Nossa Senhora das Mares was carved from Penha.) Most of the older *freguesias*—Sé, Conceição, São Pedro, Santana, and Passo—were located in the central area of the city; the commercial neighborhoods of the *cidade baixa;* and the civil, religious, and monarchical administration buildings of the upper city. These were also the earliest settlements (together with Vitória) and the locations of some of the oldest residential structures. The other *freguesias* were of a more "suburban" character—the location of *roças* (small farms) and fishing communities. An additional ten rural *freguesias* lay at the outside edges of the urban and suburban districts of Salvador. These too were locales of *roças* and of larger plantations as well as extensive uncultivated *mato* (woods or forest).

Residential patterns in Salvador did not generally assume an appearance of racial segregation. In one *freguesia,* on one block, a wealthy white merchant might live in close proximity to a free *pardo* bureaucrat and several free *negros de ganho* or artisans might share an adjacent living space with slaves. Nevertheless, the population of *libertos* was concentrated in a few of the urban *freguesias.* This seems to have been due to the fact that many *libertos* were involved in some form of commerce (street vendors, transporters, artisans) and the central *freguesias* were the ones where most commercial activity occurred. Also, *libertos* tended to form alliances with their fellows and with slaves with whom they often shared occupations, living space, and Candomblé community. These forms of connection may help explain the congregation of *libertos* in specific areas of Salvador. According to Mattoso's examination of testaments of freed slaves, the majority of freedpeople living in Salvador had their dwellings in the following districts, in order of prominence: Santo Antonio, Santana, Conceição, Sé, and São Pedro.[9] Among the Candomblé communities identified in the police documentation and located within Salvador's city limits, twenty-eight (50 percent) were found in these five *freguesias.* The archival records suggest that the more suburban of the urban *freguesias*—Santo Antonio, Victoria, and Brotas—along with Pirajá (a rural district of the capital city bordering Santo Antonio and Penha) and Sé (a central urban *freguesia* with a large *liberto* population)—were the areas most commonly cited as locations of Afro-Brazilian religious activity within Salvador. Forty-two (75 percent) of the positively identified Candomblé activities identified within the city limits occurred in these five districts. The archival records thus indicate that in Salvador, rural districts and the *freguesias* with high concentrations of African *libertos* were the areas where Candomblé ceremonies were most commonly held.

In the districts of the Recôncavo, plantation slaves were the most common participants in Candomblé. But in urban Salvador people arrested in *candomblés* and other forms of Afro-Brazilian drum-and-dance gatherings represented a wide variety of occupations. Among those listed in the archival documentation were: a variety of *ganhadores* and street vendors, laundresses, domestic servants, a shoemaker, a sculptor, cabinetmakers, tailors, a cook, soldiers, stonemasons, a butcher, a fish-seller, a public-illumination worker, a gravedigger, carpenters, barbers, and a goldsmith. Material objects related to Candomblé were identified in raids on gatherings and in the homes of Africans. Many of the items were destroyed by police—some were broken, others burned. Among the objects listed in various documents were: large and small gourds holding ritual ingredients; cowrie shells; powders; ground-up roots; animal skulls; copper coins; wooden sculptures; bottles, vases, and pots of herbal decoctions; a live snake; dried frogs; percussion instruments (especially drums and rattles); *figas;* beads and beaded necklaces; ritual dolls; and a wide variety of ritual costumes that included decorated clothing, tin and wooden swords, belts, and headdresses.[10]

Furthermore, the documents illustrate a variety of activities occurring within the context of Candomblé communities: initiation rites (*fazendo santo*); drum-and-dance ceremonies of invocation of deities; divination; magico-pharmacopoeic healing; ritual offerings and *despachos* (special offerings to Exú); refuge for slaves and efforts to obtain freedom; resistance to police harassment; storage of ritual items of the deities; and storage of the personal belongings of participants. The sites of Candomblé ceremony were not only ritual centers but were also the homes of priests, priestesses, and participants; they were infirmaries; and they were places of social gathering for the Afro-Brazilian community. In this wider context Candomblé's meaning as a space of alternative orientation becomes most clear.

6

Healing and Cultivating *Axé:* Profiles of Candomblé Leaders and Communities

Candomblé in nineteenth-century Bahia was a complex of interrelated elements and experiences composing an Afro-Brazilian orientation to ultimate meaning. Its predominantly African-born leaders and their African and Brazilian-born constituents created responses to an existential situation of extraordinary personal and collective disaggregation and oppression. Central to these responses were the conjoined emphases of healing and cultivating *axé*.[1] In fact, in many senses these particular elements could be understood as dual aspects of a single phenomenon—that of maintaining "right relationship" between human beings and among humans, the natural world, and the community of Spirits.

African leaders of Candomblé communities were instrumental in efforts to address the imbalances occasioned by the experience of New World slavery. These imbalances were understood in physical, social-political, ecological, and spiritual terms and their remedies often took a variety of factors into account. This practice had its roots in traditional African understandings of the causes and cures of illness. As scholar of African religion and philosophy Kofi Opoku writes, in traditional African societies "both the organic and spiritual aspects of disease are taken into consideration" when a cure is sought. The perspective is based in the understanding that human beings are "a compound of material and immaterial substances, which makes the maintenance of a balance between the spiritual and material . . . a condition for sound health."[2]

Nineteenth-century police records and newspaper accounts refer repeatedly to the dual role of Afro-Brazilian religious leaders, known in the parlance of the time as *curandeiros* (healers) and/or *feiticeiros* (sorcerers). In a society where university-trained medical doctors and pharmacists were few and far between, African and Afro-Brazilian healer-sorcerers served as physicians and as conduits between human and natural/divine energies. Pai João, an African living in the Recôncavo town of São Felix, for example, was accused in 1874 of "divination, drawing the devil out of the body, curing, etc." and a warrant was issued for his arrest. Especially disconcerting to the police authority who filed the report against Pai João was the fact that people of some status and respectability were among the African's clients.[3] While Rodrigues noted that recourse to black healer-sorcerers was widespread among Bahia's general population in the nineteenth century (albeit often surreptitious), it appears that especially in the Recôncavo region—outside the capital city—where the dearth of medical doctors was greatest, *curandeiros-feiticeiros* were often the principle caretakers of the health of the region's inhabitants, including wealthy landowners and their families.[4]

These individuals were generally held in great esteem by other black Brazilians. Karasch writes that in nineteenth-century Rio, black religious leaders commanded the respect and fear of all: "Often of African birth, they were the priests, diviners, herbalists and healers, imams, mediums and leaders of their people."[5] Their work was essential to the life of Afro-Brazilian communities and to the creation of alternate spaces of black being. Candomblé leaders and *terreiro* communities used a variety of measures in the process of healing personal and collective imbalances, cultivating life force, and creating an alternative orientation to meaning. These included the following:

> • *The establishment of new forms of relationship emphasizing a distinct and collective African-inspired identity.* This was effected through initiation, the structure and hierarchy of Candomblé leadership and participation, respect for *terreiro* leaders, and mutual support among Candomblé members. Also, the establishment and cultivation of ritual relations between deities and devotees helped create the basis for a new understanding of family and lineage among blacks in Bahia. This process and the concomitant development of pan-ethnic alliances among Africans helped replace blood linkages which had been severely dislocated by the slave trade and by the practice of slaveholders who disregarded black family ties.

> • *The use of cosmic forces and their material manifestations in redressing the disequilibrium represented by slavery.* The prior discussion of *feitiçaria* in colonial Brazil and the profiles following here demonstrate that Afro-Brazilian religion was centrally concerned with finding means to bring some measure of "right relationship" into the exceptional imbalance of the master-slave dynamic. The use of ritual, magico-pharmacopoeic means to alter the extreme inequalities of power in colonial and slave-based societies must be understood as a principal form of black resistance to slavery in Brazil.

•*A close attention to the physical, psychic, and spiritual needs of Candomblé participants.* Theologian Dwight Hopkins emphasizes "knowing about oneself and
taking care of oneself" as part of the slaves' understanding of God in Afro–
North American religion.[6] Similarly, Candomblé—in divination, initiation,
and a variety of other forms of ritual and relationship—represented a space
for the discovery and cultivation of connection to the divine. Among the
major roles of Candomblé in nineteenth-century Bahia was that of remind-
ing blacks of an alternative, ontological identity based in intimate, reciprocal
relationship to cosmic forces.[7] This identity inherently and profoundly contradicted the identity assigned to blacks by the dominant society. Additionally, Candomblé represented a space of rejuvenation. Escaped slaves sought
refuge in *terreiros,* and people who were ailing came to be treated for the
variety of distresses causing their illnesses.

•*Making room for joy in resistance.* Hopkins further articulates the idea of a
"theology of pleasure" in Afro–North American slave religion.[8] In comparison, a similar emphasis can be seen in the spaces of nineteenth-century
Candomblé and in Afro-Brazilian religio-cultural manifestations more generally. The music and dance of ceremony functioned not only to invoke and
celebrate the deities but also to provide a space of pleasure, transformative
pleasure, for participants. In the 1808 Christmas gatherings in Santo Amaro,
African slaves came together in various ethnic congregations to feast and
dance in the days of respite occasioned by the holiday. When "in the greatest
intensity of their dance" the Yorubas and Hausas were admonished by a local
prelate and ordered to disband their gathering, they refused to obey and
defended their right to joy. The slaves responded to the priest "with less
decent words and finally they told him that their masters had the whole week
in which to enjoy themselves and that they [the slaves] had in it one day only
and for him to go away."[9]

All of the above elements of Candomblé may be understood as
means to healing, the cultivation of *axé,* and the creation of alternative
orientations in the context of a slave-based society. The invocation, ritual
feeding, and embodiment of Spirit in Candomblé ceremony served to
bring the generative and transformative power of deities into the community of devotees, such that spiritual energy could benefit those who
were in need and could be increased and acknowledged as a renewable
resource. In a reciprocal manner, the attentions of devotees to the divinities helped ensure the continuation of a cycle of relationship—an inter-
dependency between the human community and the community of
Spirit. The profiles gathered here offer insights into the organization
and functioning of early Candomblé communities, a sense of the commitments and concerns of leaders and participants, and glimpses of the
repression *terreiro* members suffered over the course of the nineteenth
century. They also reinforce the role of Candomblé as a generative force
in the alternative orientation of Africans and their descendents in Bahia.

Profiles

The *Quilombos* and the *Calunduzeiro*

The town of São Francisco sits on the east bank of the Santo Amaro River which feeds into the north end of the Bay of All Saints. It was the first Recôncavo city founded after the capital, Salvador. In the heart of the Bahian sugar-growing region, cane was its principal commerce in the early nineteenth century. The town boasted a large, ornate mother church and the buildings of the municipal council and the district jail were situated at portside. Prisoners in the São Francisco jail suffered not only the normal privations of confinement, but also the plagues of *maruins,* clouds of tiny, virulent mosquitoes which bred in the swampy pools of salt floodwater formed along the river's banks by the vagaries of the tide.[10]

The Recôncavo jails were busy in 1807. The governor of Bahia, João Saldanha da Gama, had ordered the extinction of the many *quilombos* which surrounded the region's settlements. He authorized local *capitães do mato* to conduct raids in the hills and woods, confiscate incriminating evidence such as weapons and items of *feitiçaria,* and to assault, imprison and/or send into forced labor the individuals found in the illegal outlying communities. Saldanha da Gama, better known as the Conde de Ponte, understood the *quilombos* as an important alternative space for blacks in the Bahian Recôncavo. He blamed the existence of these fugitive communities for slave indiscipline and frequent escape, describing them as

> innumerable assemblages of . . . people who, led by the hand of industrious charlatans, enticed the credulous, the lazy, the superstitious, those given to thievery, criminals, and the sickly to join them. They lived in absolute liberty, dancing, wearing extravagant dress, phony amulets, uttering fanatical prayers and blessings. They lay around eating and indulging themselves, violating all privileges, law, order, public demeanor.[11]

Quilombos were spaces where slaves, *libertos,* and other marginalized people took refuge, however temporary and assailed, in order to (re)-create an environment where they were able to rest their overworked and castigated bodies, a place to tend to their needs for physical and psychic healing. African healer-advisors were frequently present in these make-shift communities.[12] These men and women were sought not only for their medicinal and curative abilities but because they were also a source of connection to African deities and ancestral traditions. In fact, the co-functions of physical healing and cultivation of relation to African spiritual energies were the common marks of Candomblé's leadership in the nineteenth century. The African *curandeiros, feiticeiros, pais e mães do terreiro,* and the *crioulos* who followed in their wake practiced an understanding of healing as the adjustment of discordant relations—physical, spiritual, ecological, and social-political. Their prescribed remedies were often a combination of appeal to cosmic principles (*orixás, voduns,* etc.) and the application of extensive knowledge of a pharmacopoeia that contained African, indigenous Brazilian, and Old World European elements.

In April 1807, several *quilombos* on the outskirts of the city of Salvador were discovered and attacked by armed troops. A month later, in the urban districts of the city itself, a rebellion of slaves and freedpeople was planned to occur during the Corpus Christi festivities. With foreknowledge gained from a slave who denounced the plans, the governor ordered the encirclement and search of the suspected house. A meeting was interrupted, a cache of munitions found, and although a few of the conspirators initially escaped, thirteen people were eventually punished for their participation in the conspiracy. The two men identified as leaders—one a slave and one a *liberto,* both Hausas—were executed.[13]

Later still, in June and July, twenty-one black men and women were imprisoned in the São Francisco jail under suspicion of conspiracy, participation in *quilombos* and other gatherings of blacks, and for the possession of "suspect" items. A report of interviews with the prisoners, conducted by local *capitães do mato* and forwarded to the governor, indicates that fifteen of the prisoners were slaves and six were *libertos.* Most lived on plantations in the vicinity of São Francisco and the town on the other side of the river, Santo Amaro. There were fourteen men and seven women. All but two of those arrested were African born, and the two Brazilians—*crioulas*—were married to African men.

Among the São Francisco prisoners was a freed Jeje man called Francisco Dosû, or simply Dosû. He was arrested in the slave quarters on the Paramerisso sugar *engenho* where it seems he was staying temporarily with an acquaintance, as he did often while traveling throughout the Recôncavo. Dosû's permanent residence, on the Garogaipequena *engenho,* was shared with his companion, Maria Francisca, also Jeje. Dosû was widely recognized as a healer and spiritual leader. A "great calunduzeiro," in the words of Maria Francisca, he was sought by people of all colors and status, male and female, for counsel and for healing. Asked to name the people who consulted with him, Dosû declined, saying that he didn't recall the names other than that of a *crioula,* Euzebia, who lived in the town of São Francisco and who, in the company of the town notary, José Anacleto Pinheiro, would visit him on the Garogaipequena place when he was staying there. Other times, Euzebia sent Pinheiro on horseback to bring Dosû to her house, where he would reside for weeks at a time. Once, when she was suffering with a great swelling in her stomach, Dosû cured the woman with roots. And, he explained, in a show of gratitude, Pinheiro "treated him well and gave him some gifts." Perhaps in response to a question about his participation in drum-and-dance gatherings, Dosû told his interrogators that he "frequently danced drums so as to heal." And in her own testimony, Maria Francisca elaborated, declaring that Dosû "has traveled around to heal, and is for this summoned from throughout the Recôncavo. . . . [H]e dances drums and on these occasions many people make offerings—flasks of wine, *aguardentes,* money, chickens live and cooked, and many other gifts." The police had in their possession a box of wasps, roots, and the skulls of male goats which they presented to Dosû during the questioning asking if the objects belonged to him. He answered affirmatively and his affirmation was seconded by the later testimony of his companion. As he completed his statement, Dosû emphasized again that he traveled widely in the Recôncavo as a healer and that he in fact stayed for a time in the house of the notary he had mentioned before, José Anacleto.[14]

Dosû and Maria Francisca's ignorance or selective recall of the names of most of his clients suggests an important element of Candomblé's nineteenth-century life. Association with persons of some status—particularly whites—was often a means by which communities and leaders sought to protect themselves. Euzebia, a Brazilian-born black woman, was well remembered by Dosû and Maria Francisca, but it seems that the approbation of her boyfriend—the town notary, a white man—was envisioned as especially useful evidence of Dosû's acceptability. Other blacks, who perhaps did not share Euzebia's intimate association with a person of unquestionable status (who himself had benefited from Dosû's services) were not mentioned. Their names were forgotten as much for their own safety as for the fact that they would not have been able to vouch for Dosû's respectability, since their own was in question or denied.

Dosû and Maria Francisca's testimonies are illustrative of many of the central aspects of Candomblé leadership in the nineteenth century. First, Dosû was an African-born man who was able to obtain the limited freedom of *liberto* status. Either through their own industry or through the combined efforts of a group of supporters, African religious leaders were often able to achieve manumission in Bahia. While the number of freedpeople in Brazil was proportionately higher than in some other slave societies, such as the United States for example, it is important not to overestimate the ease of self-purchase or the frequency of gratuitous manumission by slave-owners. Katia Mattoso estimates that in 1819 about 2.75 percent of Salvador's slave population received manumission. In 1839 and 1840 the percentage rose to 4.04 percent and in 1869 and 1870 6.62 percent of the slaves were freed each year. According to Mattoso, the acceleration was related to Bahia's worsening economic situation and to the gradual disintegration of slavery in the Brazilian northeast.[15] It is generally understood that *alforrias* (manumissions) were more common in urban areas than in rural zones.[16] Female slaves were freed more often than males, lighter-skinned blacks more often than darker-skinned blacks, *crioulos* more often than Africans, older slaves more often than younger, and domestic slaves more often than agricultural workers. The fact that Dosû, an African-born male in the Recôncavo region (where most workers were involved in agricultural labor), could secure his liberty was not an insignificant accomplishment. In any case, regardless of gender, color, age, or situational proximity to masters, black slaves who achieved manumission most often did so by paying for their freedom with cash earned and saved through years of extra labor in addition to the ordinary tasks required of them by their owners. Many also had the assistance of *irmandades, juntas de alforria,* and networks of relatives and friends who could lend or give monies toward the purchase of freedom. *Liberto* status, as tenuous and contested as it often was in Bahia, provided a basic level of independence and a sense of self-determination which seemed an essential element in the work and personalities of many Candomblé leaders. Furthermore, the increasing proportion of freedpeople in Bahia as the nineteenth century progressed helped ensure an enduring foundation for Candomblé.

The explanation that Dosû "danced *tabaques* so as to heal" underscores the use of music and movement as elements of transformation in Afro-Brazilian religious ceremony. It also emphasizes the interconnection between healing and the cultivation of relation to cosmic energies. The ritual use of drums in Candomblé, as in *calundu,* is particularly important as a means of communication, invocation of the presence of Spirit, and transformation of the quality of being in any given physical or psychic situation. As Rodrigues wrote, music in Afro-Brazilian religion is the means by which the "state of being in-the-saint" (possession) is created.[17] Dosû danced to the sound of drums in order to transform himself or to transform his milieu, or both. In any case, as with Luzia Pinta, his goal was to effect a qualitative change in order to cure. E. Bolaji Idowo suggests that there is an intimate association between religion and medicine in traditional African societies. According to Idowo the proper consecration of the healing implements (human and natural) is presumed necessary for efficacious cure.[18]

The element of Dosû's work which both he and his companion emphasized most strongly was healing and advising. In fact, it appears that for this *liberto*, being a *calunduzeiro* was his primary employment. From Maria Francisca's statements we learn that Dosû danced *tabaques* at large gatherings where a variety of offerings were brought. Certainly participants consumed many of the items and others were likely kept by Dosû as payment for his services. But the objects listed included materials commonly used in offerings to Aja-Fon (and other West African) deities. Chickens in particular, notes Suzanne Preston Blier, are identified with religious sanctification and spiritual empowerment. Goats too, the skulls of which Dosû maintained in his possession, are important elements in Fon, Ewe, and Yoruba ritual. Goats serve as a "primary symbol" for empowerment objects in the Fa divination system of West African Vodun and related rites, their skulls and fur appearing frequently on Vodun ritual sculpture.[19]

Most of the Africans listed in the archival documents related to Candomblé were referred to solely by their Portuguese names. Dosû is an important and interesting exception. Bastide and Herskovitz noted that Dossou or Dosû was one of the names of King Agadja who reigned in Dahomey at the end of the eighteenth century. It was also a name given to the child whose birth followed that of twins.[20] Given that Dosû is identified as a Jeje freedman, his name further corroborates his origin among Dahomean people and assists in the attempt to interpret the bases of his work as a healer-sorcerer. That Dosû was publicly known by his African name also suggests a strong connection to his African identity, of which his responsibilities as a *calunduzeiro* were undoubtedly a part.

Finally, at the end of Maria Francisca's interrogation she made a statement that Dosû, under the influence of his own medicines and in jealousy, once killed a man and a woman—slaves on the Colonia *engenho* of José da Veiga Sampaio. Maria Francisca explained that the woman, called Ilasia, had been Dosû's lover and the man was a *mestre d'açucar* on the sugar-cane plantation. It isn't clear from the report whether Maria Francisca was specifically asked by her interrogators for this information. Was she perhaps fearful of her own safety with Dosû? Had they perhaps had a discordance of their own recently? He wasn't staying at the house they shared when he was arrested. While it is impossible to know the answers to these questions from the documents at hand, the incident Maria Francisca relates is perhaps a representation of the sources of fear and respect that many people in nineteenth-century Bahia felt for *curandeiro-feiticeiros*; it was believed that the energies they were able to manipulate could be used for ill as well as for good.

Santa Barbara and the Police

One of the most intriguing and suggestive documents I was able to locate in the Bahian state archives related to Candomblé in the nineteenth century is also perhaps the most frustrating. Unlike most of the others whose language and script indicate that they were prepared by literate persons, this document contained a great many misspellings and grammatical errors which—in addition to its generally deteriorated state—made it difficult to read. The document is neither signed nor dated although it is clearly a matter of correspondence from a police official in the *freguesia* of Santo Antonio alem do Carmo to the chief of police. The letter is located in a *maço* which held documents dated between 1823 and 1846, and its specific mention of an Angolan *boçal* (newly arrived African slave) helps affirm that it was likely written during this time period. After midcentury, the presence of just-arrived, completely unassimilated Africans would have been unusual. Also the document refers to the *Entrudo*—a pre-Lenten celebration which was on the wane in the second half of the nineteenth century as Carnival took its place.[21]

The letter was written to complain of a *candomblé* in Cabula, a neighborhood of Santo Antonio where *terreiros* were frequently noted. Santo Antonio was among the principal locations of *candomblés* in the nineteenth century as well as one of the districts with the largest population of African *libertos*. In fact, according to the records at my disposal, Santo Antonio was the most commonly cited *freguesia* for Afro-Brazilian religio-cultural gatherings—23.6 percent of all assemblages discovered within the city of Salvador occurred there.

Near the beginning of the year, around the time of the Festival of Kings and the Entrudo, a *crioulo* named Manoel Pedro planned an attack on police. Manoel Pedro was a leader of the Candomblé community in Cabula and his *terreiro* had suffered harassment from local authorities. The letter describes the plan "that on the days of the entrudo all the *candombleizeiros* [Candomblé participants] would be there, they would be lying down, armed with clubs, with the lights out, so that as soon as the police came they would be attacked; as this *negro* Manoel Pedro was in the Estrada das Boiadas ready to give the signal as soon as any troop marched." Manoel Pedro was also accused of having sequestered a fourteen- or fifteen-year-old black girl named Sunsão [possibly short for Assunção], daughter of a *crioula* slave, and keeping her in the *candomblé* under his tutelage and influence without the permission of her masters. The document further states that Santa Barbara of the *terreiro* "divines, makes marriages, and punishes the police" who come to raid the ceremonies.[22] In one such raid, an Angolan *boçal* was caught and imprisoned but Manoel Pedro and Sunsão escaped. The letter asks the chief of police to make an order for the arrest of the Candomblé leader and his protégé so that the young woman could be returned to her legal owners and the *feiticeiro* deported.

In the document, the *terreiro* is understood not only as a space of refuge for slaves but also as a community of active resistance. It seems not accidental that Santa Barbara is identified as the patron of this *terreiro*. Rodrigues noted that Santa Barbara was universally perceived as the warrior deity Xangô among *candomblés* in Bahia.[23] Xangô is one of the most popular of the African deities of the diaspora, and at the end of the nineteenth century his presence was ubiquitous in Bahian *terreiros*.[24] Every *candomblé* Rodrigues visited had at least one stone—often a meteorite—in which Xangô's essence was housed and nurtured.[25] As the god of justice, Xangô was an apt choice for protector and vindicator of the Cabula *candomblé*. Santa Barbara's role in the ritual community is indicative of a sense of concrete interaction between *orixás* and the Candomblé faithful. Divination, an essential element in Candomblé, is interpreted here as emanating from the deity. It is Xangô (in this particular instance) who advises his devotees on matters of health, ritual responsibility, relationships, and destiny. And the revelation that it is the *orixá* who serves as ritual conductor of marriages strongly implies that some Candomblé communities had their own means of consecrating black unions, in spite of the paucity of legalized, church-based weddings among blacks in nineteenth-century Bahia.

Another element of this Candomblé community which echoes Rodrigues's findings is that the leader lived and worked away from the *terreiro*. Originally from the town of Santo Amaro, Manoel Pedro resided in the Xica Bixenta alley in front of the Franciscan nun's retreat (Os Perdões) and worked as a craftsman in a goldsmith's workshop. The *candomblé* itself was located much further from the center of the city on a *roça* known as Serralho. Rodrigues observed in the 1890s that many Candomblé leaders lived in the urban areas of Salvador while the locations they used for large ritual gatherings were in suburban, semi-rural areas where access was difficult and where there was a greater likelihood of being able to conduct rituals undisturbed. Also, the *candomblés* located in semi-rural areas were assured proximity to the plants, trees, springs, rivers, hills, and other elements of the natural world so central to the cultivation of the cosmic energies and the realization of rites of purification, healing, and consecration.

Quinta das Beatas

Antonio da Silveira, another African *liberto,* had a house in the district of Brotas, in an area called Quinta das Beatas (roughly, Estate of the Devoted Ones), where he gathered blacks of all colors and statuses to dance. At ten o'clock on July 7, 1849, the subdelegate of the *freguesia* encircled the house and arrested twenty-one people who were found dancing "against the active orders." Ten men and eleven women were imprisoned in the Aljube jail—seven African freedwomen, seven African freedmen, one *cabra,* two free *crioulas,* one enslaved *crioula,* and three enslaved African men.[26] Four years later, in February 1853, Antônio was again under suspicion and his house under surveillance. A *parda,* Carolina Pereira, appeared to have taken ill after ingesting some of his remedies. When police went in search of Antonio, he was not at home but a man and a woman, both *crioulos,* were found there. The man, Domingos Francisco do Rosario, was in an adjacent building—Antonio's infirmary, according to police. It seems he was staying there while being treated by the healer. The police noted especially that the infirmary was maintained with "extreme care" and was furnished with beds, couches, and clothes for many people. There was also "a large quantity of herbs, bottles, vases and pots with decoctions."[27]

Brotas had the most extensive area of Salvador's urban *freguesias* and its population, predominantly people of color, was widely scattered on small subsistence farms.[28] The area where Antonio lived, Quinta das Beatas, was the property of the Franciscan order Senhor Bom Jesus dos Perdões. Religious orders frequently owned large landholdings which they rented or leased in parcels to farming tenants. A listing of the freed Africans present in Brotas in 1849, coordinated by the local subdelegate in response to a municipal order, numbered 232 people: 101 men and 131 women, all but one of whom were aged thirty or older. Ninety percent of the *liberto* men in Brotas were farmers—usually growing manioc and vegetables. Others raised dairy cattle, fished, or did artisanal work.[29] While we don't know if Antonio da Silveira was employed in any work other than that related to his responsibilities as a healer and spiritual leader, Brotas was a logical location for a Candomblé community which included an extensive infirmary. Access to medicinal and ritual herbs and roots would not have been difficult in this semi-rural area. Furthermore, because of its sylvan characteristics and sparse population, Brotas was a common destination for fugitive slaves who wanted the protection of woods and relative inaccessibility. A local judge complained regularly to the provincial president that the district was overrun with *terreiros* and *quilombos*. He bemoaned the fact that freed Africans living in Brotas often gave shelter to runaway slaves and encouraged them to leave their masters and work with them on the farms.[30] The slaves indicated in the 1849 raid on Antonio's compound may have been similarly seeking refuge in the ceremony. In my own documents, Brotas was the third most frequent location among eighteen *freguesias* and Recôncavo towns cited (probable and positive documents combined). There were nine mentions of gatherings in Brotas, and Quinta das Beatas hosted four of them.

The two recorded instances involving Antonio da Silveira indicate that the *liberto*, identified as a *curandeiro*, was involved in both healing and cultivation of *axé* with his community of clients and supporters. Again, Opoku reminds us of the essential connectedness between right relationship, spirit, and materiality in African understandings of healing. He writes, "It is generally believed that nothing can be well with men in society if good relations are not maintained between them and their fellow human beings and between them and the powers that control the universe."[31] The profound personal and collective discordance represented by slavery required extensive and repeated interventions to redress the considerable imbalances and provide healing for the sicknesses and misfortunes inherent in the situation. Opoku explains that the cures for collective misfortunes (epidemics, droughts) often include the same kind of material/spiritual coalescence used for individual illnesses—"the taking of herbs and roots as well as ritual cleansing and the offering of sacrifices."[32]

The mutual process of healing and cultivation of *axé* in Candomblé (as in traditional African religion) not only involves pharmacopoeic applications and ritual adjustment of imbalance, but also signals the need for initiation and its labored, communal realization. The infirmary house on Antonio's compound with its many beds, couches, clothes, and herbal infusions may have also served as a communal living space for members of the Candomblé community. A *crioula* found in Antonio's house during the 1853 raid, a woman called Anastácia Maria, was not specifically mentioned as a patient—as were the *crioulo* and the *parda*. Perhaps she was an auxiliary or other member of the ritual community, perhaps even a *filha do santo*.

Finally, because these documents date from the midcentury point (1849 and 1853), they evidence the increasingly multi-textured, pan-black composition of Candomblé *terreiros* in Bahia. While Africans predominated in the dance gathering, a *cabra* and three *crioulas* were also present there. In the report alluding to Antonio's pharmacopoeic healing work, a *parda* is mentioned as a client and two *crioulos* are found in the house in his absence. Even Antonio's absence is suggestive of the network of people who supported Candomblé and its leaders through the "witch-hunts" of the nineteenth century. The 1854 police report says that Antonio was in hiding. Was he somehow notified of the police's impending arrival and perhaps sheltered by sympathetic persons?[33] The fact that by 1854 Antonio da Silveira had been jailed at least once previously for his practice of Candomblé indicates that he had some idea of what to expect from an encounter with Salvador's *pedestres, subdelegados,* and local jails—all of which had a reputation for brutality.[34] This fact and the comprehensiveness of his infirmary suggest that in spite of police harassment, Antonio da Silveira took his work seriously and was supported by others who benefited from his services and/or shared in his ritual community.

The Velha Preta Revisited

Santana do Sacramento was one of the central *freguesias* of Salvador and as such was part of the city's most urbanized and densely populated area in the nineteenth century. The *freguesia* was, like most of Salvador's districts, inhabited predominantly by people of color. Many were *libertos* and free *crioulos* who were *ganhadores* and/or did artisanal work: Men were often carpenters, shoemakers, street vendors, painters, barbers, and stone masons, while women most often worked in domestic service or washed and starched clothes. There were also slaves who lived in Santana—commonly *ganhadores,* male and female, who lived away from their masters—and *pardo* small businessmen, bureaucrats, and artisans as well as a few whites, many of whom were retired politicians, military officers connected to the city's central barracks at Mouraria. Santana was also home to some of the city's best-known musicians and visual artists.[35]

Several *cantos* (work groups) of black *ganhadeiras* and *ganhadores,* slave and freed, were located in this *freguesia*. Members of the Canto da Mangueira congregated behind the central police barracks while the Largo do Guadalupe was the site of a *canto* of women. The São Miguel Plaza was home to another *canto* of *ganhadeiras* as well as the center square of a neighborhood notorious to press and police for its *batuques*.

Several newspaper notices from 1866 indicate the gatherings of large numbers of blacks "even on Sundays" whose drums and loud humming "thundered in the air."[36]

On a Sunday evening in April 1854, the home of an elderly African woman was the site of just such a gathering. The woman lived behind the wall of the Desterro Convent in the center of the *freguesia*. The convent was a few blocks away from the Fonte das Pedras, one of the many municipal water fountains at which black workers frequently congregated. A *pardo* neighbor, Manoel da Conceição, approached the large group of blacks and apparently told them to disperse. Most refused and Manoel went to the local subdelegate to denounce the assemblage. Around nine o'clock, Manoel returned with Santana's subdelegate, José Eleuterio Rocha, an inspector, and another assistant. Manoel was deputized by the subdelegate and left to guard the Ferraro Street exit of the house in order to prevent anyone's escape while José Eleuterio and his two companions entered the house. By this time, however, it was deserted except for three people: a white couple and the older African woman to whom the house belonged. The man was obviously ill. In a space described as the elderly woman's room, the raiders discovered a blood-spattered figure covered with feathers and surrounded with food.[37]

Here again we see *candomblé terreiros* as centers of a simultaneous process of healing and *axé*-cultivation. The blood, feathers, and food were most likely elements of votive offering such as would be made to one of the *orixás* or *voduns*—whose ultimate aim would be to fortify the *axé* or life force of the deity and of the ritual community. Animal blood is a component of offering widespread among traditional African peoples across the continent—as well as in many of the religious traditions of the Afro-Atlantic diaspora. Blood is understood to be a life-sustaining element and, as Blier notes, in Aja-Fon cultures, "each offertory animal's blood is identified with a spiritual energy."[38] Bastide writes that blood is a major means of connecting the world of human beings with the world of Spirit.[39] Its use in offerings to ancestral or cosmic energies is a means of transferring the vital force of the sacrificial being to the divinity and, by extension, to the ritual community. Chicken feathers are often used to indicate that rites of empowerment have been effected. In West Africa, they are commonly seen on ritual statuary such as the Aja-Fon *bocio*.[40] The plumage of chickens and other birds in ceremonial spaces, on the bodies of initiates, and among the paraphernalia of deities and priests was noted in Fernando Ortiz's early-twentieth-century writing on Cuban Santeria as well as in Nina Rodrigues's reportings on Candomblé.[41] Food and feeding is an important expression of mutual care in Candomblé. The deities are offered nourishment by their devotees—specific foods for each *orixá, vodun, inquice,* etc.[42] In turn, the human community benefits from the renewed strength and protection of the Spirit's *axé.*[43] Ortiz offers a corresponding example from Cuban Santeria in the first decade of the twentieth century. Describing an altar to an *orisha,* he writes that a bird or other animal is sacrificed and its blood dripped over the "idol" in front of which various foods are placed. "The spirit of the foods and offerings go to the deities; what is left is consumed by the *brujos* [*feiticeiros*] and in the most solemn feasts, by the distinguished *hijos-del-santo* [*filhos-do-santo;* initiates]."[44]

The case of this Santana Candomblé community offers insight about perceptions of Candomblé in the larger society and about the participation of whites. The police documents tended to equate Candomblé with Africans and Africanness almost exclusively until the second half of the nineteenth century. In the 1829 raid on the Accú Candomblé *terreiro* in Brotas, the Juiz do Paz who reported to the provincial president expressed dismay at the participation of a large number of *crioulas* in the ceremonies.[45] Later, in 1843, the subdelegate of Victoria expressed a similarly unsettled attitude toward the involvement of Brazilian-born people in African-based drum-and-dance gatherings; although this time there was a recognition that such participation was increasing. The subdelegate specifically asked the chief of police what the punishment should be for the arrested Brazilians, since the laws seem to have been created with Africans in mind (or for slaves—which often, but not always, was a coterminous identity). He acknowledged that "today drum dances which were employed by Africans are substituted by the native sons."[46]

The ritual gathering in Santana was initially described by the denouncer as composed of "a great number of Africans." Whether or not the people who evaded police detection were all actually Africans is impossible to know at this juncture. Nevertheless, it is clear that there were at least two non-Africans, in this case whites, present at the gathering who were not discovered until the police searched the house. Because the dominant discourse overwhelmingly identified Afro-Brazilian religio-cultural manifestations with Africans, at least prior to the end of the slave trade, my sense is that in cases where large groups of black people gathered—but were not actually arrested—*crioulos* and other darker-skinned Brazilian people may have been misidentified by observers as Africans.[47]

The presence of whites in the ceremonial spaces of Candomblé during the nineteenth century was not nearly as common as that of

Brazilian-born blacks and Africans. The fact that the white man discovered in the house was ill points to the phenomenon of Afro-Brazilian religion as a resource of alternative healing in Bahia—a resource that did not necessarily entail full participation in the life of the ritual community and could simply be accessed from a position of clientage. That this couple was actually in the house of the Candomblé leader during a ceremony suggests either that they were indeed active participants in the ritual community or that they were clients whose presence was required as part of the procedure for the man's healing. Rodrigues noted the common occurrence of this kind of patronage of black healer-sorcerers at the end of the nineteenth century, writing that whites, mulattos, and others consulted "black feiticeiros in their times of affliction, in their disgraces." Some clients, he suggested, publicly believed in the religions, others publicly lambasted them, but the great majority of Bahians, in private moments of distress, turned to the black healer-sorcerers for help.[48]

Neither the white couple nor the black priestess were arrested by police. The African woman was admonished by the subdelegate and warned to discontinue her gatherings under pain of imprisonment. Because Africans (and especially the ritual leaders) were almost always jailed in raids on *candomblés* one might speculate that the presence of the whites in this instance served to soften the punishment. However, this was not always the case.

As a final reflection on this profile, the *pardo* denouncer signifies the internal tensions of Bahia's multi-faceted black population. Pardos, the lightest and often relatively more privileged sector of Bahia's black residents, were less active in Candomblé than *crioulos* during the nineteenth century.[49] There are, nonetheless, many instances of their participation indicated in the archival documentation. The extent to which Brazilian-born blacks identified with African-based religion and culture depended very much on the environment in which they were raised and the people who raised them. *Crioulos* who had at least one African parent (especially an African mother), as well as *crioulos* and *pardos* who were raised in the company of Africans, seem to have more easily shared an identification with *coisas do Africano* (African things; African cultural elements). Oliveira emphasizes that legal status, relations with white masters, and the effect of being raised as a *cria da casa* (a somewhat privileged child house slave) also helped determine the manner in which Brazilian-born blacks connected with an African-based identity.[50] The influence of the dominant anti-black ideology was always a countervailing force. It consciously and subconsciously sent the message that Africans could be accepted in Brazil only insofar as they repudiated their Africanness and that their children and grandchildren's own limited acceptance within the structure of white hegemony in Brazil depended on their distancing themselves (literally in terms of "whitening" and figuratively in terms of racial/cultural identification) from African roots. That Candomblé created and maintained a firm connection to multiple African-identified rites and traditions while embracing ever-larger numbers of Brazilian-born black participants suggests its role in the development of a more inclusive Afro-Brazilian identity and a redefinition of the meanings of blackness in a racist milieu.

The House of Independence

The *sobrado* at number 7 Santa Theresa hill in São Pedro had vases of flowers in four of its windows. On every Monday and Friday of July 1862, people gathered there—especially slaves—for meetings organized by Papai Domingos. "Daddy Domingos" was the name by which the *liberto* Domingos Sodré was affectionately known among the many African men and women who came to him for advice and for assistance in securing their freedom.

Theodolinda, a Yoruba slave, was one such woman. She was owned by José Egydio Nabuco, a customs clerk, and she was a frequent visitor to Papai Domingos' house. José Nabuco complained that the woman stole items and money from him and carried them to Papai Domingos' residence "under the pretext of obtaining freedom by means of feitiçaria."

Domingos Sodré owned his house and, according to Nabuco and the chief of police, he worked in combination with two freed African women—*ganhadeiras*. These three (and perhaps another African *liberto*, Antãe) shared responsibilities as diviners and "luck-changers"[51] and were known to encourage slaves to make offerings to modify the behavior of masters and mistresses and to use magico-pharmacopoeic and ritual means to free themselves from bondage.

The chief of police ordered the local subdelegate to raid the Candomblé house, arrest anyone who was there, and forward any objects discovered. When the subdelegate and his block inspectors arrived at Domingos Sodré's house, the African was there, perhaps awaiting their arrival, in the uniform of the Independence War veterans. A vast array of items were found in the house, most out of immediate view of visitors. In the front room of the house (the *sala*, living room) were paintings of Catholic saints and a small Catholic altar. Away from this more public display however, the subdelegate reported finding a variety of materials related to Candomblé: "four metal *chocalhos* [rattles, shakers], a box of various wooden figures, and other objects such as beads and cowrie shells; a blunt-edged and point-less tin sword. An iron object with cowries and a wooden sword . . . a white belt with cowries . . . fourteen items of clothing with cowries . . . a gourd with *cão da costa* and various miscellaneous things." Police also located Domingos Sodré's testament, a jacaranda-wood dresser containing clothing marked with initials "D. S. D. C.," and a large supply of jewelry: a gold rosary and crucifix with eighty-nine beads, a six-chain gold necklace with a cross, two gold cuff-links, two diamond rings, six gold rings, and a variety of earrings and necklaces and other sundry items made of precious metals and coral. The subdelegate reported that those African slaves who brought objects to the *candomblé* house received "drinks and mixtures" which they then gave to their owners in order to mollify them. Domingos Sodré and his partners were blamed for the loss of the labor of many Africans and the police recommended an "urgent and proficient remedy" to rid Bahia of such individuals "so harmful in our country, the larger part of whose fortune is completely in the possession of slaves."[52]

The correspondence related to this case suggests that Sodré's major activity was to advise and assist Africans who wanted to secure their freedom. Once again Candomblé is evidenced as a space in which redress could be sought for the inequities of slavery. Sodré's community became a point, in fact, for a kind of redistribution of the wealth gained through black enslavement. While Sodré himself seems to have benefited materially from the redistribution he and his assistants orchestrated, the subdelegate and local slave-owner indicate that slaves who sought Sodré's help were often able to lessen the burdens of their own captivity or even to escape it altogether. The indication that slaves used stolen items of value as offerings to help them obtain freedom suggests an idea of ritual as agency in Afro-Brazilian resistance to slavery. Rather than a passive act of "superstitious" desire, the use of ritual means to effect a substantive change in the nature of master-slave relations should be understood as a process of co-creation of a transformed reality which involved the slave, the healer-sorcerer, and the cosmic energies (*orixás*).

The subdelegate reported that Sodré had been freed in 1836 and had worked as a diviner and "luck changer" for many years. He appears to have been more prosperous than most freedpeople in Salvador at the time. Sodré owned his multi-story townhouse at a point when the majority of *libertos* rented smaller spaces or owned single-level wattle-and-daub dwellings. The fact that he had a *testamento* (a will; a testamentary statement), which he guarded carefully in a small varnished box (which was confiscated by police), suggests he had some personal wealth that he was concerned to distribute according to his wishes at his death. In her study of *libertos* based on an analysis of nineteenth-century *testamentos*, Oliveira confirms that those freed Africans who left these official instructions for the disbursement of their belongings and the ordering of their funereal arrangements were generally better off than their fellows and represented an elite among the African community.[53]

The two *ganhadeiras* mentioned in the documents may have shared the house with Sodré (as well as with others—especially other women). Among the items discovered there were "five boxes . . . containing used clothing of black women and some in good condition" as well as a merchandising box of the sort associated with street vendors. The fact that most of the clothing found was women's clothing corresponds to the quantitative analysis of the police records which testifies that the majority of people in Candomblé communities were women.

The arresting officer, the subdelegate of São Pedro, reported that Domingos Sodré "had the nerve" to wear the Independence War veteran's uniform when he was taken to jail. This particularly incensed the officer because he noted that Sodré was freed in 1836 and was still a slave "at the time of our Independence." We do not know whether Sodré participated in the war as a soldier. Those slaves who did fight were generally given freedom in return. If Sodré was not a veteran of the independence war, what might he have been trying to convey in wearing the uniform "on the occasion of his confinement to the House of Correction"?

Sodré seems to have been a fascinating personage. As a respected leader of a Candomblé community and a relatively well-to-do *liberto* who owned his own townhouse, he appears to have had a very secure sense of himself, his own authority, and his capacities. Perhaps the *farda* (uniform), which he had also worn on other occasions according to the subdelegate, was his way of embodying a spirit of independence, of honor, or self-determination. It may also have been a symbol of his sense of belonging to the Brazilian polity; wearing it to encounter the police was perhaps a way to remind the arresting officers, the society at large, and himself that he claimed (and indeed was owed) a stake in the emerging independent nation. In the "simple" audacity of wearing a veteran's uniform, this man who must have been at least in his mid-forties (considered old in nineteenth-century Brazil) conveyed an air of seriousness. At least he took himself seriously; and apparently from his reputation and the amount of material amassed in his house from constituents, a number of other people did as well.

Also, if indeed Sodré dressed in the *farda* because he knew the police were coming, might that indicate that he had the choice to try to evade them and decided against it? In a similar situation, it seems

Antonio da Silveira hid from the police. Once more, perhaps a clue can be taken from Sodré's choice of garment. The police record offers no direct verbal or written statement from Sodré, from the *velha preta* in Santana, or from most of the other Candomblé leaders who confronted officers who raided their homes which were sacred sites. When we recall the injunction of Reis and Silva to be sensitive to the actions of blacks whose words are missing from the official record, the posture and decisions elected by Sodré and the old African woman may tell us something of value.[54] Domingos Sodré wore his uniform to jail and the *velha preta* remained in her house with the sacred objects of her religion even after all but the least vulnerable of her constituents had left. It seems to me that in the emplacement of their bodies—inside an Independence War uniform and in the company of the African deity, respectively—both these leaders were indicating what was most important to them; and how they oriented themselves toward the encounter with oppression. In different ways they were each demonstrating their commitments, their independence, and their authority.

The Makers of the Saint

Rosa Lima de Oliveira, Maria do Carmo, and Joanna Valeria da Purificação, three young black women, had been secluded in initiation for two weeks when the subdelegate of Brotas, Antonio Fernandes Leal, led a raid on their Candomblé *terreiro* in the morning of February 2, 1887. The *terreiro* was the house of Domingas Maria do Rosario, a priestess and the young women's initiator. From all appearances, she was not at home at the time of the raid. The initiates, *crioulas* all, were discovered together in a room, semi-nude and with shaven heads. The subdelegate estimated their ages at between seventeen and twenty years old. He ordered the women taken to the police station for interrogation.

This disruption must have been especially troubling to the *crioulas* as they explained that they were in reclusion in the Candomblé in order to *fazerem santo* (undergo initiation; "to make the saint") and that they dared not leave the *terreiro* grounds for fear of going crazy. According to Leal, the women explained that their heads had been shaven "by order of the Saint" and that the *mãe-de-santo* obligated them to do household tasks and remain in rigorous submission to her during their period of initiation. She had informed them that they were to remain in the *terreiro* for a period of six months to a year in order to complete the necessary rituals and apprenticeship.

While the subdelegate was interrogating one of the *crioulas*, two men rushed into the room complaining vehemently of Leal's impropriety in abducting the young women. One of the men was Peregrino Sermita Bittencourt, an employee of the Monte Soccoro bank who was identified as the *mãe-de-santo*'s lover. He was carrying books for the second man, Evaristo de Santa Anna Gomes, from which Gomes was citing proof that the subdelegate "had committed an abuse in taking possession of the makers of the saint." The two men insisted on the illegality of Leal's actions, and in the subdelegate's words "became so importune and bothersome" that he ordered them removed from the premises, threatening to imprison them for disobedience and other infractions. Leal directed the young women to return to their homes and ordered them not to go back to the *terreiro*.[55]

In his final comments to the chief of police, Leal referred to the priestess and the two male defenders of the *candomblé* as "maliciously sly people, who in this way make a lovely fount for their expenses, thereby feeding the repugnant vice of their long, lazy lives." Aside from the particular verbal flourish of the subdelegate's disdain, his comments are representative of the view elites maintained and disseminated regarding leaders of Afro-Brazilian religious communities. In spite of the bias of his perceptions, Leal's report suggests significant aspects of initiation and community formation in nineteenth-century Candomblé—much of which resonates clearly in practices that continue to the present day.

Leal's letter, as well as the undated correspondence regarding Manoel Pedro and Sunsão in Santo Antonio (see "Santa Barbara and the Police" in this chapter) and a third document from the Sé *freguesia* in 1876 are three archival records which directly allude to matters of initiation in Candomblé. The 1876 document mentions the *crioula* slave of an African freedwoman who was "condemned to spend a year" in a Candomblé in Boa Vista "with other companions of misfortune."[56] In all three cases the individuals specifically mentioned as people undergoing initiation were black Brazilian-born females—*crioulas*. These examples recall the fact of women's majority participation in nineteenth-century Candomblé and are suggestive of the process by which females in Bahia have come to represent ever greater proportions of the leadership of the tradition—as it is from the ranks of initiates that priests and priestesses are selected.

In both the 1876 and 1887 cases, initiation in Candomblé was a group experience; initiates lived together at the *terreiro* for as long as a year. (This time frame is considerably longer than the one- to three-month seclusion common in present-day Candomblé initiation rituals.) Furthermore, both documents implied a sense of the "helplessness" of initiates which corresponded to their novitiate status and their seclusion from outside influences.

Rodrigues's descriptions of Candomblé initiation practices from the 1880s give a fuller picture of the process—which included purification baths; shaving the head and washing it with special herbal preparations; ritually marking the body with the colors and patterns of specific *orixás;* instruction in the dances, chants, and comportment preferences of the deities; and a series of *saidas* (ritual exits from seclusion) to mark the initiate's newly emerging identity within the Candomblé community.[57] Initiation in Candomblé is, even today, a long and rigorous process in which the relationship of the new *iawo* to her or his patron *orixá* is carefully determined through divination, acknowledged in ritual gesture, and materially represented by a variety of means—from the nature and color of clothing to the consecration of natural objects associated with the energy of the *orixá.* Initiates are prepared to embody the presence of their dominant *orixá* and are taught the specific means by which the ritual relation is to be continually cultivated. The long confinement, the submission to the head priest or priestess (and to others in the hierarchy of the community), and the detailed alimentary and behavioral restrictions which help structure the initiatory process in Candomblé serve to clearly define a psychic, material, and relational space distinct from that which preceded it. Initiation in nineteenth-century Candomblé was likely a means of further emphasizing the *terreiro* community and the *terreiro* ethos as a space differentiated from the space outside—particularly the space of the dominant society.

The *crioulas* in Brotas indicated that their heads were shaven "by order of the Saint" and that they were normally confined to a single room when not involved in household tasks. Both of these factors—the shaving of body hair (particularly hair on the head) and strict seclusion—are important aspects of Candomblé initiation. The human head is the principal site of the *orixá's* being in the body. Among the most important elements of the initiatory process are rituals designed to clarify, affirm, and settle the divine presence in the head. This process is a means of constituting a new identity and recognizes the human body as the "house" of the Spirit. For each initiate there is a very particular Spirit, *orixá,* with whom she or he thenceforth maintains a special relationship of mutual obligation and a profound shared identity. The initiation room, known colloquially as the *camarinha,* provides isolation from the rest of the house and from all outside forces generally. Initiates are understood to be, in a sense, like babies or young children—in formation, strongly impressionable, and at a certain risk—and the *camarinha* is as a womb, a place of protection, gestation, and rebirth.

While no racial or color designations were mentioned for Domingas do Rosario or the two men who confronted the subdelegate in the 1887 document, at least one of the men, Peregrino Sermita Bittencourt—as an employee of the Monte Socorro bank—was very likely a light *pardo* or white. That he and his companion, Evaristo de Santa Anna Gomes, were not identified by skin color, in spite of their "impertinence" and disruption of the subdelegate's interrogations, further suggests that the men were not *crioulos* or Africans, who generally tended to be identified as such in police documentation. Whether or not the men identified with the Afro-Brazilian community in terms of their own racial or cultural sympathies, they clearly represented the kind of support that Candomblé depended on in its negotiations with the dominant order. Gomes (who it seems had some familiarity with law) and Bittencourt came to the defense of the integrity and independence of the Candomblé community in precisely the way that generations of *ogãs* have been expected to do—using whatever personal, racial, financial, or occupational leverage they might have in order to protect the *terreiros* and the devotees with whom they are associated.

Barroquinha and Alakétu: The Recognized Originators

My intention in this study is to place Candomblé in the larger context of Afro-Brazilian alternative orientations, giving special attention to the meaning of the religion as a resource for healing, community, and redress of power imbalances in a slave-based society. In addition, my archival research has led me to argue that there is a continuity between Candomblé and earlier manifestations of Afro-Brazilian religiosity and to suggest the significance of the pan-ethnic African emphases and *crioulo*/African alliances formed in Candomblé *terreiros*. So far in the text I have tried to avoid a retelling of the familiar story of the Barroquinha/Casa Branca community—widely (if not particularly critically) identified as the oldest extant Candomblé *terreiro* in Brazil. Instead, I have emphasized the less documented history of other activities, communities, and orientations of nineteenth-century Candomblé.

However, any historical treatment of the religion would be remiss without some mention of two *terreiros* usually recognized as having been established before the end of the first half of the nineteenth century. Casa Branca (first located in the Barroquinha neighborhood of São Pedro and presently located in Engenho Velho) and Alakétu, as they are popularly known, are acknowledged by scholars and Candomblé communities as among the oldest continually operating Afro-Brazilian ritual centers in the country. Both *candomblés* are of the Ketu "nation" and Casa

Branca in particular is the *casa matriz* of several others of the older and more prestigious Candomblé houses—including Gantois and Axé Opô Afonjá. As I suggested earlier, the prominence of Yoruba *terreiros* in the popular history of Bahian Candomblé is partly due to the conscious and subconscious preference these *terreiros* have received from academics and other elite observer/participants. However, the marked influence of West Africans (and especially Nagôs) in nineteenth-century Bahian culture, together with the fact that their mass arrival coincided with the last cycle of the slave trade and the last century of Brazilian slavery, combined to create an environment amenable to the distinctiveness of Yoruba-identified traditions in Candomblé. Nonetheless, even in the formation of the early Nagô Candomblés, significant pan-ethnic African cooperation occurred. Furthermore, under the direction of African and later Brazilian-born leaders, even the definitions of "nation" in Candomblé came to take on less ethnically specific and more theological/liturgical meaning. Today the idea of "nation" in Candomblé has almost nothing to do with the distinct ethnic origins of participants or their genetic predecessors; rather it denotes a conception of liturgical tradition.[58]

The Barroquinha *terreiro* was established on a plot of land on Berquô Hill or Berquô Lane behind the Barroquinha church. The predominantly male *irmandade* of Senhor Bom Jesus dos Martírios and the women's sodality (or *devoção*) of Nossa Senhora da Boa Morte have been separately and jointly cited as the founders of the *candomblé*. In any case, substantial evidence from oral tradition points to the involvement of Yoruba women, with the likely assistance of one or more men, in the establishment of the ritual community. There are also debates and discrepancies regarding the actual date of the founding of the Barroquinha *terreiro*. Many anthropologists and other scholars have followed the lead of Edison Carneiro, who estimated the establishment at around 1830.[59] Others have suggested a less specific date—"early in the nineteenth century"[60] or late in the eighteenth century.[61]

Different versions of the names of the founders also abound. Carneiro identified the early leaders as three African women: Adêta (or Iyá Dêta), Iyá Kalá, and Iyá Nassô.[62] Deoscóredes dos Santos lists the same names as Carneiro but with slightly different spellings: Adetá, Iyakalá, and Iyanassô.[63] Pierre Verger suggests that various women were involved in the creation of the *terreiro* and specifies two—Iyalussô Danadana and Iyanassô Akala (or Iyanassô Oká)—who were assisted by a man, Babá Assiká.[64] Vivaldo Costa Lima writes that Iyá Kala and Iyá Nassô were honorifics referring to the same person—Iá Nassô Oió Akalá Magbê Olodumare. He also reports that some Ketu *terreiros* recall a story that two men, Babá Assica (or Axicá) and Babá Adetá, were involved in the founding as well.[65] Whatever the specific names, Yoruba people, and particularly women, are recalled as the originators of the Barroquinha Candomblé community.

Silveira has referred to Barroquinha as the first *candomblé* in which a number of deities were jointly cultivated.[66] Although documents like that describing the 1785 *calundu* in Cachoeira—in which the presence of Jejes of various sub-ethnic groups is indicated—leave me unconvinced of Barroquinha's absolute priority as a center of multi-divinity cultivation, it is clear from the names and origins of its early leaders that the *terreiro* represented a space for the acknowledgment and ritual nourishment of *orixás* from more than one specific spiritual tradition. Likewise it is recognized as such in the oral traditions of Ketu *candomblés*. An informant told Silveira, for example, that "the Barroquinha Candomblé was eclectic, it practiced all the languages."[67] The *candomblé* was understood to be a Ketu *terreiro,* and at least one of its chief priestesses was consecrated to Oxôssi, the mythical head of the Ketu kingdom in Yorubaland. But Vivaldo Costa Lima has insightfully pointed out that the name of another of the founders—Iyá Nassô—gives unequivocal evidence of Oyo influence as well. Iyá Nassô is not a proper name, but an honorific title, an *oiê,* given to mark a person's status. It refers specifically to an extraordinarily important function in the court of the Alafin (king) of Oyo: the person responsible for ritual care of the king's private shrine to Xangô. As Costa Lima explains, "In nineteenth-century Bahia, populated by Yorubas of various origins, including from Oyo, no one would use the title Iyá Nassô if she did not have the authority to do so."[68]

Under the leadership of the early priestesses (especially Iyá Nassô) a number of important developments occurred in the life of the *terreiro.* Probably sometime in the first decades of the nineteenth century, Iyá Nassô made a trip to Africa; she returned with an *olowu*—a priest of *Ifá,* the Yoruba cult of divination—called Bamboxê Obiticô. According to Silveira's informants, this priest is credited with establishing the *xire*— the ritual order of address and entrance of the *orixás* into the ceremonial dance space.[69] The creation of such a pattern, of course, suggests the cultivation of multiple deities and the need to develop structures for their mutual existence in a shared space.

In Silveira's estimation, Iyá Nassô most likely died around 1825. He further surmises that it was in this period that the *terreiro* moved from Barroquinha, either due to police harassment or because they were evicted from the lands they leased behind the church.[70] Prior to resettling in Engenho Velho, the community had one or two intermediate locations. In their present home, Casa Branca, the physical structures of the "great political accord" occasioned by Barroquinha's joint leadership by devotees of Oxôssi (of Ketu) and Xangô (of Oyo) are visible. Oxôssi and Xangô are the principal *orixás* of the Casa Branca community. The *terreiro* itself (that is, the land and the conjunction of edifices) is consecrated to Oxôssi while the *barracão* (the central ceremonial space) belongs to Xangô.[71] This process of ritualizing and territorializing pan-ethnic alliances such that deities of several regions are venerated and cultivated jointly by a single diverse community was a major means by which Candomblé helped foster a similarly diverse and inclusive Afro-Brazilian identity among Bahia's population.

The Alakétu *candomblé* community is often juxtaposed with that of Barroquinha/Casa Branca as a similarly historic *terreiro*. Alakétu, like Casa Branca, is one of the oldest Ketu *candomblés* in Brazil. Based in a series of interviews with the priestess Olga Francisca Regis in 1960, 1965, and 1966, Costa Lima estimates that this *terreiro* was founded at the end of the eighteenth century by an African woman, originally from Ketu, who came to Brazil as a slave when she was around nine years old. According to oral tradition at Alakétu, the girl's name was Otampê Ojarô and she was renamed Maria do Rosário in Brazil. Otampê Ojarô and her twin sister were said to have been captured together by Dahomeans "at the edge of a stream near Ketu" during a predatory incursion. When the girls were being sold at the slave market in Bahia, the story continues, the *orixá* Oxumarê, in the guise of a tall, kind, and affluent man, appeared and bought the girls.[72] He freed them immediately and they remained in Bahia. Some years later, Otampê Ojarô returned to Africa where she married Babá Laji (also known by the Portuguese name Porfírio Regis). Upon returning to Brazil she purchased the land on which the *terreiro* was founded, calling it Ilê Maroiá Laji.

Fascinatingly, Costa Lima was able to corroborate the *terreiro*'s oral tradition of its origin through the story of the kidnapping of the two girls. The late-eighteenth-century wars, especially between Dahomeans and Yorubas, were indeed a source for many of the Bight of Benin slaves who arrived in Salvador. In 1963, Costa Lima conducted interviews in Ketu during which the then-Alakétu (king of Ketu), Adegbite, confirmed that during the reign of King Akebioru (c. 1780–1795) the Dahomeans stole people from the Arô family, including a granddaughter of the Alakétu called Otankpe Ojaro. Ojarô is a shortened version of the name Ojé Arô—and Arô is the name of one of the five royal families of Ketu, from among which, even today, the Alakétu is chosen. This, and several other correlations Costa Lima was able to make with the aid of African informants, gives strong support to the Alakétu *terreiro*'s claim that it is one of the earliest founded, continually functioning Candomblé communities in Bahia.[73]

7

Networks of Support, Spaces of Resistance: Alternative Orientations of Black Life in Nineteenth-Century Bahia

Black Greetings and Silences

When blacks in Bahia met each other on the street, they customarily exchanged greetings with an exacting etiquette that often startled foreign observers. Unfailingly, we are told, when greeting or passing one another in the plazas and squares or along the byways of the towns, Afro-Brazilians used polite forms of address—"Vossa Senhoria" and "Vossa Mercê." If not acknowledging each other and asking after one another's health in mannered Portuguese, they used African languages. Men often exchanged elaborate hand gestures or removed their hats in salutation. Wetherell, the British vice-consul in Bahia, noted that when a black woman passed a seated black man with whom she was acquainted, the man would rise and remove his hat. Nineteenth-century Brazilian society as a whole was much concerned with propriety and recognition of status, but the extreme consideration which many blacks extended to their fellows appears to have been particularly pronounced—especially given the fact that whites seldom extended even simple courtesies to the black slaves and freedpeople whom they considered their inferiors. European and North American visitors to Salvador and Rio perhaps expected a less exemplary conduct from people whose social status was so generally degraded. For them, the politeness of public interrelations among blacks was often remarkable.[1]

Wetherell indicated that such ubiquitous mutual consideration seemed not at all feigned, but was a form of conduct cultivated from earliest childhood. Still, it surprised him that black women seemed "to take these little courtesies as a perfect matter of course." He described the scene of an Afro-Brazilian woman landing from a boat in Salvador's lower city, concerned not to wet her clothes and shoes. Several black men vied to carefully help her ashore. For the British observer, the coquetry and attention rivaled anything he'd ever seen from "a European beauty" or "her civilized admirers."[2]

These examples of the conduct Afro-Brazilians displayed in their interactions with each other are an important entry point for a discussion of a sense of the alternative spaces of blackness in nineteenth-century Bahia. Maria Inês C. de Oliveira perceptively suggests that blacks in Bahia experienced, indeed cultivated, a separation of spheres—or a double consciousness in the DuBoisian sense—wherein they oriented themselves and their actions according to the needs and limits of a given situation. She notes, for example, that African freedpeople who left detailed testamentary statements seldom made any reference to aspects of Afro-Brazilian culture which one would assume were central to their daily lives. This absence or silence becomes particularly instructive upon recognition that among the men and women who left testaments were several who have been clearly identified as leaders of Candomblé communities; it is safe to assume that many others were also involved in some way in the religious traditions of Bahia's black inhabitants. Oliveira interprets the silence of the testaments on internal aspects of Afro-Brazilian cultural and religious life as indicative of the way in which blacks recognized and sought to maintain distinctions between the spaces of "whiteness," or dominant ideology, and those of "blackness," or the internal workings of the black community.[3]

It seems to me that these distinctions were a necessary part of the process of negotiating a sustainable relationship to the oppressive structures of power while simultaneously emphasizing—in silence, in private, in work, in family, in music, in dance—an alternative meaning of black experience, of black being. Oliveira suggests that the Africans who left testaments viewed those documents as part of the "white" or dominant space of Bahian society and therefore acted accordingly in their use of the statements. Instructions for dispersing property and monies, directions for the praying of Catholic masses and other accepted funerary concerns were included in the testamentary documents. Information about the wishes of the attestors relative to African and Afro-Brazilian religious tradition was occasionally suggested in a very vague sense, as in the case of one man who asked to be buried in the manner of the Africans, but in general such information was strikingly absent.[4]

In the example of the testaments as well as in that of the extreme consideration in practices of mutual greeting among Afro-Brazilians one sees the means by which blacks adjusted their behaviors to facilitate life in an inherently fractured and disjunctive reality. If, in the "white" legal spaces of testamentary documentation, they had to follow the dominant paradigm and keep silence about the traditions of their own communities; they could, when engaging each other at the level of interpersonal relations and daily greeting, emphasize the value and esteem in which they held one another. In this sense, it can be said that identities of blackness in Brazil were situational. In the hegemonic spaces of dominant ideology, blackness was deprecated and the identity of Africans and their descendants was closely related to subaltern status. In these situations, if blacks wanted to "get along," they had to conform (or, in Oliveira's words, "assimilate") in various measures to the dominant paradigm—a paradigm which ignored or denied the value of African identity and African-based traditions. Nevertheless, alongside the assimilative measures undertaken by blacks to negotiate the dominant structures of Brazilian society, there existed an extensive network of elements affirming alternative meanings of blackness. That network, the subject of this chapter, was the foundational support for Candomblé and is perhaps an especially apropos composite example of the idea of "religion as orientation."

Oliveira primarily limits her use of the metaphor of separate spheres or double consciousness to African-born blacks in Brazil. My sense, however, is that the lines between Africans, *crioulos,* and even *pardos* in some instances were much less rigid at the level of alternative orientation than is generally recognized. I try to suggest a variety of ways in which Africans and people of African descent in Brazil created alternative identities for themselves in the context of a slave-based society. My focus here is on culture and orientation as a force for the redefinition of identities toward pan-Africanness and pan-blackness in Brazil. Certainly there remained distinctions between *pardos, crioulos,* and Africans within the structure of the dominant society, but I suggest that in the spaces of Afro-Brazilian work, life and culture, those distinctions were mitigated by shared sensibilities and shared experiences.[5] In the measure that *pardos, crioulos,* and Africans recognized and maintained communal and cultural ties with each other, they participated in and contributed to an alternative orientation to blackness. Much of this contact was in the "silent" spaces of family, Candomblé, and street culture.[6]

Multiple awareness or double consciousness was an essential element in the lives and decisions of people of African descent in nineteenth-century Bahia. Subject to the caprice and arbitrariness of oppression, slaves, freedpeople, and the free poor were required by their precarious social and economic position to maintain heightened senses of the boundaries in which they lived and moved—racial, gender, occupational, and others. Physical and psychic survival often depended on their ability to maintain qualities of attention and motion at once flexile and refined. As Long indicates, blacks had to know what the oppressors knew and they had to know something else as well. People who were often not able to control the determinate forces of their lives had to be "doubly alert"; sensitive to what was demanded and expected of them as well as to that which enabled them to negotiate their way through the internal and external assaults on their being.[7] The sway between fight and dance in *capoeira* can perhaps be understood in terms of this double consciousness—using the same elements for amusement as for confrontation: music and movement.[8]

In one sense in Bahia, unreconstructed Africanness was a negative attribute—that is, from the seigniorial perspective. Acting from within that paradigm (or, more aptly, from an awareness of it at its margins), *crioulos, pardos,* and even Africans themselves behaved so as to align themselves as much as possible with its structures and intentions. In another sense, from the internal perspective of the black community, Africanness was a value—especially a religious value. Muniz Sodré writes that "in spite of the seductions of power" apparently available to some Afro-Brazilians who distanced themselves from Africanness, Africans were often more esteemed than wealthier *crioulos* within the communal spaces of black Bahian life.[9] Therefore, the same individuals who might disclaim Africanness and blackness in one situation often exhibited another kind of behavior when acting under the influence of a different standard. And in the reality of urban Salvador in the nineteenth century the paradigms were constantly interacting, as were people's behaviors. It should be noted, however, that the alternative model, the orientation of blackness, has been less observed and less appreciated by scholars working within the dominant structure and with the resources and documentation of that structure. From the dominant perspective the alternative orientation sounds strangely like silence.

The ceremonies of Candomblé—nighttime gatherings, months-long initiations, consultations for healing and divination—were but one aspect of the religion, the alternative orientation, created by slaves, *libertos,* and others in the context of nineteenth-century Bahian society. Other manifestations of Afro-Brazilian religion, writ large, were embodied in the myriad activities and concerns of black communities. Lay Catholic confraternities, work groups, and other mechanisms of social and occupational association as well as ethnic alliances and the orientations of black women and families were important means by which Afro-Bahians negotiated space for identities and forms of self-determination denied them by the assumptions and structures of the hegemonic ideal. Furthermore, rhythmic sensibility, interpersonal conduct, and re-elaborations of linguistic, alimentary, and aesthetic-stylistic traditions served to infuse a developing *cultura da rua* (street culture; popular culture) with alternative meanings of blackness and alternative understandings of human relations. Candomblé developed in relationship to this wider network of alliances, experiences, and alternate spaces of being. The sections below are devoted to discussions of family and children, urban work, *irmandades,* personal and communal aesthetics, and rhythmic orientation in terms of their contributions to the creation of an Afro-Brazilian orientation in nineteenth-century Salvador.[10] White supporters and protectors were also important to the development of the religion—as was the alliance that sometimes arose between Candomblé devotees and the poor, *crioulo,* and *pardo* rank-and-file police soldiers who were responsible for quelling black religio-cultural manifestations. The final section of this chapter examines the structures of repression of alternative black orientations—legislation, policing policies, and the ideology of the dominant classes.

Children and Families

In the police correspondence I examined from the Bahian public archives, I found only three references to children in the context of Candomblé gatherings. This noticeable absence in the documentation corresponds to the general impression of historians who have found that slaves in Brazil had few offspring. Reis, for example, writes that among the population of Africans in nineteenth-century Bahia—both free and slave—children were a distinct minority.[11] The reasons for the negative natural increase among Brazilian slaves are varied and likely involve a combination of contraception, abortion, infanticide, widespread overwork, and the precarious health conditions of slaves. Also important, economic policies among planters favored the periodic renewal of the slave force with new teen and young adult African labor over making the expenditures necessary to raise slave children until they were old enough to work.[12]

Certainly the structure of Brazilian slavery did not encourage the formation of permanent unions and progeny among enslaved black men and women. In general, slaves neither married nor were registered as living in consensual non-legalized unions. Many were listed in various enumerations of the time as "celibate persons." Katia Mattoso offers an explanation based in the idea that the material and moral responsibilities of partnership and family were not ones slaves wanted or were able to take on in captivity.[13] Sonia Maria Giacomini speculates that slaves may have been inhibited from marrying due to "the impossibility of mutual protection in the face of the total arbitrariness of their masters."[14] However she suggests that the onus falls more firmly on slave-owners themselves, whose economic priorities and ideological perspective constituted a particularly significant obstacle to slave marriage. In spite of the fact that the Archbishopric of Bahia (whose rulings were effective throughout Brazil) declared in 1720 that masters could not prohibit slaves from marrying, most Brazilian slave-owners were in no hurry to acknowledge attachments among slaves which might make their position as property problematic. With only one exception, Giacomini writes, the great mass of newspaper announcements she researched for her study of women under Brazilian slavery made no mention whatsoever of the marital status of slaves.[15] Mary Karasch agrees that most slave-owners in Brazil simply did not permit the people they owned to marry.[16]

Legal marriage in nineteenth-century Bahia was largely the privilege of whites. It was an expensive ceremony and not deemed absolutely necessary by social convention. Most Africans, *crioulos,* and *pardos*—when they had unions—had consensual non-legalized alliances.[17] Legalized marriages involving slaves were perhaps so rare as to seem, to some, preposterous. This is the impression left from Elizabeth Cary Agassiz's description of a marriage ceremony in Rio. A black couple—a freedman and a female slave—had obtained permission from the woman's master to marry. (The woman was subsequently freed by her owner.) To the various passersby and onlookers, the formalizing of conjugal ties between this man and woman seemed to have been more spectacle than anything else. Cary Agassiz remarked at the discomfort the bride displayed at being watched by strangers. Even worse was the obvious disdain of the officiating priest who dispatched his duties "with most irreverent speed" and in a tone "more suggestive of cursing than praying." Upon announcing his final benediction he immediately "turned the bride and bridegroom out of the chapel with as little ceremony as one would have kicked out a dog."[18]

In Cary Agassiz's recollection, the single redeeming element of the event was the gesture of the bride's mother, who tossed a handful of rose petals into the air to greet her daughter as she exited the sanctuary. A small gesture perhaps, but it was further evidence of the efforts Afro-Brazilians made to manifest what was meaningful to them in a context at turns deriding, prohibitive, and oppressive. It is likely that the mother (and the couple themselves) appreciated the legal marriage as "an institution of the white world" and a means by which the bride and groom could gain some standing in the dominant society. The mother's approval and celebration of the marriage contrasts sharply with the contempt of the priest and the curiosity of passersby.[19]

Because it was so difficult for slaves to establish the kinds of conjugal and familial bonds which were recognized and respected in colonial and imperial Brazil, ideas of family and relationship took on new forms within the experience of Afro-Brazilians. One of the earliest-established and most enduring ties among Africans enslaved in Brazil was that of *malungos* or *malembos*. These were individuals who had shared the terrifying experience of the Middle Passage together. Men, women, and children who had crossed the ocean in the same slave ship—whether of similar or differing ethnic identities—maintained strong connections whenever they could "and felt a powerful obligation to help one another."[20] Mattoso recounts several examples of *malungos* buying one another's freedom, serving as godparents for each other's children, and otherwise manifesting an extraordinary mutual devotion.[21] *Malungo* ties were a significant form of kinship created in the earliest instances of shared horror and uncertainty. Because *malungo* relationships often crossed ethnic boundaries, they were a means toward the establishment of a pan-African identity based in the common experience of American enslavement. This meaning of family emphasized a compassionate mutuality and was echoed in other reconstructed forms of black relationship.

Another important aspect of the reconfiguration of family and lineage identity in the context of Brazilian slavery was ethnicity. In many ways, those individuals who shared ethnic ties—specific as well as generalized—took on the role of extended kin for each other. Ethnicity-based kinship ties also became the basis for the idea of "nations" within Candomblé. The broader notion of *parentesco de etnia* (relation by ethnicity) was inherited and adopted by Candomblé—where today all members of a particular *terreiro* belong to the same "family," that is, the *familia-do-santo* (family-in-the-saint).[22]

Candomblé communities presently identify themselves by ethnicity—Ketu (Nagô), Jeje, Congo-Angola (Bantu), and Caboclo are the most common denominations. Basing his comments in oral interviews conducted in the 1960s with older members of various *terreiro* communities, Vivaldo da Costa Lima determined that the meaning of "nation" in Candomblé was less focused around specific ethnic identity and served more to emphasize participation in a particular liturgical tradition. His informants—priestesses, priests, and other ritual members who were initiated into the religion by African freedpeople in the late nineteenth and early twentieth centuries—repeatedly made statements that accentuated their deep personal identification with the particular Candomblé "nation" into which they were received. The Candomblé "nation," however, was not necessarily synonymous with the hereditary ethnicity of the initiates. For instance, Eugênia Anna dos Santos (Mãe Aninha), a founder of the Ketu *terreiro* Axé Opô Afonjá and one of the legendary forces in Bahian Candomblé, was the daughter of Africans of Grunci ethnicity. She was initiated into Candomblé, however, by a Yoruba priestess (a daughter of the famous Iya Nassô of Barroquinha, according to Deoscóredes dos Santos) and was proud to proclaim that the *terreiro* she led for many years was "pure Nagô."[23] Similarly, Valentiana-Runhó, an initiate in the Jeje Candomblé tradition and former priestess of the Bogum *terreiro*, delighted in what she considered the superior reputation of Jeje Candomblé and clearly identified herself with that tradition. When speaking of her biological family however, she identified them only as "African."[24]

These and other examples suggest that Afro-Brazilians who participated in Candomblé (particularly, perhaps, after the first generation) came to identify themselves by means of the religious communities to which they belonged. Religion then, represented "ethnicity" in a way that both reformulated ideas of national identity and made those ideas more pan-African in terms of the genetic inheritance of participants. People of various heredities might all be initiated into a Nagô ritual community and would then claim allegiance to the specific ritual traditions of that "nation." So while in one sense maintaining the idea of ethnic specificity within the "nations" of Candomblé, the reformulated meaning of "nation" in the context of the Afro-Brazilian experience simultaneously engendered a concept of identity that was not ethnically specific. This new meaning pragmatically embraced the increasingly pan-African and pan-black reality of Candomblé communities.

The concept of *familia-do-santo* is another aspect of the evolution of ideas of "nation" in Candomblé. In addition to the "national" identity of Candomblé devotees, those persons who belong to a particular *terreiro* community understand themselves to constitute an extended family under the guidance and protection of the patron *orixás* and the *mãe* or *pai do santo*. *Ogãs* serve as uncles, *ebomis* and *ekedis* as older siblings (or aunts if they are elderly women), *iawôs* as peer siblings, and *abiãs* as younger sisters and brothers.[25] Also, individuals who are consecrated to the same deity recognize that they share a certain elemental energy—that of their patron *orixá*—which extends across differences of liturgical language and ritual tradition among the various Candomblé "nations."

While ideas of family among slaves and freedpeople in Brazil were restructured to emphasize ethnicity, *malungo* relations, and identity within ritual community, these new configurations did not foreclose possibilities of more conventional familial relations as well. Noting the value that blacks placed on family—however they conceived it—Henry Koster wrote, "The Negroes show much attachment to their wives and children, to their relations if they should chance to have any and to their *malungos* or fellow-passengers from Africa."[26] João José Reis affirms evidence of couples and families among the Malê conspirators who looked out for one another in a variety of ways: Men cared for children while women worked; males cooked for and tended to sick female companions; women defended their jailed partners and brought them food while they were imprisoned. There were of course, interpersonal conflicts as well. Reis uses the example of Sabina da Cruz, the companion of Vitorio Sule (one of the leaders of the revolt) to demonstrate the tensions that could arise between allegiance to family and ideas about rebellion. Sabina denounced the rebellion in its final planning stages after an argument with her husband and an unsuccessful attempt to get him to disassociate himself with the planning of the uprising as she was concerned for the safety of "her children's father."[27] The general absence of conventional families among Africans in Bahia at the time of the Malê Revolt seemingly helped to make it a more feasible option for resistance. The fact that many participants probably had few existing ties to spouses and children probably lessened their ambivalence about the consequences of violence. Furthermore, the absence of traditional familial bonds placed greater emphasis on ethnicity and religion as sources of identity and strength.[28]

Although numbers of children among slaves and African *libertos* appear to have been small, what children were present were well integrated into the life of the community. Perhaps referring both to children of free *crioulos* and *pardos* as well as to those of slaves and Africans, Wetherell noted that "a great number of black children" accompanied their mothers as they worked or conducted other activities in the streets. "They seldom cry," he wrote, and were often carried on their mother's backs or slung across the women's hips while they were spoken to reassuringly. Whether amusing themselves amid items for sale in the markets or "sprawled about at play under the cover of a propped-up mat" at the side of the rivers and streams where their mothers washed clothes, children were generally found wherever black women gathered.[29] The atmosphere of collective female presence in the labor of *ganhadeiras*, *lavadeiras* (washerwomen), and others who shared work in Salvador's streets was in many ways replicated within Candomblé communities where women were the majority of participants.

Within families, whether composed of mother and children or two parents and children, women—as the primary caretakers—were especially important transmitters of the values of an alternative black orientation in Brazil. African freedwomen in Bahia were particularly responsible for passing on and reconfiguring African cultural values—in gesture, in language, in child-raising customs, in the music of lullabies, and in the lessons of folk stories.[30] In fact, the identities and orientations of Brazilian-born blacks were significantly affected by the presence or absence of African-born kin in their raising.[31]

While we do not have a preponderance of evidence from nineteenth-century police sources relating to the presence of children in Candomblé, the writings of Nina Rodrigues, oral histories of Candomblé communities, and the recollections of individual Afro-Brazilians with ties to various *terreiros* indicate the presence of children and a tradition of *terreiro* leadership passing from parent to child. Vivaldo da Costa Lima interviewed a modern *mãe-de-santo* in the 1960s who lamented the passing of the "old days" when the women devotees would come to a *terreiro* "with their children" and stay on the premises for the entire duration of the cycle of religious feasts.[32] Almost all of the priests and priestesses of the Candomblé *terreiros* Rodrigues studied at the end of the nineteenth century were Brazilian-born sons and daughters of Africans who were themselves *feiticeiros* and *terreiro* leaders.[33] This clearly suggests that within the space of the black family in Bahia, the assemblage of gestures, liturgical rhythms and languages, ritual practices, interpretations—in short, the orientation that comprised the experience of Candomblé—was carefully cultivated as an essential element in the identity and behavior of Brazilian-born children. In this way values that had originated in Africa were transferred to *crioulos* and *pardos*. Africans had developed (and were constantly developing, first by themselves and then in conjunction with their Brazilian-born progeny) ways to engage an alternative meaning of themselves in the American context. This they passed on as inheritance for future generations.

Rodrigues wrote of a *crioulo* son of African Candomblé leaders whose parents encouraged him in the ritual interpretation of dreams. In Rodrigues's account, the young man's father, who had died, tried to contact his son to request the sacrifice of a rooster for his soul. The father eventually made his wish clear through the embodied *orixá* of a young woman he had initiated; also by means of an old African man's dream, a close friend of the late father. Rodrigues was struck by the seriousness with which blacks attended to dreams and to the counsel and instruction they received therein.[34] Identifying this as an African characteristic, he used the example to indicate the way in which Brazilian-born blacks raised among Africans were influenced in their orientation to meaning. Although in Rodrigues's view, the practice among Afro-Bahians of dreaming "with excessive frequency" was evidence of a certain intellectual backwardness, the case demonstrates that African orientations helped constitute a way of perceiving and responding to the world within the Afro-Brazilian communal experience. Interpretive forms and modes of action that were created and sustained among blacks (and significantly, across generational lines between Africans and their Brazilian-born descendants) represented an effective means toward a collective alternative identity—whether or not these values were understood or approved of by the dominant society.

Martiniano Eliseu do Bomfim (1859–1943), one of the most highly respected *babalawos* of Bahian Candomblé, was visited on a number of occasions by the North American anthropologist Ruth Landes while she was researching Candomblé in 1938 and 1939. Close to eighty years old at the time Landes met him, Seu Martiniano was the son of African *libertos*. Although the venerable priest of Ifá was generally (and for Landes, frustratingly) circumspect about the nature of the information he shared with her, he did, on one of Landes's last visits to his house, allow her and a guest to see the private room where he kept the ritual objects bequeathed to him by his mother and father. "Dona Ruth," he said to her, "I have never shown you the things my parents left me, which they brought from Africa. Perhaps you . . . would like to see them?" Landes described the scene in the close, windowless room into which Seu Martiniano led her as filled with a variety of Candomblé paraphernalia such as she had never seen before:

> There were wooden and bronze statuettes of gods, with their sacred beads, fans, and swords, all made by Negro artisans of Bahia, now dead; their costumes were tossed about, and also royal scepters of bronze whose heads were carved like human bodies displaying enormous sexual organs. There were fetish stones, containing the very power of the gods, and they were swimming in oil, blood and alcohol which they had been fed and in which they had been bathed at different times. Dust lay like a blanket, since Martiniano did not allow anyone to handle the god-things, and the room stank with an old mild odor.[35]

Lifting up a statue of Iansã for Landes to see, Seu Martiniano explained that it had belonged to his father and that the deity had been the father's protectress. "So I still make sacrifices to her," he said. After briefly examining two dishes of votive offerings in an alcove of the room he hurried his guests out and locked the door. "It's just as though that room were full of dynamite," Landes recalled him saying. "You have to know how to move around in there or something bad will happen. I wish I didn't have to take care of it, but my parents left it."[36]

Probably referring to spaces such as Seu Martiniano's altar room, Rodrigues wrote in the 1890s that in addition to the recognized *terreiro* "temples" of Salvador at the time, there were many "private oratories" in the homes of Candomblé leaders and devotees, the numbers of which, he declared, "it is almost impossible to calculate." Rodrigues estimated, however, in consultation with his informants, that thousands of such personal, home-based spaces of ritual cultivation existed in the capital city and its environs.[37] Seu Martiniano's evocative example and the evidence of innumerable other private altars in the living spaces of Africans and their descendants suggests that the Afro-Brazilian family was a privileged space of connection to an alternative identity of blackness in late-nineteenth-century Bahia. These connections were maintained by means of a comportment vis-à-vis ancestrality which invoked relation to the divine as a form of relation to history—one feeding the meaning of the other. Seu Martiniano said that he would rather not have to feed these gods bequeathed to him, that there was danger in their room, that one needed walk carefully in the spaces they inhabited; but they were the strength and protection of his parents in their time of tribulation and it was in his relationship to the deities that he acknowledged that tribulation and his continued relationship to it.

The model Rodrigues describes of "small oratories or chapels in private houses" is precisely that suggested by the police documentation.[38] Many people maintained a small space in their homes for the ritual cultivation of ancestral deities. In Cachoeira and São Félix, as in Salvador, slaves and freedpeople performed limited ceremonies at family altars without the aid of ritual specialists.[39] These rites—some performed on a daily basis—formed the core of domestic worship and were common among Africans and their descendants in the Recôncavo. It was in the homes of those with more ritual knowledge, experience, and obligation that this simpler model was elaborated into a more complex communal ritual. The pattern seems to have been that the private rooms and homes of Africans and their descendants were the initial spaces for ritual cultivation of the deities and the more extensively developed *terreiros* grew out of family-based or individual worship practices. The gestures and offerings at these small personal and family altars were the means Afro-Brazilians developed to re-member an African ancestrality to a fragmented and traumatized American existence, just as the dances, sacrifices, initiations, and other *terreiro* rituals in present-day Candomblé are a means of re-membering the contemporary experience of blackness in Brazil to the history of slavery and the authority of Africa as sources of deepest personal and collective identity. In colonial and imperial Brazil, as some individuals took on greater responsibility for sustaining the connection between the African *orixás* and the New World community of devotees, their homes became the communal centers of healing, divination, refuge, resistance to slavery, and especially the circle-dance ceremonies that brought the deities and peoples of many regions into a collective black identity in Brazil.

Urban Work

Many of the slaves and *libertos* in Salvador worked as *ganhadores* in the city's streets, selling food, sundry items, and their strength as transporters of human beings and merchandise. Africans of various ethnicities who shared an occupational affinity often organized themselves into *cantos* or work groups and would gather in one of the many public plazas, near a fountain, at the docks in the lower city, on a busy street corner, or in another location of substantial transit, where they would wait for and solicit customers. While waiting the workers often did supplementary craftwork—braiding mats and hats of straw, making leather and shell bracelets, fashioning birdcages, or stringing rosaries. The places where *cantos* met often became informal centers of black cultural interaction and exchange. Ambulatory barbers would bring their razors and stylistic expertise to the *cantos* to service fellow *ganhadores* during downtimes. Women brought prepared foods to sell and other workers gravitated toward the portable, makeshift stoves and large pots of porridges, stews, and African-inspired meat, fish, and vegetable dishes to buy a meal or snack. If the location was near a fountain, scores of slaves would gather throughout the day to replenish the barrels and buckets they carried to residences, businesses, and institutions. Police were a ubiquitous presence as well; it was among their principal responsibilities to monitor and control the urban black population. They were in a sense the city counterpart to plantation overseers and, like their rural cousins, Salvador's police force was largely Brazilian-born of African descent.

Bastide has remarked that the street was an instrument of solidarity among slaves and the free and freed common people of Salvador. "Whites merely passed through" the street while slaves and non-whites generally used it as a meeting place. For blacks who were enslaved, interactions in the squares and cobblestone roads of the city represented a means and a place to escape the strict supervision of masters.[40] Like Candomblé and *irmandades,* street culture in Bahia was a space where the slave/free dichotomy was resolved somewhat. While there was no essential distinction in the kinds of work performed by slaves, *libertos*, and the free poor in Salvador (with the exception of domestic work— nearly all domestic servants were slaves), the occupational proximity created spaces for interaction and a sense of commonality. But especially after the 1830s, as the number of free workers steadily rose, tensions developed around competition for jobs. Slave labor was prohibited in certain artisanal sectors, free African labor in other occupations—particularly maritime and mechanical work.[41]

This tension was a problem inherent in the social and economic structure of Bahian society, but the alliance of slaves and *libertos* in *cantos* helped diminish it to some degree by creating a structure which could contain and transform it into a form of collective labor. *Cantos* restricted competition, helped establish solidarity, kept collective work traditions alive, and, as Reis writes, "fought back against slavery's destruction of the African spirit of community."[42] Workers in *cantos* looked out for one another and helped each other with tasks, thereby protecting their weakest and oldest members from castigation or destitution.[43] *Cantos* were also savings and mutual aid organizations. Members helped each other save money to purchase freedom and gave assistance during illnesses. The savings functions of *cantos* mirrored those of other economic associations formed by slaves and *libertos*—the *juntas de alforria* (manumission clubs) and *irmandades* all emphasized manumission as a central concern. Here too these black spaces of labor organization, economic assistance, and mutual aid shared with Candomblé the fundamental impulse toward freedom.

Rodrigues noted that women's *cantos*, in general, were not so distinguished by ethnicity as those of men were.[44] Although Rodrigues does not specify the nature of work conducted in the female *cantos*, we might surmise from knowledge about the frequent occupations of black women in Salvador that they included groups of washerwomen who gathered at the city's fountains and streams to launder clothes, food vendors who gathered in a particular plaza with other workers, and the market-women or *quitandeiras* who set up trays of fruit, vegetables, and fish at various points in the city to sell to regular customers and passersby. We know that enslaved and freed black women dominated small-scale street commerce in Bahia. In addition to fresh and prepared foodstuffs, these women often sold household items like ribbons, thread, and cloth. When not settled at a particular corner or square in the city, they carried their merchandise through the streets in wood and glass boxes or in trays upon their heads.[45]

Ganhadeiras were especially noted for their acumen and business savvy. As Cecilia Moreira Soares notes, an aptitude for commerce and communication was essential in their work.[46] In Rio, the French artist Jean Baptiste Debret was impressed by the manners and clothing of many *ganhadeiras* who consciously presented themselves and their wares to best advantage in order to win the favor of customers and ensure sales. Debret, a guest of the Brazilian court from 1816 to 1831, wrote that the Bahian *ganhadeiras* who moved to Rio with their masters in the aftermath of the independence movement were especially notable for their style and their intelligence. They introduced Bahian foods to the Rio marketplace and were among the most successful of that city's street vendors.[47]

In Salvador, the *ganhadeiras* were intimately associated with Candomblé. The police documents and the oral histories of many of the traditional *terreiros* suggest that African and Brazilian-born black women who worked in the small-scale commerce of the city's streets were among the major participants and leaders of Afro-Brazilian religious communities in Bahia. Recall the women who worked with Domingos Sodré as diviners and "luck-changers," for example. They were street vendors whose communicative abilities likely helped attract new participants and spread the news of the work and successes of Sodré's *terreiro*. And, judging from the presence of large amounts of black women's clothing in Sodré's Candomblé house (as well as several items related to the work of *ganhadeiras,* such as a merchandising box) it appears that women in particular sought community, assistance, and recognition of their leadership skills in the house on Santa Theresa hill. Many of these women were likely slave and free vendors who worked in Salvador's streets. In Cachoeira as well, black women who were involved at various levels of the city's commercial life maintained strong connections to the Boa Morte irmandade and to Candomblé.[48]

The conjunction of *ganhadeiras* and *candomblés* is an important element in the reconstruction of the history of Candomblé's formation in Bahia. Key to this conjunction is the observation that women's *cantos* were generally not organized along ethnically exclusive lines. This implies that in the spaces of shared labor in Salvador's urban landscape a kind of pan-African solidarity may have been developing among black women—slave and freed, *crioulas, Africanas,* and *pardas*—and then carried over into women's participation in Candomblé. In his thoughtful discussion of articles on Candomblé from the nineteenth-century satirical journal *O Alabama,* Dale Graden cites the example of the Dendezeiro *terreiro* whose leadership included Ana Maria, an Angolan-born woman (the *mãe-de-santo*); Antonia Fernandes da Silva, a freedwoman "responsible for the altar; the place where the saints [orixás] are present"; and Maria, a *parda* who was the seamstress of the house. Antonia was described as the "secretary" of the *candomblé* although her ritual duties mark her as an *iylaxé* (the person charged with responsibility for feeding and maintaining the *axé* of the *terreiro* and its *orixás*). While a slave she had been sold from Salvador to Rio but had returned to Bahia after securing her manumission. Two other women were identified as Balbina, who ironed the ritual garments of the *terreiro* community, and Maria dos Santos, who headed "a group which informs the people in the city [about the activities of the *candomblé*]."[49] The work of Maria, the seamstress, and Balbina, the ironer, are reminders of the continuum between labor performed by black women in the Bahian economy and the skills they brought to the maintenance of *candomblé* communities. Maria dos Santos, the leader of the *terreiro's* information network, was likely a *ganhadeira*, serving a similar role in her perambulations as that of the women who assisted Domingos Sodré.

At the very least, one can suggest that a simultaneous process of the collectivizing of Afro-Brazilian identity was occurring among women in work as well as in religious ritual. In fact, a clear distinction between "work" and "worship" was often impossible to make. Candomblé participants—especially the women, who in the present-day manifestation of the religion provide its daily sustenance by their votive labor—recognize very clearly the connections between the "work" of cultivation which they offer to the African energies and the "work" of their ancestors who preceded them in the trials and trauma of black life in the New World. The iyalorixá of the Terreiro do Cobre, Valnizia Pereira de Xangô Airá, insightfully explained to me that the tremendously physical and exhausting collective labor involved in maintaining Candomblé communities and cultivating the *orixás* is, in her mind, closely related to the unremunerated, distressed labor of the slave ancestors of modern-day Candomblé participants. As in the case of Seu Martiniano, Mãe Valnizia maintains an acute, embodied sense of a comportment vis-à-vis the divine as an orientation toward history.[50]

While *ganhadeiras* were a visible and important aspect of Bahian daily life, the work of street vending was not the primary task of the majority of urban female slaves. Most enslaved women and girls in Salvador did some form of domestic work. They were personal servants, maids, seamstresses, laundresses, cooks, wet nurses, and lacemakers.[51] Most significant for our purposes, they were under the almost constant supervision of masters and mistresses and, by and large, did not have even the limited mobility and earning possibilities of *ganhadeiras*.

Most of these women were *crioulas* and *pardas;* Brazilian slave-owners generally preferred Brazilian-born slaves over Africans for household work.

In light of arguments by some scholars that African women in Brazil had more independence than in Africa, Sonia Maria Giacomini has emphasized that even those who worked as *ganhadeiras,* if enslaved, were ultimately subject to the whims and caprices of owners.[52] And those who were freedwomen were constantly subject to the repressive power of police and the larger social-legal apparatus of Brazilian society. Others argue further that while enslaved *ganhadeiras* may have been under less strict supervision from owners and worked with the possibility of earning some supplemental money, whatever "independence" this afforded was not unprecedented in (and arguably not comparable to) the traditions of women's commerce from which many West African slaves came —often within patriarchal societies. Moreira Soares, for example, reminds us that many of the *ganhadeiras* of Bahia were originally from areas of West Africa where small-scale commerce was essentially a female occupation and a means by which women were able to nurture social and financial independence for themselves and their children.[53] Finally, although the question of the relative oppressiveness of African versus Brazilian patriarchy is outside of the scope of this study, it bears recalling that black women in Brazil, both slave and free, were aware of the precariousness of their sexual integrity and attempted to protect themselves from unwanted advances from both black and white men in a variety of ways.[54]

The vulnerability of enslaved women, however, was especially striking because as captives, their sexuality and reproductive capacities did not belong to them. This particular exploitation and its engendered suffering was "generally underestimated and at the same time quotidian."[55] Domestic service, at which the majority of female slaves worked in the cities, involved exposure to any number of daily traumas—from sexual objectification by the males of the household to the tyrannies of mistresses who served as an equivalent to the plantation overseer in the domestic sphere. Brazilian mistresses were often described as demure and mannerly ladies when interacting with social peers or superiors, but the same women, in the company of their slaves, were known to "curse them all day long" and otherwise supervise them with roughness and even violence. Furthermore, for black women enslaved in Brazil, the indignities of forced labor and sexual abuse were compounded by the absolute violability of their maternal rights and sensibilities. Giacomini provides numerous examples of women who were rented and sold for the milk of their breasts when their own babies were as young as forty, twenty, or even seven days old.[56] My own research testifies to the alarming frequency of slave suicides in Bahia—many of whom were women and some, as in the case of Lucrecia in 1847, attempted, like Margaret Garner in 1856 in Ohio, to take the lives of their children as well as their own.[57]

In such circumstances, the cultivation of spaces of support and refuge were absolutely necessary for enslaved and oppressed people. The majority presence of women in Candomblé suggests again the force of the religion as an alternative orientation. And the ritual emphasis on refuge and release from slavery further connects Candomblé with other black institutions such as *irmandades, juntas de alforria,* and *cantos* which held as central elements of their mission the gathering and sharing of resources to free enslaved people.

Other aspects of black labor and economic activity were also essential to the maintenance of alternative orientations in Bahia. One particularly notable example is the role of peddlers in the Recôncavo, most of whom were freed slaves. In Bahia of the late colonial and imperial period, where the infrastructure for ground transportation was weak and slow to develop, peddlers who carried goods between the capital and the Recôncavo (and sometimes even further into the backlands areas) were an important source of materials and information. Blacks in the more distant and isolated towns and districts of the Recôncavo were linked to a larger sense of community by the *liberto* peddlers. The vendors would stay in the homes of slaves and freedpeople during their sojourns, passing on news from neighboring and distant areas; providing ritual, culinary, and other material items obtained from the African trade; and helping to create and sustain networks of friendship, shared ethnicity, and proximity.[58]

The 1807 report from the São Francisco jail, for example, includes statements from several local slaves regarding their interactions with black peddlers from the capital. A Jeje man named Antonio and his *crioula* wife, Jeronima, were questioned about three freed Jeje traders who customarily stayed in their house in the slave quarters of the Osso-do-Boi *fazenda* when selling their wares in the area. While Antonio and Jeronima carefully emphasized to authorities that the visitors never involved them in anything untoward, the couple admitted that they shared hospitality with the peddlers. They fed the men and let them use their house in the *senzala* as a base while the vendors sold *panos da costa*[59] and bought other items, such as chickens, to resell in the city. Benedito, another Jeje slave who identified himself as Antonio's brother, was arrested at the same time (in Antonio and Jeronima's house) and was also questioned about his connections with the city vendors. Benedito was owned by a priest, Pedro Ferreira dos Santos, who imported goods from Lisbon to Bahia. The priest used his slave to deliver the imports to a customer in Salvador as well as to make weekly rounds to pay local free workers in the owner's absence. Benedito admitted that he knew the three Jeje traders well and said further that he sold *panos da costa* for them and for others. Benedito, Antonio, and Jeronima strongly denied any connection with illicit gatherings, but the extensive network of petty commerce and interpersonal relations to which they alluded suggests in itself that even in the realm of small-scale vending and distribution, Bahian blacks constructed supports for community-building and a measure of self-determination.[60]

Irmandades

Lay Catholic brotherhoods were perhaps the most widespread form of mutual aid association in colonial and imperial Brazil. It is estimated that in the 1850s, every Bahian—free and slave—belonged to at least one *irmandade* and many belonged to several.[61] These lay associations were originally organized along lines of nationality/ethnicity, color, class, and, sometimes, occupation.[62] Each *irmandade* was devoted to the veneration and celebration of a particular saint and was headquartered in a church or, as was often the case for Afro-Brazilian confraternities, in a side chapel of another group's church. The sodalities were responsible for sponsoring annual festivals in honor of their patron saint and for other regular ritual activities of veneration, such as masses and votive offerings.

For the black population of Salvador, *irmandades* served as manumission societies, assured care for sick members, provided fellowship and status, and, especially, assured a decent burial to all members. This last service was of particular concern to most nineteenth-century Brazilians. Significantly, the lay brotherhoods provided a physical and cultural-communal space relatively independent of outside control. True, *irmandades* were required to have their charters approved and regularly renewed by civil and ecclesiastical authorities. But in general, the brotherhoods were spaces recognized by the dominant society in which blacks could exercise a certain autonomy over their affairs. With few exceptions, leadership and membership in *irmandades* was not conditioned on wealth (it was based rather on color and ethnicity), so that within any particular Afro-Brazilian lay association, a slave could feel himself the equal of a small businessman and both could fulfill the same responsibilities. Also, through the *irmandades*, Afro-Brazilians enjoyed opportunities to build and decorate their own churches, sponsor chaplains, have funeral services as extravagant as those of elite whites, and display themselves "with brilliance and grandeur in the religious processions which marked the life of the city."[63]

Irmandades were very important to the maintenance, development, and reorganization of African religious traditions in Brazil. Bastide suggests that throughout Latin America, African religions survived most fully in the places where ethnically or racially segregated lay Catholic confraternities were encouraged and where blacks were allowed to dance outside the churches after mass or during processions.[64] *Irmandades* were also a space in which African language was conserved. This, of course, was a means by which African traditions and values could be developed in a new context.[65] Inasmuch as the black *irmandades* were spaces where African language, culture, and ritual knowledge could be transmitted, the Catholic church became part of "o espaço sagrado Africano."[66]

These values, languages, and forms of ritual knowledge were often even transmitted through Catholic imagery, devotions, and pageantry. In the late eighteenth century, members of the Irmandade da Nossa Senhora do Rosario dos Pretos in Salvador responded to prohibitions against the Africanness of their worship style by petitioning the Queen of Portugal to be permitted to resume use of masks, dances, and singing "in the Angolan tongue with accompaniment of instruments for hymns and praise" in celebration of their patron, the Virgin Mary. The petitioners indicated that their activities "seem to greatly please the still glorious mother of God."[67] The desire of the blacks to celebrate the Virgin Mother in their own language, music, and dances as well as the implication that she was gratified by their actions suggests that the members of the *irmandade* conceived of their relationship with Nossa Senhora in terms of their experience of relationship with African deities. Expressions of kinship between blacks and the saints that they cultivated humanized the saints and emphasized their relatedness to human beings and to the human condition in ways not unlike those associated with the *orixás, voduns,* and *inquices.* A nineteenth-century U.S. visitor to Brazil overheard a black man say, "la vem o meu parente" (there comes my relative) as a statue of his patron saint was carried in the street. Another example from a common folk saying suggests the humanization of divine personage even more vividly: "Saint Benedict is a saint whom every black adores. He drinks brandy, and when he sleeps, he snores."[68]

When the first *irmandades de cor* were organized in the seventeenth century in Brazilian towns and cities, they were organized along distinctly ethnic or racial lines. However, by the eighteenth century less exclusive confraternities were being formed and by the nineteenth century most *irmandades* made little distinction regarding African ethnicity.[69] By the early nineteenth century the membership list of Rosário dos Pretos, originally organized as an Angolan *irmandade,* indicated it was open to all people—slaves, ex-slaves, Africans of various ethnicities, women, men, *crioulos,* mulattos, and even whites. Nevertheless, positions of authority on the *mesa* (governing board) were limited by constitution to Africans and *crioulos.* The position of Procurador Geral, for example, an important role of advocate on behalf of *irmandade* members, was available only to Angolans and *crioulos.*[70] Mieko Nishida's study of Afro-Bahian sodalities includes an observation suggestive of both the developing pan-African orientation of blacks in the late colonial period and the flexibility and compatibility of various African religio-cultural orientations. By the late eighteenth century (when the Rosario dos Pretos Irmandade was petitioning Dona Maria), the "Angolan" confraternity had developed a clear majority of West African associates. In spite of this fact, it was important to the *irmandades* members that they maintain "a collective ethnic identity as 'Angolans.'"[71] This was a flexible and inclusive notion of "ethnicity" grounded neither in strict genetic heredity nor in specific regional provenance. The "Angolan-ness" of Rosario's multi-ethnic late-eighteenth-century membership seems not unrelated to the idea of "ethnicity-as-religio-cultural identity" developed in nineteenth- and twentieth-century Candomblé.

Beginning in 1811, the Irmandade dos Martírios, a black brotherhood centrally involved in the founding of the Barroquinha Candomblé *terreiro,* counted among their honorary members some of the most prestigious personalities of Bahia's elite sectors. Archbishops, *marechais-do-campo* (field marshals), *desembargadores* (chief justices), brigadiers, counts, barons, and even colonial governors—like the Conde dos Arcos, who joined in the second year of his governorship—were listed in the *irmandades* membership rolls. These illustrious men were essentially members in name only; they lent the prestige of their presence to formal ceremonies but were not involved in the day-to-day activities of the confraternity.[72] Renato da Silveira, anthropologist and scholar of Bahian Candomblé, suggests that in spite of its symbolic character, the connection of dominant elites with one of the most important institutions of the Nagô community was an important symbol of political alliance to both parties. Through their occasional participation in special solemnities the white political and military leaders offered public recognition, however timid, of the Martírios membership (and of Nagôs more broadly) as acceptable elements in Salvadoran society. These occasions became opportunities for rites of "legitimation of subaltern authority," and blacks used them to demonstrate to the wider society their own capacities for organization and leadership—"their own political power."[73] The elite honorary members in some ways prefigured the role of *ogãs* in Candomblé *terreiros*. They contributed financially to the confraternities—supporting structural repairs and alterations of buildings, funding special decorations and adornments for processions and votive celebrations, and negotiating on behalf of the *irmandades* for permission to hold *batuques* on saint's days. These were examples of situations where black space and hegemonic space intersected—each, in a sense, implicitly validating the other. Furthermore, they demonstrate how blacks used institutions of the dominant society—such as *irmandades* and traditions of patronage—to enhance their own space and participation within the larger Brazilian polity.

Lay confraternities throughout Brazil experienced a general decline in popularity in the nineteenth century. This trend was especially sharp in Bahia after 1850 as local and provincial governments began to assume more responsibility to provide basic infrastructure and social services.[74] Oliveira's analysis of African *liberto* testaments suggests an even earlier decline. Beginning in the late 1820s and early 1830s, fewer people were indicating participation in *irmandades*. Among the reasons for the decreased influence of *irmandades* were the prohibition of burial in private cemeteries and the replacement of mutual assistance functions by other associations. Burial services had traditionally been a major function of *irmandades*, and cemeteries were often located on the grounds of churches which headquartered the confraternities. Sometimes people were even buried in the churches themselves under stone slabs or in walls. For the West and Central South African peoples and their Brazilian descendants, who composed the majority of Bahia's nineteenth-century population, the question of appropriate burial and proper respect for the dead was a serious one. Africans held a high regard for ancestral forces. Ancestors were understood to exhibit concern for the daily lives of their descendants and to advocate on behalf of their unimpeded transition at death into the world of those-who-came-before. Concern for the well-being of discontent souls (especially those denied proper burial) was a notion shared equally by Africans in Bahia and by Portuguese immigrants. A primary role of the *irmandades* was to ensure a decent ceremony of death.[75]

But as Bahian elites came to be more concerned with issues of sanitation and public health (partly in response to the negative image of their city in the eyes of European and North American visitors) they moved to control burial practices more stringently. Because funereal pomp and circumstance and burial near one's confraternal "kin" were great incentives for membership in *irmandades,* the prohibition of burials on church grounds and in private cemeteries was an important factor in the decline of the city's sodalities. Also, of particular consequence to blacks, the manumission function of lay confraternities was increasingly taken over by abolitionist emancipation societies in the second half of the nineteenth century.[76]

As *irmandades* gradually declined in importance throughout the nineteenth century, the influence of the established church on urban slaves and freedpeople also decreased. As a result, the orientation of black spiritual practices moved more fully into cultivation of ancestral traditions. This tendency developed even more with the abolition of slavery and the formal separation of church and state at the founding of the republic in 1889.[77] The change that Mattoso sees as an apparent move from more Catholic-structured black spirituality toward more African-structured traditions can be interpreted in other ways as well. It seems plausible that while *irmandades* were strong and viable institutions in Bahian society generally, they could serve to organize certain aspects of African and emerging Afro-Brazilian tradition from within Catholic church structures, thus limiting resistance on the part of dominant elites. However, once the lay confraternities began to lose strength and viability due to improvements in social service infrastructures, the development of a national movement for abolition of slavery, and prohibitions against private burials, functions they originally served had to be addressed outside of Catholic church structures. One might also observe that the lessening ethnic exclusivity of *irmandades* may have been transferred to and reflected in Candomblé. Or perhaps both the greater inclusiveness of black *irmandades* and the development of structures of pan-African orientation in Candomblé were part of a general trend in the nineteenth century toward more broad-based black identities. Whatever the case, the formation and consolidation of Candomblé communities was occurring in the same time period as the decline in *irmandades,* and as *terreiros* were increasingly recognized publicly (especially after Barroquinha) there was perhaps less need for *irmandades* as a space for the cultivation of African values and traditions and the re-creation of kinship ties.[78]

Another possible connection between the emergence of *candomblés* and the decline in *irmandades* is related to the participation of women. Female membership in *irmandades* is estimated at around 10 percent for the colonial and imperial period. Women were generally permitted in black confraternities but were barred from participation in white ones. According to Patricia Mulvey, most often the women were wives, sisters, or friends of male members. Even though their numbers were small, most black *irmandades* reserved some positions on the governing board for women of African descent. Women played important roles in organizing the periodic festivals and nursing sick members of the confraternities.[79] In stark contrast, the police documents suggest that women accounted for 61.2 percent of the participants in Candomblé from 1800 to 1888. And in fact, women's participation was slightly higher in the first half than in the second half of the nineteenth century. One can perhaps surmise a connection between higher female participation in Candomblé and lower women's membership in *irmandades*. Possibly, too, as *irmandades* declined in popularity among Afro-Brazilian males, the men moved to participate more actively in Candomblé. This might help explain the slight rise in male presence at Candomblé ceremonies in the second half of the nineteenth century. In any event, in comparison to the relatively small participation of black women in *irmandades,* Candomblé appears strikingly as a women's space within the larger Afro-Brazilian orientation.

Personal and Communal Aesthetics

In general, slaves in Brazil were poorly dressed. Men wore pants and shirts of burlap and other sacking material, sometimes of rough cotton, often tattered; women wore skirts of calico with simple blouses and perhaps a shawl. Young children were often naked or covered with a simple smock. Not uncommonly, the clothing of slaves reflected the status and resources of their owners; well-to-do Brazilians tended to use one form of riches (particularly female slaves) as a means of displaying others. On Sundays, one of the few times "proper" white women were to be seen in the street, wealthy families would process to the local church to attend mass and the personal servants of the mistress would follow behind her displaying varying degrees of luxury (especially lace and jewels), depending on their household roles and the favor of the owners. But even among the majority of slaves and freedpeople who did not have access to more lavish clothing and accessories, many attempted (within their means) to cultivate and project a sense of style which emphasized their conceptions of beauty, creativity, and integrity.

For some women, this was simply a matter of wearing a flower or small piece of coral through the perforation in their ears. Black men in Bahia were often seen with bracelets in the form of an incomplete circle of twisted or thick, polished, iron. A fugitive slave in 1858 was discovered with three steel rings on the fingers of his left hand. Verger suggests that the rings were an indication of the man's Muslim identity, as such rings were often associated with Malês in Bahia.[80] Through a surprising variety of aesthetic means, blacks in Brazil cultivated an alternative sense of themselves, their community, and their relation to the material and structural elements of the hegemonic society. Choices in personal adornment, composure, and gesture were the most immediate means available to enslaved and subaltern people by which to express another orientation to the fact of their oppression. What blacks wore, how they walked, and the flair they gave to expressive gestures transformed the physical and social-structural materials at hand into new elements. They made prominent (or at least brought into visibility, into manifestation) alternative individual and communal values that marked the humanity of the bearers .

One of the most common elements of black style observed by visitors to nineteenth-century Brazil was that of hair design. Debret wrote that although black ambulatory barbers were the lowest echelon of the profession in Brazil, they were able to make a good living because Afro-Brazilians of both sexes were very style conscious and desirous of having attractive haircuts.[81] In his own illustrations, Debret recorded a wide variety of braided, twisted, and secured hairstyles for women, often with the additions of combs, beads, flowers, or other adornments. He noted that the women whose hair was most ornately embellished were usually house slaves of wealthy mistresses.[82] Debret also left an illustrated record of the various ways black men wore their hair; many of their styles involved intricate patterns created with a barber's expert razor.[83] Wetherell referred to a number of different hairstyles in Salvador too, although his descriptions lacked the extraordinary variety that Debret found in Rio. In Bahia, Wetherell emphasized, most black women wore headwraps and kept their hair close-shaven. They, like the men, could often be seen sitting at curbside having their hair trimmed by ambulatory barbers. Other women who wore their hair longer, parted it in the middle, and combed it into a puff on each side. Men in Salvador preferred either close-cropped styles or they shaved their hair in the back and let it grow longer in the front.[84]

In addition to hairstyles, blacks in Bahia used a variety of elements of personal ornamentation and general artistry to mark their bodies and the objects of their making with symbols and materials that were significant to them. Cowrie shells, for example, were in widespread use among Afro-Bahians throughout the nineteenth century. Wetherell noted their application in jewelry as well as on drums and other instruments.[85] Documents from the police correspondence also include references to cowries which were attached to ritual clothing, musical instruments, and ceremonial jewelry or were used loose in divination.[86] In addition to bracelets and steel rings, observers noted that black men in Salvador often wore brass finger rings—four to six on the thumb and second finger. Wetherell reports that grass-cutters claimed that the rings were amulets of protection against snakes. Other kinds of jewelry worn by Afro-Bahians included bracelets of iron chain (used by men), others of glass beads; and rings and bracelets of silver. A few black males wore "necklaces of beads" quite distinct from a Catholic rosary.[87] The description of these beaded necklaces is suggestive of the *colares* of contemporary Candomblé; they also recall other references to *contas* and *missangas* (beads) found in the ritual spaces of Candomblé.[88] Identifying facial marks were also common among many of Salvador's African workers.

Clothing, especially women's clothing, offers other evidence, within the available material limits, of African sensibilities of style. In common use were wide skirts of colonial Iberian style in prints and vivid colors, the ubiquitous rectangular *pano da costa*—which was often of a striped pattern—and headwraps.[89] This combination of mixed patterns —printed skirt and striped *pano*—and the practice of wrapping the head in cloth turbans is still common in Candomblé. In fact, the clothing of nineteenth-century black Bahians, particularly that of women, makes a strikingly evocative connection to Candomblé at numerous points. Habsburgo and Wetherell, both writing near midcentury, described the clothing of Afro-Bahian women in terms which, a hundred and fifty years later, offer mirror images of the ritual vestments worn by females in Candomblé communities. Rodrigues, observing at the end of the nineteenth century, further confirmed the styles.[90] Habsburg described the common costume of women slaves. It included a wide circular skirt of simple calico print, a white short-sleeved or sleeveless blouse, a shawl of open needlework, glass bead necklaces with "profane amulets" hanging in several lengths at the chest, and a white or light blue headwrap.[91] This ensemble closely resembles the less formal, day-to-day clothing of modern Candomblé ritual. In place of the shawl, a white or striped *pano da costa* would be wrapped around the upper torso as the initiate went about the daily duties of washing clothes, sweeping and scrubbing floors, cooking, making offerings to the deities, attending to visitors and consultees, and otherwise carrying out her everyday responsibilities within the *terreiro* bounds. This rather simple clothing may also be seen in the less lavish private ceremonies of individual *terreiros* where only initiates are present. Habsburgo did not mention footwear in his description, which was likely not an oversight; slaves were customarily barefoot in Brazil. Likewise, today the *filha de santo* who has not completed seven years of initiation is usually barefoot when involved in ritual activities.

Wetherell described the "gala dress of the black women" that might be worn by the domestic slave of a wealthy family or perhaps by a well-to-do *liberta* or *crioula*. He portrayed this more extravagant attire as a plain or embroidered muslin blouse, sometimes "so sheer as to barely disguise the upper body," the bodice embellished with a large lacy pattern. The blouse was generally worn loose enough that one shoulder remained bared. A very voluminous skirt formed a complete circle when extended to the floor; the bottom hem was embellished with lace and a white arabesque that had been sewn from the inside. An underskirt was also embellished with lace. Bracelets of coral, gold, beads, and other materials as well as necklaces, rings, and "curious earrings" were ever-present elements. An elegant *pano da costa* hung over the shoulders and the woman's bare feet were threaded into small, heeled sandals whose last was considerably shorter than the length of the foot, so that the woman's heel protruded over the end of the shoe and she walked in an affected manner. Finally, the head was covered with a turban of lace, white netting, or colored muslin with a lace border, "very elegantly arranged."[92] Rodrigues wrote that rich black women in Bahia adorned themselves with a multitude of bracelets reaching to the middle of the arm if not covering all of it. They wore belts with a large bunch of trinket-charms, of which a large *figa* was prominent. Their full skirts were of fine silk, their blouses of pure linen, and their *panos da costa* of rich fabric and painstaking handiwork. Rodrigues also mentioned dainty sandals which barely reached the midpoint of the feet.[93]

These nineteenth-century observations distinctly recall the clothing of contemporary *mães-de-santo* of Candomblé, especially that worn during major ceremonies for the *orixás*. The descriptions also suggest the formal dress of initiates—*iawôs* and *ebomis*—when dancing in the ceremonial circle at major *festas* to invoke the presence of the deities. Still, even in the more luxurious "gala dress," bare feet are the norm for *filhas de santo* with less than seven years of initiation. Elegant, backless, heeled sandals (while not as uncomfortably fitting as the ones Wetherell and Rodrigues described seem to have been) are the especial province of the highest-ranking priestesses during public ceremonies. In Candomblé as during slavery, shoes remain a marker of status. Bare feet in the *terreiro* are also a means to connection with the *chão*, the floor, the bare earth, which is a link to *axé* and to ancestral energy.

Candomblé became a space where black women could cultivate an awareness of their grace, their sensuality, and their unique and impressive beauty. It became a space where such cultivation was made an essential element in the larger project of re-creating one's value, meaning, and purpose. But Candomblé was not the only space for this. Elizabeth Cary Agassiz wonderfully summarized the way some black women in Rio used their garments to evoke the dignity and drama of their self-perceptions. The flair of their style, the grace of their arms in beaded bracelets, the elegance of the dark skin of their hands impressed Agassiz, who wrote of the West African slave *ganhadeiras*:

> They are a very powerful-looking race, and the women especially are finely made and have quite a dignified presence. . . . The women always wear a high muslin turban, and a long, bright-colored shawl, either crossed at the breast and thrown carelessly over the shoulder, or, if the day be chilly, drawn closely around them, their arms hidden in its folds. The amount of expression they throw into the use of this shawl is quite amazing. I watched a tall, superbly made woman in the street to-day who was in a great passion. Gesticulating violently, she flung her shawl wide, throwing out both arms, then, drawing it suddenly in, folded it about her, and stretched herself to her full height; presently opening it once more, she shook her fist in the face of her opponent, and then, casting one end of her long drapery over her shoulder, stalked away with the air of a tragedy queen.[94]

A particularly telling connection between black women of the nineteenth century and the aesthetics of Candomblé is highlighted in the Bahianas, the women of present-day Salvador who specialize in street sales of traditional Afro-Bahian foods: *acarajé, abará, vatapá, carurú,* and assorted Afro-indigenous sweets such as *bolo de aimpim* and *bolo de carimã.* Many of these foods are the ritual aliments of the *orixás.* In the nineteenth century, as in the twentieth, the women who sold them on the streets were likely the same ones who prepared them for the deities in Candomblé. In much the same way as did their *ganhadeira* predecessors, contemporary Bahianas travel daily from their homes in various parts of the city to plazas, busy street corners, bus terminals, and other points of convergence, where they arrange their portable stoves and the wood and glass boxes that display their goods and set large tin pans of *dendê* oil to heat. Often throwing the first nine *acarajés* (black-eyed pea patties, ritual food) into the street for the *orixá* Iansã, the Bahianas commence a long day that lasts from late morning into evening, serving faithful customers, attracting others with the rich and pungent smell and vivid colors of their delicacies, and enduring the vagaries of the weather and the market to provide daily sustenance for themselves and their families. The overwhelming majority of these women are black, and not uncommonly they are associated with the myriad communities of Candomblé in the capital city and its environs. The nature of their work, their clothing (more or less elaborate adaptations of the workaday dress of black slave women—long wide skirt, short-sleeved blouse, white or light colored headwrap, *colares* in the colors of various *orixás* with the protective *figa* almost always in view at the back of the neck), and the food they prepare each night and sell during the day are direct connections between the slave and freed *ganhadeiras* who helped originate the Candomblé communities of Bahia and the black women who sustain them today.

Rhythmic Orientation: Music and Dance

Whether maintaining "a loud, monotonous humming" as they carried barrels and boxes up steep slopes and through narrow roadways, keeping time with the cadence of their feet and the call and response of repetitious songs to facilitate large and cumbersome loads, chanting the virtues of the fruits and vegetables in the trays they balanced, or creating a space of community and refuge in a Salvadoran plaza at sunset in a circle dance with instruments like those from home, black men and women in Bahia entwined a profound awareness of music and movement into their orientation to work, to celebration, to sorrow, to life.

Barbers were especially noted for their musicianship—it was just one of several other skills, including bloodletting and dentistry, for which they were known. José Francisco da Silva Lima recalled that in the mid nineteenth century, small bands of barbers would play popular dance songs, including one of Angolan origin called the *lundu,* at the entrances of churches during feasts and novenas.[95] Music was a constant accompaniment to the city's black barbers as they worked, and their three principal activities often occurred simultaneously—that is to say, grooming, surgery, and musicianship. While one man attended to the barbering or doctoring of a client, Wetherell wrote, other associates played instruments "to soothe the soul, or drown the cries of pain, as the case may be."[96] The police correspondence includes several examples of the musicianship of barbers as well. In an especially detailed case from 1843, a resident of Aljube Street in the Sé *freguesia* complained of the music of a group of black barbers who lived and worked on the Ladeira dos Gatos. José Pinheiro Lisboa protested to police that "daily, from dawn until after eight o'clock at night, 'the barbers' disturb the neighborhood with their infamous instruments, and particularly they disturb the supplicant, who, even though he is a lover of music, is not of that of such barbers." Further describing the polyrhythmic tones of the black musicians, Pinheiro reported, "they accompany the disharmonious sounds of their instruments with beats they make on a board, either to supply the drum which is part of their orchestra, or to keep the beat, which they never get right."[97]

The emphasis of these and other street musicians on "the beat" and its complexity, underscores the centrality of percussive rhythm to Afro-Bahian sensibility. Whether it was used as a mechanism to regulate the expenditure of energy in collective work (through rhythmic singing and specifically patterned bodily movements and cadenced steps) or to transform the atmosphere in "sacred" or "secular" ceremony to allow the emergence of another reality, the percussive "beat" served as *materia prima* for black people creating alternative meanings of their lives in Bahia. Both organized and impromptu black dances were common occurrences in the streets of urban Brazil. Often facilitated by the festivities surrounding saint's days and holy days or in the evenings after many hours of labor or even arising spontaneously in the midst of a day's tasks, men and women gathered—most often in a circle—to combine the rhythms of their instruments and their bodies to transform the place and time they inhabited. Wetherell describes such a gathering of men in Salvador who formed a circle around one, two, or three dancers alternating in the middle who punctuated their movements with a handheld horsetail brush whose description recalls the sacred implements of the *orixás* Iansã and Oxóssi. A beaded, stringed calabash; a small drum decorated with ribbons, beads, and bits of mirror that was played like a tambourine; and short hollow bamboo sticks struck against stone were the principal instruments of the dance. Echoing José Pinheiro's comments about the percussive emphasis of the barber's gathering, Wetherell wrote that the music of the black men "had no tune, but kept time." Those who danced in the outer circle while they waited for a chance to enter the center added handclapping and singing to the chorus of instruments. The men danced together for a long time; the ones in the center remaining there until they were tired, others then taking their place, and all participating "with a great deal of spirit."[98]

The "spirit" of black Brazilian dance, particularly its transformative capabilities, was widely remarked upon by nineteenth-century observers. Although many visitors to Brazil talked about the metamorphosis which occurred in black dancers as they danced, most failed to see the development in terms of anything other than a "wildness," something uncontrollable or even demonic that both fascinated and evoked a certain wariness. European visitors Spix and Martius, for example, described seeing groups of blacks dance in the streets of Bahia as the sun went down, "elevating themselves many times to a savage enthusiasm."[99] Debret, on the other hand, was among the more thoughtful and perceptive witnesses to black Brazilian rhythmic sensibilities. Writing in the second decade of the nineteenth century, he recalled an affecting scene in a Rio de Janeiro plaza. As in Bahia, slaves in Rio customarily gathered around fountains, which were the major source of potable water. Debret's description might easily suggest one of the many *batuques* which often arose among the blacks who worked in Bahia's streets.

"Many times one of them, inspired by longing for the motherland, remembers a song": As one man begins a verse, his voice quickly draws others around in a circle. And as he who began the song calls out each strophe, compatriots reply with "a kind of strange refrain" or simply a cry articulated in two or three sounds which sometimes change their character or tone. Almost always, the song is accompanied by a "pantomime improvised or successively varied by the spectators" who move forward to dance in the center of the circle. During the drama, "the delirium of possession" passes across the faces of the dancers while others mark time with hand claps—two quick beats and one slow. Still others make perfect harmony on improvised instruments: plate shards, pieces of wood and metal, shells, rocks, and even tin. The music of the band, like the song's chorus, is in soft tones—only the original refrain rises more forcefully as the leader calls out. When the song ends, "the enchantment disappears" and each person goes his or her separate way, "coldly . . . thinking of the master's whip and the necessity to finish the work interrupted" by such a "delicious 'intermezzo'."[100]

Descriptions such as these suggest the use of dance and music to remake space and transform experience, however "temporarily," belying any convenient distinctions between the "secular" and the "sacred" in Afro-Brazilian religious experience. The "delirium of possession" is of course a hallmark of communion with the deities in Candomblé. But it seems also to represent a generalized qualitative change in the experience, the orientation, of dancers who use the movements of their bodies and the rhythms of their songs as elements of an alchemy in the creation of "other" means and spaces of existence. Whether the dancers in the plaza were experiencing the presence of the *orixás* or simply a great intensity of feeling and where a line of demarcation exists between the two, if indeed it does, seem not the most essential questions for the moment.

What is important for our understanding is that in some way, this dance and music complex, within the spaces of a repressive system of slavery, provided suffering people with a means by which to reorient themselves and their environment to an alternative experience. Sociologist Muniz Sodré writes:

> Dance is a decentering movement, a symbolic re-elaboration of space. Consider the dance of the slave. Moving himself in the master's space, he momentarily stops perceiving himself purely as a slave and remakes the surrounding space in terms of another orientation; one which has to do with a symbolic system different from that managed by the master and which breaks the boundaries fixed by the dominant territorialization.[101]

Part of "breaking the boundaries of the dominant territorialization" was the circle dance; a way, as it were, of creating new, more elastic boundaries—of community, of refuge, of transformation. Historian of Afro-Atlantic slave culture Sterling Stuckey writes that the circle dance was a unifying form for Africans from various parts of the continent who found themselves enslaved together in the Americas.[102] Karasch affirms that in all of the areas of Africa from which Brazilian slaves were taken, dance traditions were central cultural elements.[103] Partly because whites did not often recognize the meaning and power of dance in African religious and aesthetic traditions, Stuckey argues, it became "the greatest spiritual and political resource" for blacks in the unspeakable traumas of New World slavery. Dance, a practice widely shared among West and South Central Africans, and closely connected to concepts of ancestrality and transformation, was a means by which black people in the Americas were able "to recall the traditional African community and to include all Africans" in their developing conceptions of what it meant to be African in the New World.[104] In places like Brazil, where there were multiple structures of social-racial categorization, substantially greater importations of Africans, and fewer children born to African slaves, this process of the creation of pan-African identity appears to have occurred simultaneously with other impetuses toward the maintenance of specific ethnic identities. Nevertheless, the structures of community engendered by shared dance, especially in the circle, were prime sites for the re-creation of black identity toward a pan-African emphasis in the New World.[105]

Networks of Repression and Interstitial Supports

Between 1807 and 1885, no less than twenty-five municipal and provincial prohibitions were passed against black gatherings in Salvador and the Recôncavo as indicated in the Posturas ("Record of Municipal Edicts") and in the police correspondence I examined from the public archives. Most of the injunctions outlawed *batuques* in general, but others created specific penalties for African funeral gatherings, *quilombos*, *candomblés*, and "disturbances" by blacks. In Salvador, for example, the vice-president of the province issued an official memorandum on October 1, 1835, criminalizing "gatherings [of Africans] for dances of batuques which may disturb the public peace and the tranquillity of families."[106] Later, in June 1844 the municipal council of the city prohibited slaves from engaging in *batuques* and dances at any time or place on pain of eight days' imprisonment.[107] Other similar laws came into effect in Salvador in 1827, 1829, 1831, 1844, 1854, 1871, and 1885.[108] In general, when *candomblés* were raided, it was to laws such as these that police authorities referred.

The fact that it was necessary for provincial and municipal authorities to repeatedly prohibit drum-and-dance based gatherings gives a sense of the way in which Candomblé, and Afro-Brazilian culture in general, was in constant tension and negotiation with the received order. In spite of recurring attempts to destroy *candomblés* and forbid *batuques*, these essential elements of Afro-Brazilian orientation were somehow maintained. A large portion of the credit for this must, of course, rest with Afro-Brazilians themselves but it is also important to recognize that even within the dominant society there was seldom a consensus about how to respond to the ubiquitous presence of *batuques*, *tabaques*, *candomblés*, *calundus*, *sambas*, and other forms of drummed and danced black expression.

Throughout the history of slavery in Brazil, slave-owners and civil and religious authorities had deeply ambivalent responses to the tendency of African slaves and their descendants to gather together in the practice of songs and dances "in the style of their land." There were two major schools of thought among elites about this widespread custom. One side feared that such gatherings were socially disruptive and potentially dangerous to the established order. At times, several hundred blacks congregated to dance in a single, unsupervised setting and authorities feared that such gatherings were opportunities to plan plots and rebellions.[109] Certainly the prevalence of African rhythms that were unfamiliar (and perhaps disquieting) to Portuguese tastes, prolonged and energetic collective dancing, and songs and conversations in African languages could be conceived as threatening to a population of privileged whites, who found themselves vastly outnumbered by Africans and their Brazilian descendants in the plantation regions and major port cities.

In December 1808, in the Recôncavo town of Santo Amaro, during the feast days of Christmas, Africans converged from the surrounding plantations and formed three large groupings according to their "nations" to celebrate the holiday, interrupting the normal cycle of their labor. The Jejes danced and sang to the music of their drums "on the Sergimirim Place," the Angolas did likewise according to their own rhythms behind the Chapel of the Rosary, and the Nagôs and Hausas gathered "in the back road, next to the distillery." Captain José Roiz de Gomes, who reported the incidents in a communiqué on January 20 in the following year, described the Nagô and Hausa grouping as the most resplendent, mentioning a large decorated drum which figured prominently in their celebrations and indicating that their festivities lasted well into the night and included food and drink. Gomes reports that the gatherings were well attended and that no "tumult or disorder" occurred.[110] As I indicated in Chapter 6, these slaves declined to stop their celebrations when approached by a local priest, contrasting their constant labor with the leisure of their masters and insisting that they were entitled to some enjoyment.

In his report, Gomes seemed to be most disturbed by the impertinence of the slaves who "[wrapped] these insolences in the title 'amusements'," often with the consent of their masters. Later that month, such gatherings of slaves were summarily prohibited and orders were issued to imprison blacks "as soon as they come together in such disturbances, or upon leaving the *fazendas* to which they belong" without permission.[111] This kind of response that harshly condemned African drum-and-dance gatherings was typical of the repressive measures of João Saldanha da Gama, governor of Bahia in the early years of the nineteenth century. Gama, the Conde de Ponte, was notoriously severe in his views about what constituted appropriate behavior for slaves and about the need to repress religio-cultural manifestations in order to prevent rebellion.

The other side of the debate was articulated by those who believed that allowing slaves to maintain African cultural traditions would enhance ethnic divisions and release some of the tensions and frustrations of a life of enslavement. Saldanha de Gama's successor, Dom Marcos de Noronha, the Conde de Arcos, embodied the converse of his predecessor's views. Arcos believed that the most successful means of social control of slaves was to encourage the permanence of ethnic differentiations among them. He saw this as a way to limit the tendency toward mutual identification and common cause among Africans who were collectively enslaved. Arcos supported "leisure" for slaves as relief from the agonies of slavery and seemed to have believed that "slavery itself caused rebellions," which belief he indicated in some of his letters. In his view, much of the blame for slave resistance could be placed on the excessive punishments meted out by slave-owners as well as on the conditions of overwork, insufficient food, and lack of diversion under which many Bahian slaves lived.[112] Arcos came to power a few years after the Portuguese court moved to Brazil to escape Napoleon's armies in Europe. In the wake of the move, Brazil's ports were opened to international trade and a number of important political and economic changes were instituted which helped to modernize and diversify the region's economy. Silveira suggests that the certain tolerance Arcos extended to blacks and black culture was a new phenomenon in the provincial governance and that it resulted from the relatively more amenable social relations in the province occasioned by a period of economic prosperity.[113]

Changes in political office at the provincial level were often accompanied by significant differences in policing policies. This was both obvious and dramatic in the case of the Ponte and Arcos tenures, but on lower levels of the chain of authority such differences in perspective may help explain why regulations against *batuques,* gatherings, and dances were not always enforced uniformly. In the 1835 correspondence between the Juiz de Paz of Victoria and the vice-president of the province the *juiz* explained that "the policing of Africans in my district" is "my largest responsibility" and complained that the vice-president's immediate predecessor did not sufficiently appreciate the need for night patrols and other regular police presence stationed within the district. The *juiz* asked the vice-president to order a detachment of soldiers to remain stationed in a local fort so as to "send out Patrols and to be ready for whatever urgent need."[114]

In the absence of direct supervision of owners and overseers in the urban setting, the "responsibility" to which the *juiz* alluded was arguably the central role of Salvador's police force as a whole—that is to say, to control the slave and freed African populations. In this context, the prohibitions against *batuques* and other drum-and-dance gatherings were only an aspect of a larger corpus of legislation and custom which limited the mobility of slaves and freedpeople, restricted their residential options, delimited hours of appropriate presence in commercial establishments, constrained the employment opportunities and political participation of *libertos,* and otherwise sought to contain black movement within acceptable physical, cultural, political, and psychic boundaries.

In the second half of the nineteenth century, as positivism and pseudo-scientific theories of racial inequality gained currency in Brazil, Bahians of the dominant classes expressed growing concern with both the problem of black presence in their nation and their own image in the eyes of Europeans and North Americans. Increasingly, Afro-Brazilian religio-cultural manifestations were viewed as threats not only to the smooth running of the slavocratic social and economic apparatus but also to elite ideas of "Brazilian civilization." Official and unofficial positions on Candomblé in the dominant society generally alternated between a legal-hegemonic discourse of vice and criminality, occasional tolerance of the religion as a cultural "escape-valve" for slavery-based tensions, and recourse to the services of *curandeiro-feiticeiros* in moments of personal crisis. These positions were given further nuance by Afro-Bahians in the emerging *elite-de-cor* who sometimes shared family connections with Candomblé participants. Some of these colored elites helped organize and maintain informal networks of support for Candomblé, lending the prestige of their occupations and their connections to social and political leaders in the service of the *terreiros* with which they had some affinity.[115] Others of this new elite, however, were not immune to disparaging attitudes about Candomblé.

Aristides Ricardo de Santana, an Afro-Bahian who became editor of the journal *O Alabama* in 1863, used the periodical as a platform for his dissatisfaction with the proliferation of *candomblé terreiros* and rites. Graden notes that the editor and contributing writers tended to view the religion as an anti-progressive element in the life of the city. For the staff of *O Alabama*, "Candomblé became a key symbol of a past that needed to be forgotten in order to prepare for a better future."[116] Candomblé must have represented a difficult tension for individuals like Santana. Their desire to project "acceptable" images of blackness and their commitments to the ideology of the emerging liberal order urged them in the direction of denouncing and distancing themselves from practices viewed as incompatible with "civilization." Incidents of abuse (actual and imagined) by black religio-cultural leaders were additional fodder for those who would stigmatize Candomblé. In order to more fully understand the nuances of Aristides Ricardo de Santana's positions and allegiances, however, one would have to know more about how he represented himself and how he related to other Afro-Bahians apart from the pages of the newspaper he edited.[117]

Several episodes in the police documentation exemplify the concern among Salvador's authorities for the deleterious effects of Afro-Brazilian religion. In May of 1862, João Antonio de Araújo Freitas Henriques, then chief of police, complained of the widespread presence in the city of "fortune-tellers" and "removers of spells" with whom he associated the debasement of "our civilization" and the origins "of many crimes and disgraces."[118] And in March 1866, the subdelegate of Victoria wrote to the chief of police requesting "an exemplary punishment" for a black man accused of being a *feiticeiro* who had deposited a dog's head in a wall of the São Pedro fort. The subdelegate urged severe castigation of the man, who refused to give his name, as a means to decrease the incidence of practices "which loudly testify against our civilization."[119]

Indeed it seems that those individuals who were identified as Afro-Brazilian religious leaders were often punished more severely than others. Many were given long jail sentences; others, particularly Africans, were deported. And, in keeping with the role of the police as "urban overseers," slaves were also singled out for harsher treatment. In fact, slave-owners in Salvador often remanded the individuals they owned to the police barracks and jails to be chastised with whips, the *palmatória*, and other implements of torture as a means to control them. For example, in response to participation in a Candomblé gathering and for general disobedience and insubordination, Maria, a slave of Felippa Laura Maria da Conceição, was ordered by her mistress to receive thirty-six strokes on her hand with a thick wooden paddle.[120]

Most *libertos* and freedpeople who were arrested for participation in Candomblé were sent to jail for a relatively short period of time—usually between three days and two weeks. But conditions in Salvador's notoriously filthy and deteriorating prisons surely made the time in captivity seem much longer. In a city already suffering from regular bouts of epidemic fevers, infectious diseases, and a general lack of public sanitation, imprisonment could be an extraordinary health hazard. An excerpt from the travel memoir of Thomas Lindley, an early nineteenth-century visitor to Bahia, described the jail as rarely containing less than 200 people and horribly insalubrious due to "the lack of circulating air and the total negligence of sanitary materials." Lindley noted that in spite of being located next to a small hospital, the conditions of the jail led to over 100 deaths among the inmates each year. Furthermore, prisoners were responsible for their own keep and if individuals did not have family members or friends to provide them with daily food, they were at the mercy of local benevolent societies such as the Santa Casa de Misericordia, which provided soup and farinha to the most destitute prisoners. Lindley further remarked at the presence of fugitive slaves among the inmates who were kept until their masters could be located and their punishment determined. Daily, such slaves were chained to each other at the neck and sent in a coffle through the streets to collect water "from a distant place, [this] being the only article furnished by the prison."[121]

Police correspondence confirms this portrait suggested by the foreign visitor. In a particularly disturbing set of reports from the director of the House of Correction to the chief of police in November 1849, the prison administrator pleaded for assistance in repairing "all the roofs of the prison" which were in such a ruinous state that the inmates and guards were threatened by rising water and had no place to sleep. A day later, the same administrator further noted that a freed *crioula*, Eliza Maria de Piedade, gave birth in the waterlogged jail to a baby girl at three o'clock in the afternoon.[122] Earlier that same year, the African *liberto* religious leader and healer Antonio da Silveira was arrested with twenty-one other individuals for "dancing against the active orders" at his house in Quinta das Beatas. The majority of the dancers would likely have been imprisoned in the House of Correction.[123]

Confinement to the House of Correction or the Aljube jail was the fate of most Candomblé participants who were arrested in police raids. Nevertheless, some Afro-Brazilians were able to negotiate space for the celebration of their rituals and availed themselves of the protection of influential whites as well as sympathetic elements of the police force. Most rank-and-file police soldiers were free *pardos*, and some were free *crioulos*. They were also overwhelmingly poor and many had been forced into service in periodic roundups carried out in the city and the Recôncavo. In fact, individuals arrested in Candomblé gatherings were at times impressed into military and police service. After a raid on a *candomblé* in the Rua de Taboão, orders were issued to examine the participants to see if any might "be put to use as a recruit."[124] Members of Salvador's police force, who shared many aspects of class position and cultural orientation with the people they were responsible for controlling, sometimes evidenced ambiguous feelings about their role as agents of black oppression. *Pedestres* (patrolmen), *guardas* (guards), and others in the lower echelons of the chain of command not infrequently aided blacks in their encounters with authority. They were punished for their solidarity (insubordination) just as they were punished for their own participation in *candomblés* and *batuques*.

In 1855, a subdelegate and an inspector in the Sé district complained to superiors about the insubordination of a patrolman, José Gregório. The incidents they cited of Gregório's unsuitable behavior included the fact that he allowed two Africans to enter a house which he was guarding. The subdelegate had ordered that no one be allowed entrance because the house was to be searched for a stolen trunk. In another instance, José Gregório refused to arrest two African women, disobeying direct orders from the inspector and obligating him to get someone else to do the job. The patrolman was sentenced to three days in jail in the police barracks.[125] In a further example, Adão Baptista de Azevedo, an artillery soldier of the first line, insulted a patrolman who attempted to disperse a *batuque* of black youths in which Azevedo was taking part, barefoot.[126] Instances such as these suggest that rank-and-file police and military soldiers not only shared a disenfranchised economic and political position with the general Afro-Brazilian population but that these largely *pardo* and *crioulo* men were also capable of making common cause with Africans and with other Brazilian-born blacks in conflicts with the authority they themselves represented.

Even among higher-ranking officials, however, there existed a variety of responses to Candomblé and other Afro-Brazilian religio-cultural manifestations. In April and May of 1862 a series of letters passed between João Antonio de Araújo Freitas Henriques, the chief of police, and João d'Azevedo Piapitinga, first alternate subdelegate of Santo Antonio, regarding a Candomblé gathering in Pojavá, an area on the outskirts of urban Salvador. During his tenure as chief of police, Henriques was vehement in his condemnation of Afro-Brazilian religio-cultural manifestations. He issued various orders to the subdelegates of the city for the wholesale arrests of diviners, spell-removers, and *feiticeiros* and emphasized the destruction of *candomblés* and *batuques* in his policy imperatives.[127] On April 19th Henriques wrote to warn Piapitinga that a *candomblé* was planned for that day in Pojavá and that he was ordering an encirclement by police soldiers early on the morning of the 20th so as to capture any people found there "as well as all the objects suspected of having a peculiar usage." Henriques urged the subdelegate to head toward the *candomblé* site as soon as he received the letter in order to help with the raid.[128] In a response dated April 21, the subdelegate explained that he had not received the police chief's letter until that very morning and that as he headed toward the indicated place in Pojavá he met fifty-eight people (mostly *crioulos* and a few African *libertos*) in the custody of police officials. Piapitinga respectfully noted that the people and the objects found in their possession would be presented to the police chief.[129] Two days later Henriques wrote another letter to Piapitinga requiring the subdelegate to say whether or not he had had any foreknowledge of the *candomblé* ceremony—which had occurred on the Easter Sunday holiday—and which, Henriques reminded him, Piapitinga was duty bound to disperse in order to prevent "the perpetration of crimes."[130] Piapitinga responded again on the 26th of April explaining that he only found out about the *candomblé* through Henriques' April 19th letter. The subdelegate wrote that gatherings such as the one which occurred on Easter Sunday were generally simple affairs.[131] In the final letter of this exchange between the two men, Henriques expressed disbelief at the subdelegate's supposed ignorance of the Easter *candomblé*. "I cannot neglect to tell you," Henriques wrote, "that it is very extraordinary that Your Mercy only had notice of the existence of the Candomblé of Pojavá through the communiqué I sent you; living as you do in that locality for so many years, as you say, and surely knowing that these festivities, which are not customarily so simple as Your Mercy would have one believe, usually prefer to take place on Easter Sunday."[132]

Indeed Piapitinga was a long-term resident in the second district of Santo Antonio and the ambivalence of his reaction to the Pojavá *candomblé* was compatible with earlier actions he had taken as substitute subdelegate of the district in November 1855. The chief of police at that time, Francisco Liberato de Mattos, had issued a general order to all subdelegates in the city of Salvador to search the homes of Africans in their districts for evidence which might indicate plans for rebellion. The subdelegates in some areas did find "suspicious" items—particularly "objects of their religious beliefs."[133] Piapitinga, however, responded that although he had earlier requested a force of ten soldiers to help with raids, he no longer needed the men because using his own measures he had found no indication of insurrection "in spite of the fact that more than 400 Africans, free people and slaves, reside in this District."[134] In another instance a week later, Piapitinga was called to task by Mattos for not responding with greater dispatch to the complaint of a local block inspector, Francisco de Moura Rosa, who claimed to have been insulted and assaulted by a group of *crioulos* who disobeyed his orders during one of his daily rounds. Interestingly enough, the inspector assumed the "crioulos rebeldes" were heading toward local *candomblé* houses and he identified one of the men as a police musician. Furthermore, when Moura Rosa did not receive an immediate response to his complaint, he wrote to the chief of police suggesting that his assailants, especially a man known as Marcolino, were not being properly pursued because they enjoyed the favor of powerful patrons.[135]

Piapitinga's unhurried response to the inspector's charges, his disavowal of the need for soldiers to search the homes of Africans in his district, and his apparent inattention to the Easter Sunday *candomblé* gatherings may have been due to a level of sympathy with the local Afro-Brazilian population or to a paternalism regarding the people under his police control or even to possible material or other benefits he may have received for his tacit support. We can't know from the documents at hand. What we do know is that, for whatever reasons—and likely for a variety of reasons—people like Piapitinga often came to the aid (implicitly or explicitly) of Candomblé communities and participants, thus pro-

viding important protection from harassment and aiding in the development and continuance of these traditions so essential to the life of Bahia's
black population.

One of the most interesting examples of elite protection for Candomblé devotees and rituals recorded in the police correspondence
comes from October 1855. A block inspector, Aguedo Feliciano Castilho, and five other officers—including a local justice—entered the *loja*
(basement or ground-floor) of a house and found a Candomblé ceremony in progress. A neighbor had informed the inspector that on
certain days (specifically, Sundays and holy days) large numbers of
Africans gathered for meetings in the *loja,* which was occupied by two
African individuals. Entering the space, the inspector and his coterie saw
six Africans in a circle doing something contrary "to the religion of the
country." Castilho attempted to arrest the Candomblé participants but
was impeded by the owner of the *loja,* Ignacio Alberto d'Andrade e
Oliveira, who was identified as a *cidadão* (meaning citizen, connoting the
political and social legitimacy of citizenship). Oliveira confronted Castilho and the others, saying that they were legally incompetent to disrupt
the gathering in the space he owned and that they must remember that
he too was an "authority." When told that the subdelegate of the Sé
district had declared the happenings in the *loja* "offensive to the religion
of the country" Oliveira remarked that the order to raid his premises
meant "nothing but an offense to his rights as a Citizen," and that those
rights should be guaranteed by the "zealous authorities of the Constitution of the Empire." Finally Oliveira threatened the inspector that if he
tried to proceed further he would "gather all his forces, even to the point
of arming the Africans with sticks." The inspector and his associates
withdrew.[136]

Provocatively, Oliveira appears to have interpreted the raid as an
affront to his personal rights and not simply to his property rights. His
statement that the subdelegate's order was "an offense to his rights as a
Citizen" seems to have come in response to the accusation that the
activities practiced in his *loja* were against the religion of the state. Was
Oliveira suggesting (implicitly or explicitly) that he shared the religious
orientation of the Africans? Although the Brazilian constitution of 1824
did not specifically prohibit the practice of Afro-Brazilian religion, its
provisions to permit worship other than state-supported Roman Catholicism were generally not interpreted as applying to African traditions. In 1829, for instance, when the justice of the peace of Brotas,
Antonio Gomes de Abreu Guimarães, reported a raid on a Candomblé
terreiro in his district, he quoted article five of the constitution in his

argument against the Candomblé community. The article read, in part, "the Roman Apostolic Catholic Religion shall continue to be the Religion of the Empire. All the other Religions will be permitted but their practice shall be domestic, or private, in houses designated for this purpose without any exterior Temple form." Guimarães further stated that this provision was meant to apply to "the Political Nations of Europe, and never the black Africans, who, coming from their homeland to ours, are educated in the Recompense of our Religion."[137]

In his report on the raid of Oliveira's *loja,* Inspector Castilho lamented "that there are still men in the midst of a civilized City who allow in their houses such africans who are involved in such barbarous activities, and instead of restraining them, encourage them, and even protect them with the authority with which they are invested."[138] By associating himself with Candomblé and using his "authority" and resources in its defense, Oliveira challenged the general perspective of Bahian elites that Afro-Brazilian religion (and, perhaps, by extension, blacks themselves) was not deserving of the protection of the constitution. His actions also highlighted the growing tension between ideas of "civilization" in Brazil—heavily dependent on a mimicry of European ideals—and an African-influenced cultural tradition profoundly entrenched in Bahian reality. However, it should be noted that Oliveira's statements to the inspector were phrased in terms of his *own* rights as a citizen and as a man of authority and not in terms of any implied rights that the Africans had or should have had. In this sense, the support he offered the blacks who lived and gathered in his *loja* did not dramatically depart from the paternalistic model of race relations so deeply ingrained in the psyche and customs of colonial and imperial Brazilian society. Nevertheless, the help of individuals—and even families—from within the dominant sectors of the Bahian social structure was crucial to the survival of individual Candomblé communities and to the development of the religion as a whole. The *terreiros,* in turn, recognized this significant assistance and by the late nineteenth century institutionalized the status of protector-benefactors in the role of *ogãs.*

If much of the white support for Candomblé came in terms of the familiar models of patronage and paternalism, Afro-Brazilian religion nevertheless offered alternative models for the meaning of Brazilian community, polity, and humanity. Candomblé and other elements of alternative black orientation in nineteenth-century Bahia signaled the development of a collective Afro-Brazilian experience whose deeper meanings and contours were perhaps best seen in the internal spaces and relations of the black community: within families (in their various forms), in the work lives of *ganhadores* and *ganhadeiras;* in aesthetic and rhythmic sensibilities; and in the circle dances of *batuques, sambas,* and *candomblés.* The traditional historiographic emphasis on a relative lack of inter-ethnic cooperation in organized slave revolt has tended to privilege an interpretation which highlights distinctions within the Afro-Brazilian community. Clearly at the level of organized rebellion, ethnic and national differences were often accentuated. Yet it is necessary to simultaneously recognize that Afro-Brazilian religio-cultural manifestations, such as Candomblé, evidenced integration of a variety of pan-African elements and participation of various components of Brazil's black population.[139]

While Africans certainly held on to a sense of their ethnic particularities, especially when among their compatriots, it seems that specific ethnic identities increasingly shared space with a more collective orientation to Africanness and blackness in the Brazilian context.[140] As an analysis of the police documents suggests, it was the more collective dynamic of African identity that *crioulos* and *pardos* inherited as the century progressed. This was especially clear in Candomblé, where the cultivation of multiple deities, the synthesis of aspects of several ethnic traditions, the reconstitution of family lineage along devotional community lines, and the changing meaning of "nation" served to emphasize a shared Afro-Brazilian context for blackness and Africanness.

The existence of Afro-Brazilian orientations which mitigated the racist hierarchies of power in nineteenth-century Bahia, does not, however, negate the fact of those color- and status-based hierarchies and their influence on identities of blackness. What I am suggesting is that blacks in Bahia operated with an extraordinary sense of awareness about the configurations and limitations of their social and economic position. This heightened awareness was necessitated by their marginality to the structures of power and was the means by which they attempted to "sway between a dance and a fight," to situate themselves alternately in alliance, resistance, and restraint vis-à-vis the separate spheres and the often hazardous terrain between.

8

Candomblé as *Feitiço:* Reterritorialization, Embodiment, and the Alchemy of History in an Afro-Brazilian Religion

> The slave had to come to terms with the opaqueness of his condition and at the same time oppose it. He had to experience the truth of his negativity and at the same time transform and create *an-other* reality. Given the limitations imposed upon him, he created on the level of his religious consciousness. Not only did this transformation produce new cultural forms, but its significance must be understood from the point of view of the creativity of the transforming process itself.[1]

—CHARLES H. LONG (italics in original)

In an interview in the May 14, 1936, edition of the newspaper *O Estado da Bahia,* Martiniano Eliseu do Bomfim said: "My parents were slaves. My mother, I remember well, had a scar on her buttocks from a burning they gave her as punishment. All this must be studied."[2] Seu Martiniano's comment in the context of a conversation on Afro-Brazilian traditions recalls his perspective on the altar room of the *orixás* of his parents and suggests that the lived experience of his parents was part of his own religious comportment. In his emphasis on a recognition of the centrality of the experience of enslavement to the meaning of Afro-Brazilian religion, the respected *babalawo* highlighted a critical historical consciousness. This is the same kind of consciousness to which Iyalorixá Valnizia Pereira alludes in statements about the extraordinary labor intensity of Candomblé. The *mãe de santo* of the Terreiro de Cobre suggests that the vital work of Candomblé is an embodied memory of the work performed by enslaved ancestors who originated the tradition in Brazil.[3] It is a very intimate, immediate consciousness embedded in comportment which connects present activities, present orientations, with the experiences of preceding generations. The labor intensity and inevasible responsibilities of Candomblé, are a kind of communion with forebears, a continuation of the process by which *axé* (life force; spiritual force) has been cultivated and transmitted among New World devotees. In caring for the patron *orixás* of his mother and father (perhaps in the manner they themselves taught him) Seu Martiniano implicitly recognized not only the African traditions of his Yoruba parents, but also the protection necessitated by the traumas and dangers they suffered in slavery. In that sense, what the *babalawo* fed in his ritual gestures of offering to the *orixás* was not only the power and beneficence of those deities, but the alternative orientation of his parents—their identities of connection to African cosmic forces in the midst of and in spite of the subaltern status imposed upon them in slavery. Furthermore, relationships such as the one Seu Martiniano maintained to the *orixás* of his parents, to the continuation of Afro-Brazilian religion, are often articulated within Candomblé in terms of an inherited responsibility—something in the veins, in the blood.

Scars like those on the body of Seu Martiniano's mother and the years of uncompensated labor of Candomblé's earliest devotees form essential parts of the experience of the religion, the meaning of its rituals, and its central emphasis on the development of an alternative identity for participants. In Candomblé, links to the history of Brazil's black presence are both material and immaterial. Straw mats for sleeping recall the rough pallets of slaves on dirt floors. Calf-length everyday calicos and bare feet—the uniform of votive labor in the *terreiros*—are immediate reminders of the work clothing of slave and freed *ganhadeiras*. The drum voices evoking the presence of the deities in ceremony are those which gathered the African nations to diasporic communion in an earlier century. And the *orixás,* descending into the bearing-up bodies of devotees, are sometimes recognized as spirits *de herança,* an inheritance from relatives who served them lifetimes ago. Candomblé is filled with physical and spiritual manifestations of the connections between "then" and "now"—material and immaterial links to the historical past; localization points for collective memory.

Just as Candomblé supported and continues to support an alternative orientation to identity it also engenders *an-other* perspective about history. This is not an abstract, distanced, "rational" kind of analysis of the past. It is not a history to be examined objectively or transcended. Rather, Candomblé is history riding your back. Something close and demanding, passing its burdens as both gift and requisition. It is also history as alchemy, Candomblé as *feitiço*—a means of constructing an oppositional self (personal and collective) out of the materials of subjection, the materials of oppression, the history of slavery. Like the bones, blood, coins, and scraps of prayer which composed the *mandingas* of José Francisco in Portugal, the elements of black life in Bahia were among the alchemical materials of Candomblé as *feitiço*.

In the societies of the New World, blacks have used a variety of means to engage what Long calls "the structures of involuntariness, oppression, and denials" which have been determinate factors in their lives for centuries. Corresponding with the idea of African American orientations as "conjuring" or "feitiço," Long writes: "In the context of their struggles . . . they discovered a rhythm of life, a modality of experiencing and knowing that expressed a unique manner of coming to terms with what is the case by transforming negative situations into creative possibilities."[4] This emphasis on transformation and creativity is central to an understanding of Candomblé as *feitiço*. Whether in terms of the use of *mandingas, patuás,* and offerings to the deities in attempt to modify relations between masters and slaves; the manipulation of percussive sound as a means to transform bodies and spaces for healing; or the gathering of ethnic Africans and *crioulos* into an Afro-Brazilian collectivity based in shared ancestrality and the circle of spirits, Candomblé was a performance of conversion—altering the nature of reality to address the deepest needs of besieged and subjected peoples.

Black religion also represented a recognition of different *forms* of power. Slaves and freedpeople in Bahia, for example, understood that the effective social, economic, and political power was not in their hands and was not generally available to them in any meaningful sense—so attempts to challenge hegemony on its own terms were relatively infrequent. (The rash of African-led rebellions between 1807 and 1835 implies that many people were not convinced that the structural dominance of elites was impervious to threat. In these revolts Africans were more willing to challenge the hegemonic system than were *crioulos,* who were perhaps more acutely aware of the differences in power or who, as João Reis suggests, were more reconciled to the nature of life in enslavement, since they had been born into it.)[5] However, the documentation of Candomblé, *calundu,* and other forms of black religiosity in colonial and imperial Brazil indicates that Afro-Brazilians commonly recognized other sources and forms of power which could be used to address the structural imbalances from an alternative perspective. The *feitiços* of healer-sorcerers, the prayers and offerings at altars to the *orixás,* and the circle dances of *batuques* and *candomblés* were attempts to use alternative sources of power to engage the disjunctions of slavery and to strengthen the forces (the *axé*) of those who called upon and cultivated those alternative sources.

The *terreiro* community was an important physical and psychic space for what Muniz Sodré calls the "reterritorialization" of African identity in Brazil.[6] Candomblé *terreiros* were places—especially after the mid-nineteenth century, but earlier as well—where Africans, *crioulos*, some *pardos*, and even a few whites gathered in an experience of redefinition of black identity which countered that imposed from outside in a variety of ways. At a basic level, Candomblé represented a challenge to the hegemony of Catholicism—suggesting another means by which to approach relation to the divine. The fact that blacks in Brazil would maintain and cultivate spiritual traditions based in African orientations represented a threat to elite control of the black populace as well as to notions of the existence of a Brazilian "civilization" modeled on European ideals that consciously excluded African elements as undesirable. The flexibility with which Afro-Brazilian religion often incorporated elements of Catholicism, as a veneer or as a means of indigenization, was particularly disturbing to Bahian elites who viewed such adaptability as apostasy. Candomblé also countered the dominant definitions of blackness by emphasizing an identity of profound and intimate connection to the divine (more specifically, to African conceptions of divinity) over the imposition of slave and subaltern status. Through participation and initiation in Candomblé tradition, black Brazilians (and not-so-black Brazilians as well) were reintroduced to a meaning of themselves, a meaning of their own identities, which stressed a connection to valued traditions of blackness: blackness as Africanness and Africanness as a source of *axé*. Finally, Candomblé communities were spaces of collective transformation, where the deities and peoples of specific regions of Africa came to form a single community, a collective identity, derived from the shared experience of black life in Brazil. Also important to the meaning of nineteenth-century Candomblé communities is the idea Dwight Hopkins has used to discuss Afro–North American religious reterritorialization—"self co-constitution with God."[7] As in the United States, the reterritorialization of black identity in Brazil occurred most strikingly in the context of orientation to the divine.

The physical organization of Candomblé *terreiros* is a reflection of and a representation of the pan-Africanizing impulse in the religion's development. As Africans and their descendents reorganized the structures of ritual cultivation of divine energies in Brazil, they did so in such a way as to bring together various deities under the collective care of a single community. Each *orixá* is accorded a specific, delimited space—often a room, or a one-room "house"—in which the divinity is said to reside.[8] This is the place where the *orixá's* energy is ritually cultivated and where various rites for devotees are conducted. In Africa, deities were often associated with (and venerated by) particular families, ethnic groups, and geopolitical entities. The collectivizing experience of Candomblé brought the deities of various ethnic and sub-ethnic groups into a single ritual space. At the same time, a sense of each god's particular origins and the relationships among groups of deities were maintained through traditions of metaphysics, myth, language, alimentary preferences, dance and music rhythms, etc. This process modeled (and perhaps stimulated) the experience of Africans themselves.

In Candomblé the body as territory and the meaning of a body-conscious spirituality are at the heart of reterritorialization. Both Sodré and Long indicate the relationship between embodiment in African American religion and the recognition of limits, of territory. For Sodré, the idea of limitation in Candomblé issues from non-Promethean African paradigms of civilization. That is to say, paradigms "not disassociated from the Cosmic Order, not generative of radical oppositions between subject and object—rather, frankly territorialized."[9] Limitation, territorialization, or, as Long calls it, "a meaning of restraint"[10] is closely related to the nature of alternative identity in Candomblé. Candomblé is an orientation which recognized even the limitations of slavery, in a certain sense, and attempted a way to hold onto a truer self, a way to survive in the midst of siege. Maria Ines C. de Oliveira reports that through her research on African *libertos* in nineteenth-century Bahia, she has become increasingly convinced that many of them maintained a comportment vis-à-vis the dominant society that was neither characterized by open rebellion nor by passive acceptance. Rather it was an "ineffable something," a mode of being along the lines of "a third way." Here, the central issue was not confrontation (or its opposite). Rather the question was one of assessment: critical, honest, realistic assessment of the situation in which the Africans found themselves and then an inquiry (at various levels, internal and external) into what was necessary to "manage the new place."[11] The orientation represented by Candomblé (and by the general modus operandi of many African *libertos*) was a way to grow strong in assaulted territory—a way to build an alternative experience of humanity, of participation in society, of citizenship.

Ashis Nandy has similarly remarked at the way "average Indians" negotiated and adjusted within the limitations created by British colonialism. Although the non-rebellious efforts to manage an oppressive situation were sometimes mocked by colonialists who felt the Indians to be submissively, even comically, accepting of white domination, Nandy insists that the Indians were, in their apparent acceptance of the status quo, actually defending a sacred part of themselves; hiding it; protecting it. Nandy writes of the "non-heroic ordinariness" of "the average Indian" as a means to psychic survival. The apparent compromises with the colonial system were a protection from being overcome by the values of the colonialists. "Defeat," Nandy writes, ". . . is a disaster and so are the imposed ways of the victor. But worse is the loss of one's soul and the internalization of one's victor, because it forces one to fight the victor according to the victor's values, within his model of dissent. Better to be a comical dissenter than to be a powerful, serious but acceptable opponent."[12] The alternative models of power in Candomblé can be seen as instruments of dissent which follow an orientation distinctly different from that of the dominant classes. They are ways to maintain a very different sense of selfhood and identity while operating within the limitations of hostile hegemonic forces.

We return to a notion of the separate spaces of "whiteness" and "blackness" in nineteenth-century Bahia. Candomblé was a means to protect an alternative identity which then, by virtue of its existence and safeguarding, allowed "assimilation" into dominant paradigms without suffering destruction. As blacks in Brazil secured an-other identity in a safe place and found ways to nurture it privately and collectively, they were able to make the compromises with the dominant social and economic structure necessary to survive. The private oratórios described in Rodrigues's discussion of late-nineteenth-century Candomblé, the altar room of Martiniano Eliseu de Bomfim, and the collective spaces of Candomblé terreiros represented such "safe" places. These were the locations wherein a lineage of alternative meaning, of alternative identity, was recognized and fed.

The experience of slavery, of dehumanization, of objectification necessitated the development of some kind of oppositional identification which represented an alternative to "slave," but which thereby also implied a relationship to that signified identity. The Africanness of the slave class and of slave culture in nineteenth-century Bahia has led some scholars to assert that no "slave consciousness" existed among blacks there.[13] However, it seems to me that at a very important level, an Americanization (or creolization) of experience and meaning was constantly occurring through the bodies of enslaved Africans from their earliest contact with slavery which then changed the meaning and form of consciousness and culture. Roger Bastide maintained that while the minds and spirits of Africans may have held tenaciously to African values, the actions their bodies forcibly performed were Americanizing them.[14] This Americanization can perhaps be appreciated most clearly in the orientation of African bodies in work. The experience of forced labor, the physical duress, the dislocations, the commodification of the body were corporeal experiences directly related to enslavement. As the African body participated as an exploited element in the colonial and imperial project in Brazil, that corporeal experience was brought to bear on African structures of mind and culture, essentially creolizing them. Unless one sees the body as completely separate from the mind-spirit, one must recognize in some foundational way that the embodied experience of slavery indeed informed the slaves' sense of being and necessitated a response, antidote, or alternative.

The corporeality of the slave experience is further highlighted in the phenomenon of movement as an essential aspect of slave resistance. From a variety of contexts, the *movement* of black bodies can be interpreted as movement away from the signified identity of slave and toward an alternative experience of self. *Quilombos*, for example were mobile, furtive communities of alternative black orientation by means of which slaves physically *moved away* from slavery's sites. The act of *fuga* (escape) was an act of *running away*—to anonymity in the larger cities, to the density of forests, or to *candomblés* and *quilombos*. In all of these cases, the point was *moving* the body, orienting the body to another physical and psychic space, a space of alternative possibility. So too dance was a means by which the body was oriented to an alternative experience. The same body that contorted under the weight of cane-stalk bundles or barrels of rum or water or years of washing clothes by hand, the same body that worked involuntarily, unpaid, and under duress emphasized, through dance, another meaning of itself.[15] It availed itself of another way of experiencing the world—right in the midst of the ordeals of slavery. In part, this was done as a means to engage and dislodge some of the trauma; and to form in the *other* spaces—in Candomblé communities, in street culture, in *quilombos*, in *cantos*, in families, etc.—*an-other* construction of reality, of identity, of meaning. So while slave culture in Bahia was heavily influenced by African sensibilities, it must be simultaneously recognized that immediately upon imprisonment in the slave coffles and *navios negreiros* (slave ships) and certainly upon arrival in the New World, the *bodies* of enslaved Africans were being oriented to an entirely different meaning—an Americanizing orientation through the corporeal experience of enslavement. The Americanization of the African body made that body a contested site. Signified identities of blackness (subaltern, slave, inferior, etc.) and alternative orientations toward the ontological self were contemporaneously present in the same personal and collective corpus.

Candomblé, and African American alternative orientation more generally, became a premier location for the engagement of this corporeally contested identity. It is significant that so many of the alternative spaces of blackness relate to physical orientation (work, dance, escape, behavioral comportment, gesture, ritual, etc.) because the body has been the prime site of the degradation and Americanization of black identity through its commodification, enslavement, and signification. Candomblé can be understood as a ceremony, a performance of the *reclamation* of the body by a pan-African collectivity, a circle of Spirits and New World kin. This reclamation is an essential meaning of Afro-Brazilian religion and is distinct from African tradition—at least its pan-ethnic collective character and urgency is particular.

In Candomblé, as in many other religions of the Afro-Atlantic diaspora, a principal element of alternative orientation has been an intimacy with divinity evidenced most strikingly in the phenomenon of possession or trance. In any number of traditions of African American spirituality, including Afro–North American Christianity, Jamaican and Trinidadian Shango Baptism, Cuban Santeria, Haitian Vodou, Surinamese Winti, and Brazilian Candomblé, intimacy with the divine has been a hallmark of religious experience. As Sheila Walker notes, the "palpable relationship between people and their deities is a unifying feature of the Africa-to-Afro-America religious continuum."[16] In Candomblé, possession (and, by extension, initiation) expresses the fundamental nature of the relationship between human beings and deities. It is a relationship of exchange, of mutuality, of shared responsibility, and above all, of accompaniment.

This familiarity with God, rooted in African understandings of relationship between human beings and the divine, appears to have taken on especially marked characteristics in many religious traditions of the Americas. It is as if, in the experience of slavery and the consequent and subsequent struggles against oppression, there was a greater need for the presence and protection of the Spirits. Also, of course, as individuals from various regions and ethnicities were scattered throughout the plantations, mines, and cities of the New World, the original ethnic and religious communities were fragmented and new gatherings were created for the reconstructed cultivation of religion and identity. In Candomblé, the reterritorialized religion brought together deities and devotees of a wide variety of African traditions into a new "self-founding" experience of black religion in Brazil. At the same time, responsibility for cultivating relationship with the deities became increasingly personal and involved greater numbers of individuals (especially women) who were initiated in the service of the *orixás* as priestesses and priests.

Pierre Verger explained that in Africa, ceremonies for the *orixás* have traditionally been the responsibility of liturgical leaders specifically designated and trained for that work. Other members of the family or group dedicated to a deity have essentially peripheral roles—contributing to material costs and participating (if they choose to do so) in the songs, dances, and festivities accompanying the ritual celebrations. They also observe the prohibitions—such as those regarding food and sexual relations—of the particular deity, "and in so doing they are perfectly within the bounds of their obligations."[17] However, in Brazil, each member of a Candomblé community has the responsibility of attending to even the smallest needs of his or her *orixá*. As Verger suggested, this situation emphasizes the role of a competent *mãe* or *pai do santo* who can orient devotees in the appropriate ritual obligations.[18] It also highlights the greater intensity of connection between devotees and deities in the New World setting.

Africans interviewed by Nina Rodrigues at the end of the nineteenth century in Bahia expressed a certain discomfort with what they saw as the widespread susceptibility of Candomblé devotees to *cair no santo* ("fall in the saint"; become possessed by an *orixá*) in Brazil. They also indicated that in Africa relatively few people personally experienced the embodied presence of the deities. The trance state was the prerogative of the priests "or at least, of a small number of privileged people."[19]

Karen McCarthy Brown, in her discussion of Haitian Vodou, has also reflected on what appears to be the more stringent, and yet more fervent, creative, and intimate connection between deities and devotees in the New World. Brown compares the experience of Haitian refugee children coming to the United States in the 1980s with that of slaves who were newly arrived in Haiti in the colonial era. She explains that in the island nation itself, children are rarely possessed by the *lwas* (gods; divine spirits); the experience is perceived as too dangerous for them. However, many of the boys and girls who made the hazardous voyage in unseaworthy boats, although they were accompanied by adult guardians and extended kin, were separated from their grown-up companions by the U.S. Immigration and Naturalization Service. Brown notes that several of these children "responded to their fear by going into possession."[20] The relatively more common experience of possession and initiation into the service of the *orixás* and *lwas* on this side of the Atlantic is perhaps a reflection of the effects of the physical and psychic disjunction caused by the experience of the Middle Passage and of slavery. Not only did those disjunctions highlight the consciousness of ethnicity and alternative identity among Africans in the New World, but even the intensity of connection to religion was accentuated in the American context. Surviving the traumas perhaps required a stronger grasp, a tighter embrace between deity and devotee, than that which had existed previously. Candomblé tradition maintains that the ability to receive an *orixá* is an inherited trait, thus implying that the fixedness of such an embrace became embedded in Afro-Brazilians as a genetic possibility, passed on through the generations—a gift of grace, of accompaniment, inside terror.

As with the body-centered emphasis in the Pietzian idea of the fetish, Candomblé manifests its meaning in active relation to the human corpus. Dance, rhythm, and possession or trance are essential forms of the alternative orientation present in Candomblé. Possession is particularly significant because the occupation of black bodies by divine being is a stunning contestation of subalterity. Also, initiation (and the material implantation of the essence or energy of an *orixá* into the body of the devotee) is a form of marking blackness with divinity. The experience of accompaniment, of "self co-constitution with God," agitates at the center of the meaning of possession in New World African-based religion.

The historical experience of slavery transformed the meaning and experience of Candomblé into a ceremony of alternative personal and collective identity. The *roda* (circle) of multiple pan-ethnic African Spirits, the intensified emphasis on mutual obligation between all devotees and *orixás,* the greater frequency of the embodiment of divine presence, and the interpretation of the meaning of history from the perspective of religious comportment are all elements of the collectivizing and transformational impetus in Candomblé. Through the religion, black Brazilians (and others attracted by their example) engaged the elements of their oppression into an alchemy of resistance, of assessment, of recognition, and of healing.

Coda: Abolition, Freedom, and Candomblé as Alternative *Cidadania* in Brazil

By interrogating the subaltern and slave identities imposed on blackness in nineteenth-century Bahia, Candomblé offered an alternative
model for the meaning of Brazilian community, polity, and humanity.
In the last thirty years of the century, the abolition movement grew in
force and influence, the nation moved from empire to republic, and
national elites searched racist modern European ideologies of development for answers to their complexes of identity and rationalizations for
their profoundly exclusivist political ideals. In this period Candomblé
represented a means by which blacks in Brazil attempted to find/make
a place for themselves within the Brazilian totality at a moment when
their presence was increasingly questioned and marginalized.

At the beginning of the second half of the nineteenth century the
African slave trade was finally abolished in Brazil. Slavery gradually
declined in the northeast and the number of *libertos* grew as cane-
growing diminished and increasing numbers of Bahian slaves were sold
to the emerging coffee plantations of Brazil's central south. Caio Prado
Jr. noted that the end of the slave trade marked a period throughout
Brazil when resources which had been spent on the transatlantic commerce in human bodies were made available to develop infrastructure
and modernize production methods.[1] However, the development of
Brazilian industry in the wake of the end of the slave trade was decidedly
more pronounced in the southern sections of the country than in the
northeast. This was partly due to a series of economic crises which the
region endured related to the flight of Portuguese capital after Brazilian
independence, the transfer of slave labor to the developing coffee-
growing regions, the competition for sugar on the world market, and
recurrent droughts and epidemics. The situation was also related to the
deeply entrenched seigniorial culture in Bahia and Pernambuco where,
even as slavery decreased in importance as a system of labor, there was

no real impetus to move beyond the structures of patronage, patriarchy, and rural fiefdoms which had developed in the region since the sixteenth century. By the eighteenth century in Bahia, free labor and small-scale farming dependent on the largesse of plantation owners were essential elements in the region's economy. These forms of labor organization remained the norm in the northeast until well into the twentieth century.

Even Salvador, a capital city, was still very much tied to the Recôncavo ethos in the late nineteenth century; according to Mattoso, the city remained essentially a provincial entrepôt. Bahia's significance as a port declined throughout the nineteenth century as Rio and São Paulo developed into the political and industrial centers of the nation, respectively. But even without the more pronounced technological and political modernization of the country's southern cities, Salvador began to experience the effects of increased emancipation as Africans and their *crioulo* children and grandchildren swelled the ranks of *libertos* and freeborn blacks in the city. By the end of the empire and the beginnings of the republic, a significant *elite de cor* had developed which played an important role in the protection of Candomblé as well as in the emerging political and workers' movements in early-twentieth-century Bahia.[2]

The ending of slavery was essential to the development and stabilization of Candomblé. Even before final abolition in 1888, manumission in the lives of individual people was an important element in the religion and a necessity for its continuity. In order for Candomblé to develop and maintain itself in Bahia, *somebody* had to be free. And in dialectical relationship, one of the major characteristics of Candomblé was to secure freedom and refuge for those who were not yet free. In the relative autonomy of the urban environment where funds could be amassed for self-purchase or for the purchase of freedom for a spiritual leader, African *curandeiro-feiticeiros* were often liberated from the direct control and humiliation of masters. The rooms they rented or small houses they owned were spaces generally free of immediate elite supervision. These men and women used their freedom to fulfill religious obligations, serve as healers, learn and teach African traditions, and otherwise be spiritual resources for people attempting to make their way through the vagaries of colonial and imperial Bahian society. A certain amount of freedom had to exist in order for Candomblé to exist (even if initially there was just enough internal autonomy to carry out the ceremonies and rituals of remembrance), and Candomblé was fundamentally about making more freedom. There was a connection between the psychic/spiritual reclamation of selfhood in Candomblé participation and the physical reclamation of selfhood in *liberto* status. Each was a kind of freedom, one facilitating the other, both a means of moving black identity out of contestation.

Unlike the abolitionist movement in the United States whose arguments were largely articulated in moral and religious terms, the development of Brazilian anti-slavery ideology among elites drew heavily from latter-nineteenth-century European intellectual trends that emphasized technological modernization and a concomitant pseudo-scientific racism. Positivism, for example, which favored scientific social engineering and authoritarianism as a path to progress, was attractive to elites concerned that their society advance economically and politically along European lines but equally concerned that these advances not take place with the full participation of the *plebe* (common people). As Thomas Skidmore notes, positivist philosophy provided "a model for modernization which rationalized the continued concentration of power in the hands of the elite."[3]

Especially after the abolition of slavery in the United States and in the wake of the Paraguayan War (1864–1870), the dominant classes of Brazil grew acutely conscious of the perception Europeans and North Americans held of their slave labor–based society. And as calls for the final eradication of slavery grew in the 1870s and 1880s, many clearly evidenced an overriding concern with the question of how to modernize a society that was predominantly illiterate, predominantly disenfranchised, and predominantly colored. Returning from a visit to Europe in 1881, physician Manuel Vitorino (who later became governor of Bahia and vice-president of the Republic) explained the development of his own abolitionism as directly related to European opinions about Brazilian slavery: "[O]ne experience made me politically militant—my trip to Europe showed me just how far they were slandering us and how our reputation had bedeviled us, the fact that we were a country that still had slaves. After returning home my abolitionist feelings became insistent and uncompromising and on this issue I never again conceded."[4]

This was the atmosphere in which positivism and related theories such as Darwin's biological determinism became important motivations for the abolitionist movement among elites in Brazil. They represented ways to conceptualize and structure an "advancing" economy, society, and political system without fundamentally disturbing existing power relations. And they corresponded to a growing concern for "whitening" the population by encouraging European immigration and outlawing immigration from Asia and Africa. Progress was associated with abolition and abolition was associated with whitening. (And in a circular manner it was clear that poor white immigrants were hesitant to come to a country where enslaved workers undercut the value of their labor—especially when other alternatives like the United States were available.)

It was in this context that Candomblé communities, which had served as locations for the redefinition of black identity in Brazil in the late colonial and imperial period, represented spaces where Afro-Brazilians continued to create alternative meanings for their lives. The years following abolition and the establishment of the republic saw a substantial increase in the formation and public recognition of Candomblé *terreiros*. Police persecution of the communities continued as well. While the dominant society did not conceive of newly freed slaves and the mass of poor, disenfranchised Brazilians as valued members of the new polity, Candomblé communities practiced what Julio Braga has called an alternative *cidadania* (citizenship),[5] a model of human relations and of participation in society within a paradigm strikingly different from that embraced by the nation's elites. For Candomblé as well as for other contemporary Afro-Brazilian religions, such as Umbanda and Xangô, Braga notes that police repression has been a component of the resistance the dominant society organized toward "the presence of cultural values distinct from those of the occidental model-ideal."[6]

Indeed throughout its history, Candomblé has nourished at the center of its life "cultural values" distinct from those of the dominant society. Where the hegemonic ideal emphasized the degradation of blackness and distinctions among various classes of Brazilians of African descent, Candomblé was a mechanism for the (re)creation in diaspora of a collective Afro-Brazilian identity based in shared African ancestry and the gathering of various regional deities and devotees into the circle of communal celebration. Where the dominant ideology viewed rituals of drum-dances and the cultivation of *orixás* as "witchcraft" and "uncivilized" behavior, Candomblé insisted on its creation of identities of depth and integrity for enslaved and oppressed people and on its determination to keep the Spirits of Africa in close proximity to those who depended on them for protection and blessing in the midst of great physical and psychic danger. And where Bahian elites feared the conflagration of resistance and religion among blacks, Candomblé served as a central element in fugitive slave communities as well as in individual efforts to wrest freedom from the tenacious hold of a society structured on slave labor. As an alternative orientation in Brazilian society, Candomblé has represented an important model of resistance to the status quo. Its black- and female-led multi-racial participation suggests possible models for other aspects of Brazilian society, intimating the contrasting ideas of citizenship articulated by Braga and others.

Paul Gilroy asserts that as blacks have moved from slave to citizen status in the Americas, their constant searches for ways to be justly and productively engaged in the political and social life of the nations in which they live have contributed profound insights into the nature and limitations of contemporary societal configurations. In this sense, he says, black people have assumed the role (abdicated some time ago by Western practical philosophy) of inquiry "into what the best possible forms of social and political existence might be."[7]

Candomblé, and other alternative orientations in nineteenth-century Bahia enabled the recognition, engagement, and transformation of life in the context of tremendous trauma. Within the limitations of the time and place, blacks in late colonial and imperial Bahia used the materials at their disposal to try to make sense of the disequilibrium in which they found themselves. In the attempts, they created new meanings of community and new identities of blackness which have continued to serve generations of their descendants in the Americas still struggling with questions of how to transform shock and woundedness into something that saves.

Glossary

abiã: one who is at the pre-initiate stage in Candomblé; an individual who has been recognized as a potential *iawô* but who has not yet been fully prepared to ritually receive an *orixá*

advinhador: spiritual guide; seer; diviner; counselor

aluguel: rental

axé: life force; spiritual force

babalawo: priest of Ifá, the god of divination

babalorixá: "father-of-the-orixá"; high priest; foremost male spiritual leader of a given Candomblé community

banzo: "fatal nostalgia"; a kind of wasting-away due to homesickness considered by colonial and imperial observers to be a major cause of death among African-born Brazilian slaves

batuque: Afro-Brazilian drum-dance

boçal: newly-arrived African slave

bolsa de mandinga: "mandinga pouch"; a body-centered manifestation of Afro-Brazilian and Afro-Portuguese religiosity popular in the colonial period

branco/branca: white person

caboclo/cabocla: Indian

cabra: term used to indicate a darker-skinned person of mixed African and European descent; a *pardo* and *crioulo* or *pardo* and *preto* mixture

calundu: a general term used to describe Afro-Brazilian religion in Bahia prior to the nineteenth century

canto: work group of slaves and freedpeople generally organized around shared ethnic identity

capitão-mor: rural militia leader

chocalhos: rattles; cowbells

cidade alta: upper city

cidade baixa: lower city

crioulo/crioula: Brazilian-born, dark-skinned black person

curandeiro/curandeira: healer

degregados: convicted criminals

desembargador: appellate judge; chief judge, judge at the High Court

ebô: offering

ebômi: filha-de-santo who has ritually marked seven or more years of initiation

ekedi: female assistant to *iawôs* during their possession by the *orixás*; *ekedis* do not themselves incorporate the deities

engenho: sugar mill or sugar plantation, depending on the context

escrivão: notary; (court) clerk

fazenda: farm

fazer santo: undergo initiation; "to make the saint"

feitiçaria: sorcery; witchcraft; general term used to describe Afro-Brazilian religious and ritual healing practices in colonial and imperial era

feiticeiro/feiticeira: sorcerer; witch; witchdoctor

feitiço: spell; magic object; fetish; "a made thing"

figa: a closed-fist symbol with thumb between the index and middle fingers that represents protection from negative influences and physical harm

filhas-de-santo/filhos-de-santo: "daughters-of-the-saint"/"sons-of-the-saint"; initiates; members of Candomblé communities

freguesia: district; subdivision of city

ganho: "earning"; the system by which slaves would work outside of the immediate supervision of masters (often as street vendors or transporters of goods and people) and be required to return a percentage of their earnings to their owners *iawô: filha-de-santo* who has been ritually prepared (initiated) to receive an *orixá*

ilê: house; Candomblé temple

irmandade: lay Catholic confraternity

iyalorixá: "mother-of-the-orixá"; high priestess; foremost female spiritual leader of a given Candomblé community

Jeje: term by which Africans of Aja-Fon and Ewe cultural-linguistic groups were collectively known in Bahia

juíz ordinário: local judge

junta de alforria: manumission club

liberto/liberta: freedperson

loge: "a sort of basement that can still be seen in some of Salvador's colonial buildings" (Reis)

loja: variation on *loge;* a ground-level or basement-level living space often inhabited by poor people or slaves

mãe-de-santo: "mother-of-the-saint"; see *iyalorixá*

massapé: rich, clayey soil of the Bahian Recôncavo, ideal for growing sugar cane

mata-marotos: "kill the rascals"—rebellions of Bahia's poorer sectors during the food shortages that followed Independence; directed against Portuguese merchants who were perceived as exploiters

mestre de açucar: "sugar master"; director of operations for a sugar *engenho*

moleque: often derogatory term for a black child

Nagô: term by which Yorubas of various subethnicities were collectively known in Bahia

negro/negra: black person; term used to collectively refer to African and Brazilian-born dark-skinned blacks

ogã: an honorific title given to certain male members of Candomblé communities who act as protector-benefactors of the *terreiro* and its members

orixá: cosmic energy; deity; representation of elements of the natural world; prototypical aspect of human personality; also, divinized ancestor

padrões: stone markers used by Portuguese merchants and colonists as navigational landmarks and as claims of possession

pai-de-santo: "father-of-the-saint"; see *babalorixá*

palmatória: a wooden paddle with which slaves were beaten as punishment

pano da costa: West African-style cloth; "cloth woven in small strips of coloured cotton from two to four inches wide in striped or checked patterns, and the slips sewed together to form a shawl." (Wetherell)

pardo/parda: "brown-skinned" person; a term indicating an intermediary skin-tone between black and white; *pardos* were also called *mulattos*

posturas: edicts

povo-do-santo: "people of the saint"; the larger community of Candomblé adherents in Bahia

preto: the color black; term used to indicate African-born blacks in nineteenth century Bahia

pureza de sangue: "purity of blood"; signified absence of African or Jewish ancestry

quilombo: fugitive slave community

Recôncavo: the immediate area surrounding the Bay of All Saints; in the colonial period and nineteenth century it was largely dedicated to the cultivation of export crops—specifically sugar, tobacco, and later cotton—and some subsistence farming

reco-reco: percussion instrument whose sound is produced by stroking a stick across a striated surface

roça: tract of cleared land; plot of land; small farm plot

roda: a circle; specifically, the danced circle of Candomblé ceremony

safra: harvest; especially sugar-cane harvest

senado da câmara: town council; municipal-level governing body

senhor/senhora: master/mistress (also, sir/madam)

senhores do engenho: sugar plantation/sugar mill owners; Bahia's economic, political and social elite in the colonial and imperial era

senzala: slave quarters; also individual slave house

sobrado: townhouse of several stories

tabelião: notary public; official charged with recognizing signatures and making or registering lawful documents

terreiro: the physical space of a *candomblé,* the ritual grounds; can also refer to a community of devotees

Appendix
Selected Documents from the Arquivo Público do Estado da Bahia (The Public Archives of the State of Bahia)

Item A. Correspondence from Joaquim Ignacio Siqueira Bulcão, Captain Moor, to the Conde de Ponte, Governor and Captain General of Bahia

July 4, 1807
Arquivo Público do Estado da Bahia
Maço 417–1: Capitães Mores—1807–1822

Circumstantiated Report of the Blacks Found in the Vila de São Francisco Jail

Circumstantiated report of the pretos found in the jail of this village of S. Francisco, accounts, and motives of their imprisonments, and what the blacks themselves have to say about it[;] Releases of some, and remittance of others, all in observance of the Orders of the Most Illustrious and Most Excellent Judge Conde da Ponte Governor and Captain General of this Captaincy.

Question
1
The preto Manoel[,] of the Angola nation, slave of Gaspar da [Cena?] e Araújo, arrested by Captain Antonio José de Santa Anna.

Response
Released
That he is the same declared above, arrested by the said Captain, and that with respect to all that he was specifically asked he knows nothing, and neither has news, because he has always been occupied in Labor and agricultural work for His Master, in light of which he was Released.

Question
2
The preto João Benguela[,] slave of the same Gaspar da [Cena?] e Araújo, arrested by the said Captain Antonio José de Santa Anna.

Response
That he is the same above indicated, and arrested by the Captain and that with respect to all about which he he was Circumstantiatedly interrogated, knows nothing, _____ he was arrested finding himself in the Senzala of the fazenda of the said his Master, and _____ nothing more said, and for this [reason] goes Released.

Question

3

The preto [Vemeilaû?], gege, slave of Leuitenant João d'Oliveira Carneiro, arrested by Captain Joaquim de Santa Anna.

Response

Released

That he is the same indicated above, and that he was arrested for not having carried a pass from his said Master, coming from the Engenho do Saco he descends to the other of Macaco,[1] and that he knows nothing regarding that which he was Specifically asked, and for this [reason] goes Released.

Question

4

Released

The preto Rafael, gege, slave of the same Lieutenant João D' Oliveira Carneiro, arrested by Captain Joaquim de Santa Anna.

Response

That he is the same declared above, slave of the said Lieutenant João d'Oliveira, and for lack of a pass from [the master] he was arrested by the same Captain, coming from the Saco Engenho and [accompanied?] by others his fellows, toward the said Macaco of his aforementioned Master, and that he knows nothing more of all that he was asked, and for this [reason] goes Released.

Question

5

Released

The preto Constantino, tapa, still boçal, slave of the aforementioned Lieutenant João de Oliveira Carneiro, arrested by Captain Joaquim de Santa Anna.

Response

Responded nothing[,] as the said preto is entirely boçal, bought _____ and for this [reason] goes Released.

Question

6

Released

The preto Francisco gege, slave of José Manoel de O, arrested by Captain Antonio José de Santa Anna.

Response

That he is the same declared above, and that he was arrested by the said Captain Antonio José, in his own Senzala, and that in it never were allowed gatherings of other blacks, and that _____[2] dances and in other times drummings, it has been

---

1. The Engenho do Macaco.
2. If *posto,* the phrase could suggest *embora que,* as in "even though [there were] dances and in other times drummings."

more than six years that it has not been done, and to everything else that he was asked, responded nothing, and for this [reason] goes Released.

Question

7
Released
The preta Anastacia, Criola married to the preto Francisco, slave also of José Manoel de O, arrested by Captain Antonio José de Santa Anna.

Response

That she is the same declared, and that she was arrested at the Senzala of her husband the preto Francisco, and knows nothing about which she was asked, investigated on this occasion and for this [reason] goes Released.

Question

8
Remitted to
the Captain Mor of Santo Amaro[.] The preto Anastacio, gege, slave of João Pedro [Fuiza?] Barreto arrested by Captain José Gonçalvez da Camara Paim.

Response

That he is the same declared above, slave of the aforementioned João Pedro [Fuiza?] Barreto, arrested by Captain José Gonçalvez da Camara Paim, that he the said preto, was never Invited by anyone to a gathering, but that he knows that in the woods of the Terranova Engenho of his said Master, towards the part of the fazenda of the son [of the Master] Francisco [Monis?], called Trigueiro, there exist, and still will be on today the 3rd of the current July, three weeks, that in that woods are various slaves reaching the number of 20, refuged in the said woods, where they have a House of straw, and in it a preto gege from the City, a preta also from the City, and many others, whose names he doesn't know, but that one of these pretos would go out, and later return through the said woods, whose place he the deponent knows, because he went there twice, where thereby he saw arms such as bows and arrows, lances, and that also in this lot was found a _____, and that is all he knows regarding that which he was asked.

This preto as _____ on the 4th of the current July was remitted to the Captain Mor of the Village of Santo Amaro, with a Copy of this his response, to whose district belongs the execution, _____ of this fact, to enter into the inquiry, and examination of him.

Question

9
Released
The preto Joaquim Nagô, slave of João Pereira do Lago resident of the [Cazumba?] Engenho, arrested by Captain José Gonçalvez da Camara Paim.

Response

That is he is same declared above, slave of the said João Pereira do Lago, that was arrested by Captain José Gonçalvez da Camara Paim, on the Road to the House of his said Master, for not having carried [with him] a pass [from the Master], and that he knows nothing of anything else about which he was Questioned on this occasion, and for this [reason] goes Released.

Question

10
Released
The preta Joanna, old gege slave of Antonio Ferreira Pacheco, resident in Cobê, arrested by Captain Antonio José de Santa Anna with a small gourd.

Response

That she is the same declared above, slave of the said Antonio Ferreira Pacheco, resident in Cobê, on whose Place, and Senzala of the fazenda of her selfsame Master, was arrested by the said Captain Antonio José de Santa Anna, and that she knows nothing of that which she was asked, and [being] examined and that _____ was found [with her] a small vase, or gourd, and inside of it a small bone which appears to be of an animal, a small cowrie shell, a little powder, and a bean-of-the-woods, all of these Things which were contained [in the gourd] were applied by her, in her use in defense of snakes not biting her, and for a pain, which habitually attacks her, all of which was given to her as Curative by a Cabocolo[3] of the Sertão[4] called Antonio, and to everything else she said nothing with absolute negation, and for this [reason] goes Released.

Question

11
Released
The preta Leonor, old gege freedwoman, arrested by Captain Diogo Alvarez Nunes with a straw bag, and inside of it some ground[5] roots, and the rest found inside insignificant.

Response

That she is the same arrested by the said Captain Diogo Alvarez with the afore-mentioned straw bag, and that everything found in it, she recognizes as hers[;] her husband, the preto gege Antonio, now dead, having left it for her, but that none of this was used against anyone and that [even less?] did she give refuge in her house to pretos, nor give luck,[6] and to everything else she responded nothing, being carefully interrogated, and examining all that was found in the said straw bag, nothing is of Circumstance, and for this [reason] she goes Released.

---

3. Caboclo, or Indian.
4. The interior, the backwoods.
5. That is, "powdered," *moida*.
6. *Dar venturas*, also "tell fortunes."

Question

12

Released

The preta Anna gege, old freedwoman, arrested by Captain Diogo Alvarez Nunes on the same occasion, and in the House of the preta Leonor.

Response

That she is the same Anna Gege who was arrested by the said Captain Diogo Alvarez in the House of the preta Leonor for having requested of this one [Leonor] shelter, and that she doesn't know, and doesn't even recognize, what are the Things existent in the straw bag of the said preta Leonor, to whom they belong, and she is ignorant of everything else she was asked, and for this [reason] she goes Released.

Question

13

Released

The preta Tereza[,] of the gege nation, old freedwoman, arrested by the same Captain Diogo Alvarez Nunes.

Response

That she is the same preta Tereza, arrested by the aforementioned Captain Diogo Alvarez in a Senzala on the Madrugacedo Engenho of Dr. Francisco Vicente Vianna, and that she was around there for reason of walking doing some business, buying beans, and more to feed herself, and that she Knows nothing of all that she was asked, and for this [reason] goes Released.

Question

14

Remitted

The preto Antonio gege, slave of Manoel Pereira Mimozo, resident on his fazenda Osso do Boi,[7] arrested by Captain Vasco de Britto, e Souza.

Response

That he is the same preto Antonio, slave of the aforementioned Mimozo, arrested by the said Captain Vasco de Britto, e Souza, and that it is true that some time ago in this part, they searched his Senzala, and in it slept three pretos from the City of his same nation, called José, Agostinho, and Benedito, who were arrested on the fazenda of his said Master by the Captain of the Freguesia of Santa Anna of Cattû, Manoel Pereira d'Oliveira, and that the said pretos walked around the farms of his

---

7. Ox-Bone.

neighborhood, Crûs das Almas, and _____, selling panos da Costa,[8] and Buying other Things, and that they never said anything to him, regarding that which he was Circumstantially Questioned[;] being True, that he was formerly the slave of Manoel Pereira Gallo, Owner of the Pop___ Engenho, who sold him to his present owner the said Mimozo, because of [an argument?[9]] he had with a Sugar Master[10] of the said Engenho; before that he was the Captive of a white man resident of the City[,] called Antonio, and this one sold him to the said Gallo [because?] he didn't want to Carry the Chair of his Master Antonio resident of the City, and he responded nothing else.

Question

15
Released
The preta Jeronima Crioula, slave of Manoel Pereira Mimozo, married to the preto Antonio gege, slave of the said, and arrested by the same Captain Vasco de Britto, e Souza.

Response

That she is the same declared above, married to the preto Antonio gege, both slaves of the aforementioned Mimozo, arrested by the Captain Mor Vasco de Brito, when her husband was also arrested; and that this one [the husband] Said nothing to her. Neither does she know of involvements he had With the pretos Benedito, Agostinho, and José who were arrested by Captain Manoel Pereira d'OLiveira on the fazenda of the said Mimoza, his Master. And being true that these sheltered themselves, and slept in her Senzala, the same as that of her husband, they never involved him in anything that she witnessed, though they ate there, and stayed there when they came from the City; they organized the panos da Costa they had brought to sell, and purchases of chickens that they made, and the other things they brought from the City, which was their livelihood, and to nothing else did she respond of that which she was carefully questioned, and for this [reason] goes Released.

Question

16
Remitted
The preto Benedito, gege slave of Padre Pedro Ferreira dos Sanctos, absent in Lisbon, arrested on the fazenda of Manoel Pereira Mimoso, by the same Captain Vasco de Brito e Souza.

Response

That he is the same declared above, and that he was arrested by the said Captain Vasco de Brito on the fazenda of the aforementioned Manoel Pereira Mimoso, where he [was present?] in the House of his Brother the preto Antonio gege, slave

---

8. Striped African cloth.
9. Or a debt.
10. One who directs operations on a sugar *engenho*.

of the same, on the circuit in which he walked to pay weekly workers by order of his master Father Pedro Ferreira dos Santos after [the master] went to Lisbon; whose imports he delivered to the Cabra Efigenia, resident of the Sitio da Palma in Bahia, and that it is true that he knows and has much friendship With the pretos, José, Benedito, and Agostinho, all freedmen, from whom, and others of the City, he accepted panos da Costa to sell, as they too did, as they insinuated that this was a good business, but that the said pretos communicated nothing to him, absolutely denying all that on this occasion was carefully interrogated of him.

Question

17
Remitted
The preto João Angola, slave of Custodio José Pereira Coutinho, arrested by Captain Pedro Jorge Gomes.

Response

That he is the same indicated above, slave of the said Custodio José Pereira Coutinho, arrested by the same Captain Pedro Jorge on the fazenda of the Ilha das [Fontes?],[11] where resides his said Master, and he said nothing About that which he was interrogated, and being present Captain Antonio Francisco d'Mello, he said in the presence of this preto that he already had a denunciation of him, for having formed a dance of drums on the day of the Eve of São João, the night which was tumultous, and [that] he went around armed with a sharp knife, with which he wanted to injure the Criolo Victorianno Gomes, resident of this village; to which the aforementioned preto João Angola denied nothing, confessing all that was told by the said Captain.

Question

18
Released
The preto Pedro Congo, old slave of the widow Anastacia, resident of São Estevão Point in this area, and arrested by Captain Pedro Jorge Gomes.

Response

That he is the same above mentioned, arrested by the said Captain Pedro Jorge in the House of the same His Mistress, and to nothing else did he respond regarding what he was asked, and for this [reason] goes Released.

Question

19
Released
The preto João of the Angola nation, old freedman, resident of São Estevão, arrested by the said Captain [Pedro] Jorge Gomes.

---

11. Isle of Fountains?

Response

That he is the same above indicated, arrested by Captain Pedro Jorge Gomes, and that he Knows nothing of all that he was interrogated [in this act?], With all the Circumstances, and that he is old, and never had communication, nor any participation, for he just [Cares?] for work, and due to his incapacity and age, he goes Released.

Question

20
Remitted
The preto Francisco gege freedman, known popularly as Dosû, arrested by Captain Manoel Gomes de Mendonça.

Response

That he is the same above declared, and known to the common people as Francisco Dosû, and in effect was arrested by the said Captain Manoel Gomes in the Senzala of a preto, whose name he doesn't say of the [Paramerisso?] Engenho, where he was being sheltered, and being particularly and carefully interrogated in this act, said that many people came to him for help, whites, pardos, blacks, of one and the other Sex, for advice,[12] and Healing, and that he did it, but that he didn't Remember now the names of the said persons, other than that of the preta Euzebia Criola, resident of this village, who went to His House when he lived on the Engenho Garogaipequena Place, and that with certain roots he made her well of a great volume that she had in her belly. Also, in the Company of this preta, would come José Anacleto Pinheiro, notary public of this village, and that from the house of the said preto, [Dosû], he [Pinheiro] would Conduct him by Horse, to this same village, and that he stayed in her House for a time of three Weeks, in which space he Communicated With the said Pinheiro, that he treated him well, and gave him some gifts. And Being presented to him at this point the Skulls of male goats, roots, a Box of wasps,[13] he recognizes that all the things are his, and confessed that he danced *tabaques* many times, so as to Heal, went about in many parts of this Recôncavo, staying also for a time in the House of the aforementioned José Anacleto, and nothing more did he respond to what he was Questioned. For these facts, and activities, a communiqué was directed to the Mayor of this Village on the date of 3rd of the Current July to proceed as falls to him and his mayoral jurisdiction by law.

Question

21
Remitted
The preta Maria Francisca gege, who lived in the House, and Company of the preto

---

12. The literal translation of *dar venturas*, is "to give luck," but it seems to have a meaning of spiritual advisement, advisement regarding one's destiny [luck] and what should be done to alter it for the better.
13. Or bees, perhaps, or hornets.

Francisco of the same nation, popularly known as Dosû, arrested by Captain Antonio Francisco de Mello.

Response

That she is the same, above declared, arrested by the said Captain Antonio Francisco de Mello, in the house that the preto Francisco Dosû had in Garogaipequena, who, being present, the same preta added that the Box of wasps, skulls of male goats, and the roots, were all belongings of the said preto, which he did not deny. She Continued confessing that the same [Francisco Dosû] was an extraordinary Healer, and that he gave advice, to which end many people sought him, whites, pardos, blacks, of both Sexes, that due to the great number she doesn't know their names, with the exception of the preta Euzebia, resident of this village, who would go there to be Healed in the Company of her lover, a white man, also resident of this village, whose name she doesn't know, to the house where he [F.D.] was. She also declares that the said preto Dosû, has traveled around to Heal, and is for this summoned from throughout the Recôncavo, and that he is an extraordinary Calunduzeiro, he dances *tabaques*, and on these occasions, there are the offerings[14] of many people, flasks of wine, aguardentes, money, chickens, live and Cooked, and many other gifts. That the said preto—either by medicines, or due to that which these [remedies] have a Habit of doing—in jealousy killed a Crioula named Ilasia, his lover, slave of the Colonia Engenho of the Captain Mor José da Veiga Sampaio, and that in addition to her, he killed another preto slave of the said Captain Mor, who served as Sugar Master of the same Engenho, and she responded no more, neither augmented anything of herself, nor of the said preto Francisco Dosû. This preta is the same Maria Francisca referred to in the first report of the Captain Major of the Ordenances of the Village of Santo Amaro, and about whom, as [also] the said preto Francisco Dosû, was included in the communiqué of the Local Judge of this Village on the 3rd of the current July, to proceed with his communiqué, and as the Law requires.

Villa of São Francisco 4th of July 1807
Joaquim Ignacio de Siqueira Bulcão Captain Major.

Item A (Portuguese). Correspondência do Capitão Mor, Joaquim Ignacio Siqueira Bulcão ao Conde de Ponte, Governador e Capitão Geral da Bahia

July 4, 1807
Arquivo Público do Estado da Bahia
Maço 417–1: Capitães Mores—1807–1822

Relação Circunstanciada os Pretos Q' Se Acharão na Cadea da Vila de São Francisco

Relação Circunstanciada dos pretos q' seachão na Cadea desta Vila de S. Francisco, partes, e objectos de suas prizões, e o que sobre ellas referem os mesmos pretos,

---

14. The word I've translated as "offering" here is *mimo—coisa delicada que se dá ou se offerece; presente; affago; carinho; primor; delicadeza; belleza* (from Silva Bastos, *Diccionario da Lingua Portuguesa*, Lisbon: 1928).

Solturas de huns, e remessas de outros, tudo em observancia das Ordens do Illmo e Exmo Juiz Conde da Ponte Govern^or, e Cap^m General dessa Capitania.

Pergunta

1

O preto Manoel de nascão Angola escravo de Gaspar da [Cena?] e Ar°, prezo pelo Cap^m Antonio Jozé de S. Anna.

Resposta

Solto

Que ele he o proprio acima declarado, prezo pelo d° Cap^m, e que a respeito de tudo quanto lhe foi perguntado com individuação nada sabe, e nem [tem?] noticias, por q' ele sempre tem estado ocupado no Serviso, e lavoura do Seu Senr, a vista do q' foi Solto.

Perg.

2

O preto João Benguela escravo do mesmo Gaspar da [Cena?] e Araujo, prezo pelo dito Cap^m Antonio José de S. Anna.

Resp.

Que ele he o proprio acima indicado, e prezo pelo d° Cap^m e que a respeito de tudo quanto lhe foi interrogado Circumstanciadam^te; nada sabe, _____ ele fora prezo achando se na Sanzala[1] do d° seu Sn^r, e _____ mais nada dise; e por isso vai Solto.

Perg.

3

O preto [Vemeilaû?] gege escravo do Ten^e João d'Oliv^a Carneiro, prezo pelo Cap^m Joaquim de S. Anna

Resp.

Solto

Que ele hé o proprio asima indicado, e q' fora prezo a falta de trazer bilhete do d° seo Snr; vindo do Eng° do Saco desce para o outro do Macaco e q' nada sabe du quanto Circumstanciadam^te lhe foi pergunto e por iso vai Solto.

Perg.

4

Solto

O preto Rafael gege escravo do mesmo Ten^e João D'Oliveira Carneiro, prezo pelo Cap^m Joaquim de S. Anna

---

1. *Senzala*

Resp.

Que ele é o proprio asima declarado, escr° do d° Ten° João d'OLiveira, e por falta de bilhete deste fora prezo pelo mesmo Cap^m; vindo do Eng° do Saco e Comp^a de outros seus parceiros, p^a o d° Macaco do d° seu S^r, e q' nada mais sabe de tudo quanto lhe foi perguntado, e porisso vai Solto.

Perg.

5
Solto
O preto Constantino tapa inda² busal³ escr° do referido Ten° João de Oliveira Carneiro, prezo pelo Cap^m Joaquim de S. Anna.

Resp.

Nada responde por ser o dito pretto inteiramente busal, comprado _____ e porisso vai Solto.

Perg.

6
Solto
O preto Francisco gege, escr° de Jozé Manoel de O prezo pelo Cap^m Antonio J° de S. Anna.

Resp.

Que ele é o mesmo asima declarado, e q' fora prezo pelo dito Cap^m Antonio José, em sua mesma Sanzala, e q' nella nunca admitio ajuntamentos de outros pretos, e q' _____⁴ dansas e em outros tempos tabaques, haverá mais de Seis an^s q' o não fas, e a tudo mais do q^to lhe foi perguntado, nada respondeo, e porisso vai Solto.

Perg.

7
Solta
A preta Anastacia, Criola Cazada Com o preto Francisco, escr^a tambem de Joze Manoel de O, preza pelo Cap^m Antonio J° de S. Anna.

Resp.

Que ela é a mesma ja declarada, e q' fora preza na Sanzala do seo marido o preto

---

2. *ainda*
3. *boçal*
4. *por isso,* or *posto?*

Francisco, e nada sabia do quanto lhe foi perguntado, endagado nesta a Cazião, e p^r iso vai Solta.

Perg.

8
Remedito ao
Cap^{mor} de S.Am^{ro}
O preto Anastacio gege escravo de João Pedri [Fuiza?] Barreto prezo pelo Cap^m J^e Glz da Camara Paim.

Resp.

Que ele é o proprio asima declarado, escravo do referido João Pedro Fuiza Barreto, prezo pelo Cap^m Joze Glz da Camara Paim, q' ele d° preto, nunca fora Convidado por outro alguem p^a ajuntamento, más q' sabe, q' nas matas do Eng° Terranova do d° seo S^r, para aparte da fazenda do filho deste Francisco [Monis?], chamada do Trigueiro, existem, e ainda havera no dia deoje⁵ 3 do Corr^e Julho, tres Semanas, q' nadita mata estavão varios escr^{os} q' chegarão ao numero de vinte apozentados nadita mata, onde tinhão hua Caza de palha, e nela hum preto gege da Cidade, hua preta tãobem da Cid^e, e outros muitos, Cujos nomes não sabe, mas q' hum desses pretos, sahia fora, eao depois entrara p^a a dita mata, cujo lugar ele sabe, porq' fora aele duas vezes, onde p^riso vira armas Como arcos com frexas, lansas, e q' tãobem nesse lote seachava hum _____, e he quanto sabe a respeito de tudo q' lhe foi perguntado.
Este preto como ficso⁶ de 4 do Corr^e Julho foi remetido ao Cap^{mor} da V^a de S. Amaro, com a Copia desta sua resposta, a cujo districto pertence a execução, _____ desse facto, p^a entrar na averiguação, e exame delle.

Perg.

9
Solto
O preto Joaquim Nagô escravo de João Pereira do Lago m^{or7} no Eng° [Cazumba?], prezo pelo Cap^m Jozé Glz˜ da Camara Paim.

Resp.

Que ele è oproprio asima declarado, escravo do dito João Per^a do Lago q' fora prezo pelo Cap^m Joze Glz˜ da Camara Paim, hindo em Caminho da Caza do dito seo Snr˜, p^r não levar bilhete deste, e q' nada sabe de tudo mais quanto lhe foi endagado nesta ocazião, e p'iso vai Solto.

---

5. *de hoje*
6. Or *com o ficso* [*fixo?*].
7. *morador*

Perg.

10
Solta
A preta Joanna gege velha escrava de Antonio Ferra Pacheco mor no Cobê, preza pelo Cap^m Antonio José de S. Anna com huma cabasinha.

Resp.

Que ela ê a mesma asima declarada, escrava do d° Antonio Ferr^a Pacheco m^or em Cobê em cujo Citio,[8] e Sanzala da fasenda do mesmo seo S^r. fora preza pelo d° Cap^m Antonio J^e de S. Anna, e q' nada sabe do quanto lhe foi perguntado, e examinado e q' [posto?] lhe foc^e9 achado hum pequeno vazo, ou Cabasinha, e dentro dela hum ofo[10] pequeno que mostra ser d'algum bixo,[11] um pequeno buzio da Costa, hum pouco depô,[12] e hua fava do matto, todas estas Couzas q' em si [tinha erão] aplicadas p^a ella, eseu uzo em defeza de lhe não morderem Cobras, e de hua dôr, q' a custuma atacar, o q' tudo lhe dera Como por Curativo hum Cabocolo do Certão chamado Antonio, e a todo mais nada dise com absoluta negação, e p'iso vai Solta.

Perg.

11
Solta
A preta Leonor gege forra, velha, preza pelo Cap^m Diogo Alz' Nunes com hum balaio, e dentro delle huas raizes moidas, e o mais infignife,[13] q'nele se acha.

Resp.

Que ela é amesma preza pelo dito Cap^m Diogo Alz' Como referido balaio, e q' tudo quanto nelle seacha, reconhece ser seo, p^r lhe deixar seu marido o preto Antonio gege, ja falescido, más q' de nada diso, fazia uzo contra pessoa algúa e q' _____[14] na sua Caza dava azilo a pretos, nem venturas, e a todo mais nada respondeo, sendo-lhe interrogado miudam^te, e examinando se todo q^to selhe achou no dito balaio, nada hè de Circumstancia, e p'iso vai Solta.

Perg.

12
Solta
A preta Anna gege velha forra, preza pelo Cap^am Diogo Alz' Nunes na mesma oCazião, e Caza da preta _____[15] Leonor.

---

8. *Sitio*
9. *fosse*
10. *fosso*
11. *bicho*
12. *de pô*
13. *insignificante*
14. *menos*, or *menor*
15. This appears to be a mistake.

Resp.

Que ela hé apropria Anna gege q' fora preza pelo dito Cap^{am} Diogo Alz' na Caza da preta Leonor por pedir a essa hum agasalho, e q' não Sabe, e menos Conhece, q' as Couzas existentes no balaio da d^a preta Leonor, de q^m Sejão, e a todo mais q' lhe foi perguntado ignora, e por ifo vai Solta.

Perg.

13
Solta
A preta Tereza denasção gege, velha forra, preza pelo mesmo Cap^{am} Diogo Alz' Nunes.

Resp.

Que ela è a propria preta Tereza, preza pelo referido Cap^{am} Diogo Alz' em hua Sanzala do Eng° Madrugacedo do Dr Francisco Vicente Vianna, e q' ai portara em razão de andar fazendo algum negocio, comprar feijões, e mais p^a Se alimentar, e q' nada Sabe de tudo quanto lhe for perguntado, e p'iso vai Solta.

Perg.

14
Remetido
O preto Antonio gege, escravo de Manoel Pereira Mimozo, m^{or} na sua fazenda do Ofo do boi, prezo pelo Cap^m Vasco de Britto, e Souza.

Resp.

Que ele è o proprio preto Antonio, escr° do referido Mimozo, prezo pelo dito Cap^m Vasco de Britto, e Sz^a, e q' hê verdade q' a tempos a esta parte, buscavão a sua San-zala, enella dormião tres pretos da Cid^e da sua mesma nasção chamados Jozé, Ag-ostinho, e Benedito, q' forão prezos na fasenda do d° seu S^r pelo Cap^m da Freg^a de S. Anna do Cattû, M^{el} Pr^a d' Oliv^{ra}, e q' os ditos pretos andavão pelos Citios da sua vezinhança, Crûs das Almas, e _____, vendendo panos da Costa, e Comprando outras Coizas e q' nunca eles lhe communicarão nada, de tudo quanto Circunstan-ciadamte lhe foi indagado, sendo Certo, q' elle fora escr° de M^{el} Pr^a Gallo Proprietr° do Eng° *Pop*, o qual o vendera ao feo[16] [posuidor?] atual d° Mimozo, porbulhas[17] q'tivera com hum M^{e[18]} d'afucar[19] do d° Eng°, antes do q' fora Cativo de hum homem branco m^{or} na Cid^e chamado Antonio, e esse o vendera ao d° Gallo [p^r?] elle não querer Carregar Cadr^a do [p^{ro}?] Seo Sr Antonio m^{or} na Cid^e, e a nada mais respondeo.

Perg.

15
Solta

_____

16. *seo*
17. *por bulhas* [?]
18. *mestre*
19. *açucar*

A preta Jeronima Criola escr^a de M^{el} Per^a Mimozo, Cazada Com o preto Antonio gege escr° do d°, e preza pelo m^{mo} Cap^m Vasco de Britto, e Souza.

Resp.

Que ela è a mesma afisma declarada, Cazada Com o preto Antonio gege ambos escravos do referido Mimozo, preza pelo Cap^{mor} Vasco de Brito, quando igualm^e foi o d° Seu marido, e q' este nada lhe Comunicou, nem ela sabe de participações q' ele tivese Com os pretos Benedito, Agostinho, e Jozê q' forão prezos pelo Cap^m M^{el} P^{ra} d'OLiv^{ra} na fasenda dele d° Mimozo seo S^r, e sendo verd^e q' estes se apozentavão, e dormião na sua Sanzala, a mesma do d° seu marido, nunca a este participarão Coiza algúa, q' ela prezenciase, posto q' ahi Comião, e estavão quando vinhão da Cidade, recolhião as vendas q' eles trazião de panos da Costa e Compras degalinhas q' fazião, eo mais q' levavão p^a Cid^e, emcujo negocio geravão, e a nada mais respondeo de tudo q^{to} miudam^{te} lhe foi perguntado, e p'ifo vai Solta.

Perg.

16
Remetido
O preto Benedito gege escr° do P^e Pedro Ferreira dos Sanctos auz^e em Lisboa, prezo na fazenda d' M^{el} Per^a Mimoso, p^{lo} m^{mo} Cap^m Vasco de Brito e Sz^a.

Resp.

Que ele hé o mesmo asima declarado, e q' fora prezo pelo d° Cap^m Vasco de Brito na fazenda do referido Manoel Per^a Mimoso, onde [asistia?] em Caza de seo Irmão o preto Antonio gege, escr° do mesmo, no giro em q' andava de pagar Semanas por ordem de seo S^r o P^e Pedro Ferr^a dos Santos depois q' este fora p^a Lisboa, cujos importes entregava a Cabra Efigenia m^{ora} no Citio da Palma na Bahia, e q' hè verdade q' ele conhece, e tem m^{to} amizade Com os pretos, Jozè, Benedito, e Agostinho, todos forros, dos quais, e outros da Cid^e [aceitava][20] panos da Costa p^a vender, como eles tãobem [o?] fazião poes q' insinuado p^r eles, [esse][21] era hum bom negocio, mas q' os d^{os} pretos, nada lhes Comunicava, negando abfolutam^{te} tudo quanto nesta oCazião miudam^{te} lhe foi interogado.

Perg.

17
Remetido
O preto João Angola escr° de Custodio José Per^a Coutinho prezo pelo Cap^m Pedro Jorge Gomes.

Resp.

Que ele hè o mesmo afisma indicado, escr° do d° Custodio J^e Per^a Coutinho, prezo pelo m^{mo} Cap^m Pedro Jorge na fasenda da Ilha das [Fontes?], onde reside o d° seo Snr', e nada dise Sobre quanto lhe foi interrogado, e sendo prezente o Cap^m

---

20. *afeitava*
21. *efe*

Antonio Francisco d'Mello, dise em presença deste preto q' ja dele tivera malsinação, p^r haver formado dansa databaques em o dia Vespera de S. João, a noite q' era re-voltozo, e andava armado Com hua faca de ponta, com a qual quizera ofender ao Criolo Victorianno Gomes, m^{or} nesta V^a, ao que nada negou o referido pretto João Angola, confesando tudo q^{to} pelo d^o Cap^m asim foi ditto.

Perg.

18
Solto
O preto Pedro Congo, velho escr^o daviuva Anastacia m^{ora} na Ponta de S. Estevão deste termo, e prezo pelo Cap^m Pedro Jorge Gomes.

Resp.

Que ele hè o proprio afima referido, prezo pelo d^o Cap^m Pedro Jorge na Caza da mesma Sua Snr^a, e a nada mais respondeo do q^{to} lhe foi perguntado, e p^r iso vai Solto.

Perg.

19
Solto
O preto João de nascão Angola, velho forro m^{or} em S. Estevão, prezo p^{lo} d^o Cap^m [Pedro] Jorge Gomes.

Resp.

Que ele ê o mesmo afima indicado prezo pelo Cap^m P^o Jorge Gomes, e q' nada Sabe de tudo quanto [neste acto?] lhe foi interogado, Com todas as Circumstancias, e q' ele ê velho, e nunca tivera Comunicacões, nem participações alguás, pois só [Cuida?] em trabalhar, e pella sua incapacidade e velhice, vai Soltar.

Perg.

20
Remetido
O preto Francisco gege forro Conhecido vulargm^e Dofû,²² prezo pelo Cap^m Manoel Gomes de Mendonça.

Resp.

Que ele hê o proprio afima declarado, e Conhecido p^{lo} vulgo por Francisco Dosû, e Com efeito fora prezo pelo dito Cap^m M^{el} Gomes na Sanzala de hum preto, cujo nome não declara do Eng^o _____ ²³
onde seachava refugiado, e sendo interrogado particular, e miudam^{te} neste acto, dife²⁴ q' aele recorrião muitas pessoas, brancos, pardos, pretos, de hum e outro Sexo

---

22. Dosû is the proper pronunciation.
23. *Paramerisso?*
24. *disse*

pª dar venturas, e Curar, o q' elle fazia, mas q' senão Lembra agora dos nomes das ditas pefoas, mais do q' da preta Euzebia Criola moradora nessa Vª, a qual hia a Sua Caza quando ele morava no Citio do Engº [Garogaipequena?], e que com certas raizes apozera boa de hum grande volume, q' tinha na barriga, e q' por Companhia a esta preta, hia tãobem Jozé [Anacleto?] Pinhrº Tabelião desta Vª, e q' da Caza dele dº preto²⁵ à Conduzia de Cavº, pª esta mesma Vª, e q' na Caza dela estivera ele portempo de tres Semanas, em cujo espafo se Comunicara Com o dito Pinheiro, q' lhe fazia todo o bem, e lhe dava alguas dadivas. E Sendo-lhe apresentado neste acto as Caveiras de bodes, raizes[,] Caixa de marimbondas, reconhece q' são suas todas estas Couzas, e Confessou q' ele dansa tabaques muitas vezes, afim como q' pª Curar, andava em muitos partes deste Recôncavo, estando tãobem algum tempo em Caza do referido Jozè [Anaceleto?], e nada mais respondeo a quanto lhe foi interrogado. Por estes factos, e participações, foi dirigido hum oficio ao Juis Ordinrº desta Vª em data de 3 do Corrᵉ Julho pª proceder como lhe Compete pela Lei, e sua jurisdição Ordinaria.

Perg.

21
Remetida
A preta Maria Francisca gege, q' morava na Caza, e Compª do preto Francisco da mesma nasção, chamado vulgarmᵉ Dofû, preza pello Capᵐ Antonio Francisco de Mello.

Resp.

Que ela è amesma, asima declarada, preza pelo dito Capᵐ Antonio Francisco de Mello, na Caza q' tinha na Garogaipequena o preto Francisco Dosû, o qual estando prezente, [dilatou?] a mesma preta, q' a Caixa de marimbondas[,] Caveiras de bodes e mais raizes, era tudo proprio do dº preto, o que ele não negou, Continuando ela a fonfesar q' o mesmo era insigne Curador, e dava venturas, a Cujo fim o procuravão muitas pefoas brancas, pardos, pretos, de ambos os Sexos, q' pelo grande numero não Conhese, [e só tem?] presente a preta Euzebia moradora nesta Vila, q' la hia pª a Curar na Companhia de seo amazio hum homen branco, tãobem morador nesta Vila, cujo nome não Sabe, na Caza do qual ele estivera. Demais declara q' o dito preto Dofû, tem andado a Curar, e hè para ifo chamado por todo o Reconcavo, e q' hè insigne Calunduzeiro, danfa tabaques, enestas ocasioens tem mimos de muitas pesoas, de frascos de vinhos, d'aguas ardentes, dinheiros, galinhas, vivas e Cozidas, e outros muitos brindes. Que elle dito preto, ou por meizinhas ou pelo q' estas Custumão fazer, com zelos, matou a hua Criola chamada [Ilasia?] sua amazia escrava do Engº Colonia do Capᵐᵒʳ Jozê da Veiga S. Paio, e q' alem desta, matara outro preto escravo do dº Capᵐᵒʳ, q' Servia de Mestre d'afuscar do mᵐᵒ Engº, e mais não respondeo, nem dilatou de si, e do dº preto Francisco Dosû.
Esta preta ê amesma Maria Francisca Comtemplada na primeira relação do Capᵐᵒʳ

---

25. Or *preso.*

das Orden^as da V^a de S.Amaro, e a Cujo respeito Como d° preto Francisco Dosû, foi incluida no oficio do Juis Ord° desta V^a de 3 de Corr^e Julho, p^a proceder de seo of°, e na forma da Lei.

V^a de S. Fran^co 4 de Julho 1807
Joaquim Ignacio de Siqr^a Bulcão
Cap^am Mor.

Item B. Correspondence from Captain José Roiz de Gomes to another Captain Moor

January 20, 1809
Arquivo Público do Estado da Bahia
Maço 417–1,Capitães Mores, 1807–1822

Gathering of Slaves

Most Illustrious Sir Captain-Moor
According to the information given me by the Lieutenant Commander of the 2nd Company of the new Regiment, José Francisco da Silva, in consequence of the order which Your Excellency gave to personnel to investigate the occurrence of a gathering of slaves which took place in this town, on the occasion of last Christmas, I was informed of the following: that on the aforementioned Holy days of Christmas, various slaves of all nations descended from the Engenhos of the district of this town, and uniting themselves in three large groupings with many from this town, according to their nation, formed three different *ranchos*, of drums, and went about their customary games, or dances; to whit, the geges, on the Sergimirim Place, the Angolas behind the Chapel of the Rosary, and the nagos and Haussas in the back road, next to the distillery which Thome Correa de Mattos patrols, this *rancho* being the most resplendent, dressed in *meio corpo*, with a large drum and some adornments with gold pieces, and they continued with their dances, not just during the day but also a large part of the night, feasting themselves in a nearby house which they found vacant, on the same back road, and in that place there was much to drink, supplied by the same pretos _____[1] of the aforementioned recreation, and they were [justly] expectant, many people [came] of all qualities and sexes, and finally without there occurring any tumult or disorder, each one retired to his domicile, [some time before?] the two previously mentioned *ranchos* or groups of geges and Angolas had retired with the night and it is not known if these feasted themselves or did anything notable. It is certain that on the afternoon of one of the aforementioned days, as the group of nagos and Haussas were in the greatest intensity of their dance, the Reverend Father Ignacio dos Santos directed himself to them with Apostolic zeal in order to impede the said dance, his diligence was useless as the said pretos did not obey him, responding with less decent words and finally they told him that their *senhores* had the whole week to enjoy themselves and that they [the slaves] had in [the week] one day only and for him to go away, that is, _____,[2] and at last the said father went away appealing to God; they say that the author of this response was the slave of Captain-Moor João Pedro, whose name I was not able to verify.

This disorder, Sir, is not new in this town, as ordinarily in similar days and times, these individuals are accustomed to gathering in order to form dances, with those damned instruments from their land, the disgrace is such that they practice [these acts] in the plain view of the magistrates themselves, who govern the republic wrapping these insolences with the title of recreation, and it is even given the

1. [missing in original]
2. [meaning unclear]

consent of the *senhores* [of these slaves] on their own Engenhos and fazendas, with the exception of a small number, as Your Excellency does not ignore, [this] requires prompt attention which Your Excellency will give as it seems to you correct. God guard Your Excellency many years. Villa of Our Lady of Purification and Santo Amaro[.] 20 of January 1809

José Roiz de Gomes
Captain Mor

Item B (Portuguese). Correspondência de Capitão José Roiz de Gomes ao outro Capitão Mor

20 Janeiro 1809
Arquivo Público do Estado da Bahia
Maço 417–1—Capitães Mores—1807–1822

Ajuntamento de Escravos

Illmo Senr Cap^{mor}
Pella informação que me dá o Alf^{es} Commd^e da 2ª Comp^a do novo Terço, José Fran^{co} da S^a, em consequencia da ordem que V.S^a. lhe deo peçoal para averiguar o precedim^{to} de hú ajuntam^{to} de escravos, que ouve nesta Villa, pelas _____ [1] do preterito Natal, fui informado do que se segue:—que naqueles ditos dias S^{tos} do Natal, descerão dos Engenhos do destrito desta V^a varios escravos de todas a naçoens, e unindoce em tres corporaçoens com m^{tos}, desta V^a, segundo a sua nasão, formarão tres diferentes ranxos, [2] de atabaques, e fizerão os seos costumados brinquedos, ou danças; a saber, os geges, no Sitio do Sergimirim, os Angolas p^r detras da Capella do Rosario, e os nagos e Uças, na Rua de detras, junto ao Alambique q˜ tem de ronda, Thome Correa de Mattos, sendo este ranxo o maiz luzido, vestidos em meio corpo com hú grande atabaque, e alguns adereçados com alguas peças de ouro, e continuarão com as suas danças, não só de dia mas ainda grandes partes da noite, banquetiarãoce em hua caza vizinha ad^a situação, q˜ se axava vazia, na m^{ma} rua de detras, e ahi ouve muito que beber, a custa dos mesmos pretos _____ [3] do d^o brinquedo, e forão expectadores, muito povo de toda a qualidade e sexo, e sem que afinal ouvesse tumulto, ou dezordem se retirarão cada hum ao seo domicilio, a tempo que os dois preditos ranxos, ou adejuntos de geges, e Angolas setinhão retirado com a noite, e senão _____ [4] que estes sebanquetiarem, ou fizeram couza notavel. He certo que estando a corporação dos nagos, e Uçás no mayor calor da sua dança, na tarde de hum dos referidos dias; se aderçou a elles com zello Apostolico O R^{do} P^e Ignacio dos Santos, p^a empedir a dita dança, cuja deligencia foi inutel, pois os ditos pretos o não atenderão, respondendo-lhes com

---

1. [Partially missing due to deterioration] Maybe *ocasioens*.
2. *Rancho = "grupo de pessoas, especialmente em marcha ou em jornada. Magote de gente. Reunião de marinheiros que comem juntos. Comida que se fornece a soldados e marujos. Comida para muitos, paga por quota"* (Silva Bastos, *Diccionário da Lingua Portugueza,* Lisbon: 1928).
3. [Missing due to deterioration]
4. *saiba* or *sabe* [?]

palavras menos desentes, e que afinal lhe diserão q̃ seos senhores tinhão toda a semana pᵃ se devertirem, e q̃ elles tinhão nella hum só dia, e que se retirace alias levaria o que lhe decem,[5] e a fim se retirou o dito Pᵉ apelando pᵃ Deos; dizem q̃o autor desta resposta era escravo do Capᵐᵒʳ João Pedro, cujo nome se não pode averiguar.

Esta dezordem Sᵒʳ não hé nova nesta Vᵃ, pois de ordinario em semᵉˢ dias e tempos, custumão ajuntarce estes individos para nela formarem danças, com aqueles malditos instrumentos a uzo da sua terra, hé tal a desgraça q~ afsim que o *pra*[6] a vista e face dos mesmos Magistrados, q~governão a *rep ica*[7] capiando estas insolencias com o titulo de brinquedo, e athe hé consentido pˡᵒˢ proprios senhores nos seos Engenhos, e fazendas, a exepção de hú pequeno numero, como V.Sᵃ não ignora, no q̃ preciza pronta providencia a qual dará V.Sᵃ como lhe parecer asertado. Deos guarde a V.Sᵃ muitos anos. Vᵃ de Nossa Senrᵃ da Purifᵃᵐ e S. Amaro[.] 20 de Janeiro de 1809

Jose Roiz de Gomes
Capᵐᵒʳ

---

5. *decem* = *dessem*[?]
6. [Partially missing in original] Probably *praticãõo*.
7. [Partially missing in original] Probably *república*.

Item C. Correspondence from a police authority in the freguesia of Santo Antonio alem do Carmo to the Chief of Police of Bahia

No date[1]
Arquivo Público do Estado da Bahia
Maço 6470, Policia: Assuntos, 1823–1846

Police Threatened by a Candomblé in Cabula

Most Illustrious Sir Doctor Chief of Police

With all due respect I come before Your Honor to denounce "the occurrence and lack of respect for the laws and justice which are entrusted to Your Honor's high and wise administration" in this Capital of Bahia[.] Most Illustrious Sir, the following fact is that in this freguesia, of Santo Antonio alem do Carmo[,] a crioulo, by the name Manoel Pedro de Santo Amaro[,] craftsman in the goldsmith workshop, presently a resident in the alley called Xica Bixenta in front of the [Nun's Retreat?][;] this crioulo individual, already having practiced various illegal acts of robbery[,] now close to the festival of Kings [and?] the Entrudo, he did the following as a medium of the candomblé of cabula, in which this said crioulo has a black girl by the name of Sunsão[,] daughter of a crioula slave of a family which lives in the calçada de Bonfim, that is[,] this negro, feiticeiro, has the said black girl of 14 to 15 years old, in his power away from the house of her legal mistresses without negotiating with her[;] It is Santa Barbara of the terreiro [who] divines, makes marriages, and punishes the police, who went to imprison them in the festival of kings[.] On this occasion I saw imprisoned[2] that boçal negro Africano angola but that Manoel Pedro, and his black girl Sunsão escaped from the grasp of the police[;] however days after they were released, the subdelegacy and the whole force of the troops of the Battalion and Urban soldiers were [disgraced?] with the shame of thieves[,] who went there in the Seralho roça of black feiticeiros indeed went to steal gold watches[,] money[,] from the pockets of the same individuals[.] That Manoel, medium of the black girl Sunsão, is the one who preaches this doctrine. This *nego* made a plan that on the days of the entrudo there would be all the *candombleizeiros,* they would be lying down, armed with clubs, with the lights out, so that as soon as the police came they would be attacked; as this negro Manoel Pedro would be in the Estrada das Boiadas ready to give the signal as soon as any troop marched[.] In light of the above, we ask Your Honor to make come to your presence the mentioned Manoel Pedro and that black girl Sunsão, with the aim of Your Honor handing over that black girl to her legal masters[;] as this black pilferer is a great seducer of others' slaves[.] It is a great justice and rectitude that Your Honor give whatever fate to this feiticeiro goldsmith negro aboard some warship

And You Will Receive Mercy

---

1. Various elements, including the mention of a *negro boçal* and the *Entrudo* festivities, suggest that this document was written before 1850.
2. That is, "I imprisoned," "I was able to imprison."

Item C (Portuguese). Correspondência entre um policial da freguesia de Santo Antonio alem do Carmo e o Chefe de Policia da Bahia

Sem Data
Arquivo Público do Estado da Bahia
Maço 6470—Policia: Assuntos 1823–1846

Policia Ameaçada por um Candomblé do Cabulla

Illmo Snr' Dotor Xefre[1] de Policia

Com todo devido respeito venho denuciar a VS "o prosidimento i falta de respeito as leyes i justissa ás quais estão comfiadas á alta i saiba[2] deminstração[3] de VS" nesta Capital da Bahia, Illmo Sr o seguinte, fauto[4] he q' eziste na freguizia, de S[to] Antonio Alem do Carmo hum criolo, de nome Manoel Pedro de Santo Amaro ofial[5] de cravador, da oficina, de ourives, morador prezentemente no beco denominado de Xica bixenta de fronte, do recolimento dos perdoes, este endivido,[6] Criolo ja tendo, praticado diversos atos de ladroeiras imjustissas ágora de proximo, das festas de Reis á o intrude,[7] praticou o seguinte como medio, do candoblé, do cabulla, no qual tem este referido criolo huma negrinha de nome Susão[8] filha de uma criola escrava de huma familia moradores na calçada do Bomfim digo tem este negro, fitiçeiro;[9] á tal negrinha de idade de 14 a 15 annos, em seo poder fora da casa dos suas competente sinhorar;[10] sim[11] elle negosea com ella, hé Santa Barba-do terreiro adevinha,[12] faz cazamentos, e castiga á policia, q' os fourão[13] prender nas festas do reis, nesta ocazião vejo prezo o tal bozá[14] negro Africano angola mais o tal Manoel Pedro, i á sua negrinha Sunsão fogirão das gara[15] da policia porem dias depois q' fourão soltos hera á sobdellegasia e toda folsa[16] de tropa do, Batalhão e Urbanos fourão se vandegados com o labeo; de ladrais os q[s] fourão áli na rosa[17] [Seralho?], de negros feiticeiro sim fourão fultar[18] relogio de ouro dinheiro; das algibeira dos mesmos,

---

1. *Chefe*
2. *sabia?*
3. *administração*
4. *fato*, or *facto*
5. *official?*
6. *individuo*
7. *entrudo*
8. Probably short for *Assunção*.
9. *feitiçeiro*
10. *senhoras?*
11. *sem?*
12. *advinha*
13. *foram*
14. *boçal*
15. *garra*
16. *força*
17. *roça*
18. *furtar*

endevidos q^m prega esta dotrina o[19] tal Manoel médio da negrinha Sunsão. [E]ste nego deo hum plano p^a q' nos dias de intrude estivesse, todos ós cambombrezeiros,[20] estivessem deitado, armados; de caceites de luzes apagadas, p^a q' logo q' foice[21] ahi á policia fouse[22] esta; agredida; p^s estes _ Negro Manoel Pedro, estava na estrada das bojadas[23] de prontidão p^a dar signar[24] logo q' marxáxe[25] q^{l}quel[26] folça de tropa; á vista, do esposto[27] pidimos a V.S. fassa[28] vim á prezença de V.S. o mencionado Manoel Pedro i a tal negrinha Sunsão á fim de V.S. intregar á tal negrinha, á os seos competente sinhores p^s este negro larapio hé um grande sedutor de escravos, alhejo[29] hé grande justissa é iquidade[30] V.S. dar q^{l}quer destino á este negro urives feiticeiro á bordo de algum navo[31] de guera[32]

E.R.M.

---

19. Or *do*.
20. *candomblezeiros*
21. *fosse?*
22. *fosse?*
23. *boiadas*
24. *sinal*
25. *marchasse*
26. *qualquer*
27. *exposto*
28. *faça*
29. *alheio?*
30. *equidade*
31. *navio*
32. *guerra*

Item D. Correspondence from José Eleuterio Rocha, of the Subdelegacy of Santa Anna to the Chief of Police of Bahia

April 24, 1854

Arquivo Público do Estado da Bahia
Maço 6230

Gathering in the House of an Africana; Objects and Persons Encountered

[Note: The first part of this letter refers to the arrest of a woman for stealing. The transcription below begins after that section.]

Most Illustrious Sir

. . . I also bring to Your Honor's attention that yesterday around nine o'clock at night, denounced by Manoel da Conceição, pardo, resident of Fonte das Pedras, that in the house of an Africana, behind the wall of the Nuns,[1] a great number of Africans have gathered at night, the majority of them declining to leave[;] judging it my duty to take measures, I went to the indicated house, bringing in my company the Inspector Joaquim da S^{a2} *I*.Lopez, the Citizen Luiz Alvares [Taderna?], who entered with me, and the denouncer, whom I ordered to get into uniform, leaving him in the road in order to prevent the escape of anyone, if, by chance there was anyone, since the yard of the house let out to the side of Ferraro street; the investigation made, solely was found a white man, in [one] of the rooms, sick, and a Senhora, who said she was his wife, and in the room of the black woman (already an elderly woman), a figure covered with feathers, spattered with blood and surrounding it some food, due to which I believed, that in fact there had been a meeting, and for this admonished her not to continue allowing gatherings under pain of being imprisoned. This, therefore, I communicate to Your Honor as is my duty.
May God Keep Your Honor[.]
Bahia Subdelegacia of Santa Anna[.] April 24 1854

Most Illustrious Sir Doctor Chief of Police of this Province

José Eleuterio Rocha
[of the Subdelegacy of Santa Anna]

---

1. That is to say, the wall of the Desterro Convent.
2. *Silva* or *Souza*.

Item D (Portuguese). Correspondência de José Eleuterio Rocha, da Subdelegacia de Santa Anna ao Chefe de Policia da Bahia

24 Abril 1854
Arquivo Público do Estado da Bahia
Maço 6230

Reunião em Casa de Africana; Objectos/Pessoas Achados

[Nota: A primeira parte desta carta refere á apreensão duma mulher por furto. A seguinte transcrição do documento começa depois daquele ponto.]

Illmo S^r

... Mais levo ao conhecim^{to} de VS^a que ontem p^{las} 9 oras da noite, denunciado p^r M^{el} da Conceição, pardo mor^{or} a Fonte das Pedras, de q' na caza de uma Afr^a, p^r detras do muro das Freiras, havião-se reunido gr^{de} n^o de Afr^{os} á noite, deixando de sahir a maior p^{te} delles, julgando do meo dever providenciar, dirigí-me a indicada caza, levando em m^a comp^a o Insp^{or} Joaquim da S^a Lopez, o Cidadão Luiz Alz' [Taderna?], q' com^{o1} entrarão, e o denunciante, q' m^{dei2} fardar-se, deixando-o na rua p^a evitar a fuga de algum, si p^r ventura existissem, visto q' o quintal da caza deita p^a o lado da rua do Ferraro; feito o varejo apenas encontrou-se um homem branco, em [um] dos quartos, doente, e uma Senr^a q' disse ser sua m^{er3} e no quarto da preta, (m^{er} já idosa), uma figura enfeitada de pennas, salpicada de sangue e ao redor algûa comida, p^{lo} q' cri,^{4} q' de facto tivesse havido o adjuncto, e por isso admoestei-a, p^a q' não continuasse a admittir ajuntam^{to} sob pena de ser presa. Isto p^{s5} comunico a VS^a p^{lo} dever q' me assiste.
D^s G^e a VS^a
B^a Subdelegacia de Sta Anna[.] 24 de Abril 1854

Illmo Sr Dr Chefe de Pol^a desta Prov^a

José Eleuterio Rocha
[da Subdelegacia de Santa Anna]

---

1. *comigo*
2. *mandei*
3. *mulher*
4. *crei*
5. *pois*

Item E. Correspondence from Chief of Police of Bahia, J.A.A.F. Henriques, to the Subdelegate of São Pedro

July 25 1862
Arquivo Público do Estado da Bahia
Maço 5754, Policia: Registro de Correspondencia com Subdelegados, 1862–1863

African Fortunetellers and the Problem of Robbery for Witchcraft; Domingos Sodré

July 25 1862
1st _
5173
Private   To the Subdelegate of São Pedro

The Citizen, José Egydio Nabuco, Customs Clerk, came to my presence to complain of the behavior of an Africano liberto by name Domingos, resident of Santa
Thereza hill, house[1] number 7 with four windows where there are vases of flowers,
and whose rear connects with the houses of the lower road, on the sea side[;] which
Africano, in combination with two Africanas also libertas, ganhadeiras, have constituted themselves diviners and luck changers, encouraging the slaves to steal as
much as they are able to steal from their Masters' houses, and bring it to them, under
the pretext of obtaining freedom by means of feitiçaria[;]such cunning strategy of
which the said citizen has been victim, from whose house a Nagô slave of his by
name

Theodolinda has carried to this den many objects of value as well as monies.
And as this Department is convinced that in many points in this Capital there exist
such speculators, who rob and get rich from the credulity of the imprudent, and [as
it] has the desire to put an end to such rapacity, to guarantee the property of others,
and to prevent the sad consequences which result due to the tolerance of such dens
of immoralities and thefts, I am going to recommend to Your Mercy that, commu-
nicating with the Lieutenant Colonel Commanding General of the Police, you give
search this afternoon in the said house, and keeping guard over the backyards, so
that the special mission is not thwarted, apprehend the persons who are to be found
in the said house, who should be immediately taken to the House of Correction—
before the people gather, as happens in such occasions.

Finally I caution Your Mercy that the aforementioned Africanos hold their sessions
in this house on Mondays and Fridays, _____ which the result of the special
mission which I entrust to you, will satisfy the _____[2] of this Division, which
well-foundedly [is reimpelled?] to see such superstitions eradicated, especially
harmful in a country in which a large part of whose fortune is occupied in slaves.
July 25 1862.

J.A.A.F. Henriques

---

1. Specifically, *sobrado* means "a two-story house."
2. Likely, "plans" or "intuitions."

Item E (Portuguese). Correspondencia do Chefe de Policia da Bahia, J.A.A.F. Henriques, ao Subdelegado de São Pedro

25 Julho 1862
APEB
Maço 5754—Policia: Registro de Correspondencia com Subdelegados (1862–1863)

Africanos Adivinhadores e o problema de furto para feitiçaria

25 de Julho de 1862
1ª_
5173
Rezervado   Ao Subdeleg^do de S. Pedro

O Cidadão José Egydio Nabuco, Empregado d'Alfandega, veio a minha prezença queixar-se do procedim^to de um Africano liberto de nome Dom^os morador á ladeira de Sta Thereza, sobrado N° 7 de quatro janellas onde ha vasos de flores, e cujos fundos se communicão com as casas da rua debaixo lado do mar, o qual Africano de combinação com duas Africanas tambem libertas, que vendem caixinha se teem constituido adivinhadores e dadores de ventura, alliciando os escravos que da casa de seos Senr^es furtão quanto podem pilhar, e lhes vão levar, á titulo de pr meio de feitiçarias obeterem liberdade, ardil este de que tem sido victima o referido cidadão, de cuja caza uma sua escrava Nagô de nome Theodolinda tem levado p^a efse covil immensos objectos de valor alem de dinheiros.

E como esta Rep^am esta convencida de que p^r muitos pontos d'esta Capital existem taes especuladores, q' roubão e se locupletão com a credulidade dos incautos, e tem todo o desejo de por termo a sem^e ganancia, de garantir a propriedade alheia e de prevenir as tristes consequencias q' rezultar devem da tolerancia do taes covis de immoralidades, e roubos, vou recommendar a VM^ce que entendendo-se [com o?] T^e Cor^el Com^e Geral da Policia, dé hoje a tarde busca na dita caza, e fazendo vigiar os quintais p^a q' se não malogre a deligencia apprehenda as pefsoas que forem encontradas na referida caza, as quais deverão ser incontinente conduzidas p^a a Corr[1] —antes que se aglomere povo, como succede em taes occassiões.

Previno finalm^e a VM^ce de que os supraditos Africanos fazem nessa caza suas _____[2] nas 2as e 6as feiras, _____ que o rezultado da diligencia que lhe confio, satisfará as v____[3] desta Rep^am, q' com m^to fundam^to reempenha em ver extirpadas sem^es supersticões, tanto mais nosscivas n'um pais em que uma grande parte de sua fortuna está empregada em escr^os.
25 de Julho de 1862.

                                                     J.A.A.F. Henriques

---

1. Provavelmente, *Correição.*
2. *sefsões? [quer dizer, sessões]*
3. *vistas?*

Item F. Correspondence from Chief of Police of Bahia, J.A.A.F. Henriques, to the Subdelegate of São Pedro

July 26 1862
Arquivo Público do Estado da Bahia
Maço 5754, Policia: Registro de Correspondencia com Subdelegados, 1862–1863

Domingos, Africano Liberto and Search of his House

1st _
26
5222   To the Subdelegate of São Pedro

Satisfied with the good result of the special mission which yesterday I secretly entrusted to the Lieutenant Colonel Commanding General of the Police Force, and about which ___[1] communiqué of this date speaks, I report to you that in the presence of the Africano liberto Domingos, who I send to you, and of the witnesses, the inspection of the house on Santa Thereza hill continues, the objects encountered being forwarded to me by the blacks I command, and that Your Mercy [understand?] that [the objects] must be forwarded to me in order to give them the appropriate fate.

This done I order Your Mercy to retire the said Africano Domingos to the house of Correction until my further deliberation.
26 of July of 1862.

J.A.A.F. Henriques

Item F (Portuguese). Correspondencia do Chefe de Policia da Bahia, J.A.A.F. Henriques, ao Subdelegado de São Pedro

26 Julho 1862
Arquivo Público do Estado da Bahia
Maço 5754, Policia: Registro de Correspondencia com Subdelegados, 1862–1863

Domingos, Africano liberto; e Busca em Sua Casa

1ª _
26
5222   Ao Subdelegado de S. Pedro

Satisfeito pelo bom rezultado da deligencia de que hontem encarreguei de intelligencia como T^e Cor^{el} Com^e Geral do Corpo Policial, e sobre o q' trata o seu officio desta data, tenho a dizer-lhe que em prezença do Afric^o liberto Domg^{os} que lhe envio e de test^{as} continue o varejo na casa á ladr^a de Sta Thereza, remettendo-me pelos pretos q' m^{do} os objectos encontrados, e q' VM^{ce} [entender?] q' me devão ser remetiddos p^a se lhes dar conv^e destino.

---

1. "His" or "your"; unclear from sentence construction.

Isto feito m^do VM^ce recolher a caza de Correção o referido Africano Domingos até m^a ulterior deliberação.

26 de Julho de 1862.

J.A.A.F. Henriques

Item G. Correspondence from Pompilio Manuel de Castro, Subdelegate of São Pedro Velho to the Chief of Police

July 27 1862
Arquivo Público do Estado da Bahia
Maço 6234, Policia: Delegados, 1861–1862

Search in the House of Domingos Sodré; Items Found (Auto da Busca)

Subdelegacy of the Freguesia of São Pedro Velho, 27 of July of 1862

Most Illustrious Sir

Yesterday I finalized the inspection-inventory of the house of the africano liberto Domingos Sodré, as Your Honor will see in the *auto da busca*,[1] which I remit by copy. In addition to the objects which I have already sent to Your Honor, [self-same] or used for the evil-doings and venturas, which this african was accustomed to give to the people who due to __ stupidity or credulity went there to know of their future, found in the sitting room for such _____, various paintings of the [supposed?] saints, and even an *oratorio*,[2] meanwhile it is in the [other] rooms[3] that he has the mixtures, clothes and emblems of his superstitious traffic. It seems to me that the clothing found, whether of men, or largely of women, should always be taken to the Secretary of Police to there be examined again. I am informed that this african for a long time lives by this means, and has a partnership with an African named Antãe[,] also liberto, who I am told, lives in this Freguesia, but I have not yet been able to learn anything of him, and in this mission I am prepared to find out more.[4] I am also told that this african Domingos was freed by the late Sudré in 1836, nevertheless he has the nerve to dress himself in the Independence War veteran's uniform, and __ of the campaign habit, as he wore on the occasion of his confinement to the House of Correction, when at the time of our Independence he was a slave, and found himself much later at the [Engenho?] of the same late Sudré. The gold objects found, are deposited in this *Juizo*, which will be forwarded to Your Honor, if it is so judged appropriate. This african is known as Papa[5] Domingos, and has constituted himself seer[6] and giver of fortune, and to whose house, I am told many seduced africanas and africanos, take to him objects stolen from their Masters, in order to under the pretext of offerings, obtain their liberty, and that with the use of drinks and mixtures, which they give them to drink are able to mollify their Masters, and other inanities which impress such stupid persons, and in this way such swindlers go on enriching themselves from the credulity of the incautious, and contributing to the loss of many africans who today live useless—their

---

1. Search report.
2. "Small chapel" or "altar."
3. As in *bedrooms*, or *back rooms*.
4. Literally, *fio da meada* is a clue to a puzzle or a problem.
5. Or "Daddy."
6. "Diviner," "counselor."

masters unable to count on their services. Having shown yourself to be so solicitous in the prosecution of crime in whatever [position?] the individual is found, as has been demonstrated by statistics; may Your Honor also contribute to the extirpation of a canker which [pervades?] this capital, and which has been so harmful in our country, the larger part of whose fortune is completely in the possession of slaves, and that an urgent and proficient remedy must be given, freeing society of such speculators who have already done us so much harm. Finally from the search report Your Honor will see, and if more informations are needed, I am ready to give them. May God Keep Your Honor

Most Illustrious Sir Doctor Chief of
Police in this Province

Pompilio Manuel de Castro

Item G (Portuguese). Correspondencia de Pompilio Manuel de Castro, Subdelegado de São Pedro Velho ao Chefe de Policia

27 Julho 1862
Arquivo Público do Estado da Bahia
Maço 6234—Policia: Delegados 1861–1862

Busca na Casa de Domingos Sodré; Itens Achados (Auto da Busca)

Subdelegacia da Freguesia de S. Pedro Velho, 27 de Julho de 1862

Illmo Senr'

Hontem finalizei o varejo na casa do africano liberto Domingos Sodré, como virá VS^a do auto de busca, que remetto por copia. Alem dos objectos que já enviei a VS^a [proprios?], ou usados para os maleficios e venturas, que costumava dar este africano ás pessôas que por ___ estupidez ou credulidade ahi hião saber de seu futuro, encontrase na salla para assim _____, diversos retratos dos [supor?] santos, e mesmo um oratorio, entretanto que nos quartos é que elle tinha os mixtos, roupas e emblemas do seo trafico supersticioso. Sou de parecer que das roupas achadas, quer de homem, quer de mulher em grande copia, que estas sempre fossem levadas a Secretaria de Policia para ahi serem examinadas de novo. Sou informado que este africano á muito vive desse mister, e tem sociedade com um africano de nome Antãe tambem liberto, que me consta, morar n'esta Freguezia, mas que ainda não me foi possivel saber delle, e nesta deligencia estou para melhor entrar no fio desta miada.[1] Consta me tambem que este africano Domingos fora liberto pelo finado Sudré[2] em 1836, entretanto que tem a expertesa de se cobrir com a farda de veterano da Independencia, e ___ do habito de campanha, como se revestio[3] na occasião de seu recolhido a casa de Correção, quando na epocha de nossa Independecia era elle escravo, e se achava m^to depois no [Engenho?] do mesmo finado Sudré. Os objectos

___

1. *meada*
2. *Sodré*
3. *revestiu*

d'ouro encontrados, estão depositados n'este Juizo, que todavia serão remettidos a VSª, se assim julgar conveniente. Este africano é conhecido pelo papai Domingos, e se tem constituido advinhador e dador de venturas e para a casa d'este, consta me que muitas africanas e africanos, alliciados levarão objectos furtados de seos Senhores ao mesmo, para á titulo de ofertas, conseguirem sua liberdade, e mesmo com bebidas e mixtos empregados, e que lhes dar a beber conseguirem amansar seos senhores, e outras frioleiras, que impressionão a taes pessoas estupidas, e assim vão taes especuladores se locupletando com a credulidade dos incautos, e concorrendo para perda de muitos africanos que hoje inutilisados vivem sem que seus senhores possão contar com seus serviços. Cumpre pois que VSª, que tão solicito se tem mostrado a perseguir o crime em qualquer [posição?], que se ache o individuo, como ja ha demonstrado pelo estatisca,[4] concorra tambem em extirpar um cancro que [paira?] n'esta capital, e que tão nocivo tem sido em nosso pais, cuja maior parte de nossa fortuna está toda na posse de escravos, e que um remedio profícuo e urgente, cumpre dar se, livrando a sociedade de taes especuladores que ja tanto mal nos ha feito. Finalmente do auto de busca verá VSª, e mais informações que necessitar, estar eu prompto a dar las.
Deus Guarde a VSª

Illᵐᵒ Senr' Doutor Chefe de
Policia n'esta Provincia
Pompilio Manuel de Castro

---

4. *estatistica*

Item H. Search Report Submitted by Clerk José Joaquim Meirelles— Addendum to Correspondence from Subdelegate of São Pedro Velho to Chief of Police

Copy of the Search Report and Found Items

On the 25th day of the month of July of the Year of the Birth of Our Lord Jesus Christ, of one thousand eight hundred and sixty-two, in this Loyal and Valorous City of São Salvador Bay of all the Saints and Freguesia of São Pedro Velho, in the street of the Hill of Santa Thereza, House number 7, residence of the Africano liberto Domingos Sodré, where the Alternate Subdelegate was going. The citizen Pompilio Manuel de Castro, like me clerk of his Duty, signed below, the Quarteirão Inspectors Adriano José Pinheiro, José Thomas Muniz Barretto, being there [at the behest of?] the said Subdelegado[,] in the presence of the owner of the house the aforementioned Domingos Sodré the Search proceeded, opening drawers, leather-covered wooden chests, and trunks, the following objects were found. Four metal rattles. A box with various wooden figures, and other objects such as Beads, and Cowrie Shells. A blunt-edged and point-less tin sword. An iron [object] with cowries and a wooden sword. Two wall clocks. A Jacaranda-wood dresser with a portion of clothing with initials "D.S. D.C." Various paintings of Saints on the walls. A white belt with cowries; underpants. A box with [soiled?] women's clothing. A leather-covered wooden chest with the said silver Necklace with diverse objects. Fourteen items of clothing with cowries. Four conical caps. A gourd with *cão da costa* and various miscellaneous things. A small varnished box containing his testament. A Gold Rosary with a Crucifix also Gold, containing eighty-nine large beads. A six-chain necklace of gold with its cross of the same. A pair of gold buttons for shirt cuffs, two rings with diamonds. Six rings of Gold, two pairs of earrings, one of golden silver, and the other of gold. A necklace with nineteen corals and thirteen gold beads; another necklace with eighty-five Corals and twenty-two beads of gold. [An antiquated measure] of silver chain, regular, four silver rings, a silver key-ring, two broken gold rings, a Carton also of silver, and two small coral *figas*. Five boxes which were broken open containing used clothing of black women and some in good condition including one [box] with some new cloth items belonging to the small merchandising box. One small merchandising box with cloth items. Excepting the furniture of the house, I mean[,] all objects mentioned here remaining in the same House, Except the wooden Saints and Objects belonging to Candomblé which are to be directed to the Secretary of Police. Remaining however deposited in *Juizo*, the Box with the Gold Objects declared above, and the testament of Domingos Sodré recognized by the Notary Lopes da Costa. And there being nothing else he ordered the Subdelegate to record the present statement, which goes via the same Subdelegado signed, like me Clerk José Joaquim de Meirelles, which I did and wrote and signed, _____ witnesses José Thomas Muniz Barretto, José Paulino de Campos Lima, [Franciscano?] Alvez da Palma, José Joaquim de Meirelles.
Is in Conformation [with the original]

The Clerk José Joaquim de Meirelles

I declare that the Original is signed by the Subdelegate and by the witnesses. Meirelles

Item H (Portuguese). Auto de Busca e Achado Preparado por o Escrivão José Joaquim Meirelles—Suplemento à Correspondência do Subdelegado de São Pedro Velho ao Chefe de Policia

Copia de Auto de Busca e Achado

Aos vinte cinco dias do mes de Julho do Anno do Nascimento de Nosso Senhor Jesus Cristo, de mil oito Centos e Sessenta e dous, n'esta Leal e Valerosa Cidade de São Salvador Bahia de Todos os Santos e Freguesia de São Pedro Velho, na rua da Ladeira de Santa Thereza, Casa n° 7, morada do Africano liberto Domingos Sudré, onde foi vindo o Subdelegado Supplente. O cidadão Pompilio Manuel de Castro, comigo escrivão de seu Cargo, abaixo assignado, os Inspectores de Quarteirão Adriano José Pinheiro, José Thomas Muniz Barretto, sendo ahi pelo dito Subdelegado em presença do dono da casa o referido Domingos Sodré, se procedeo a Busca, abrindo-se gavêtas, bahús, e Arcas, se encontrou os seguintes Objectos. Quatro chocaios[1] de metal. Uma caixa com diversas figuras de pau, e outros objectos como Contas, e búzios. Uma espada de latão sem corte, e sem ponta. Um ferro com búzios, e uma espada de pau. Dous relogios de parede. Uma comoda da Jacarandá com uma porção de roupa com os inciais D.S. D.C. Diversos quadros de Santos pelos paredes. Uma cinta branca com buzios; uma calçola. Uma caixa com roupa de mulher, [servida?]. Um Bahú com dita uma Corrente de prata com diversos objectos. Quatorze peças de roupa com buzios. Quatro Carapuços. Uma Cuia com Cão da Costa e diversos misticos. Huma caixinha emvernessada[2] contendo o seu testamento. Um Rosario de Ouro com um Cruxifixo igualmente d'Ouro, contendo oitenta e nove contos grandes. Seis voltas de colar de Ouro com sua Crúz de dito. Um par de botões de ouro para punho, dous aneis com diamantes. Seis ditos de Ouro, dous pares de argolas um de prata dourada, e outro d'ouro. Uma volta com desenove Coraes e treze Contos d'Ouro; Outra volta com oitenta e cinco Coraes e vinte duas contas d'Ouro. Uma vara de corrente de prata, regular, quatro aneis de prata, uma argola de prata para enfiar chaves, dous aneis d'ouro quebrados, um Cartão tãoebem de prata, e duas pequenas figas de coral. Cinco caixas que se arombarão[3] contendo roupa usada de pretas e algumas em bom estado inclusivel uma com algumas peças de fasendas novas pertencente a Caixinha. Uma caixinha de mercadejar com fasendas. Excepto a mobilha da casa, digo ficando todos os objectos aqui mencionados na mesma Casa, Excepto os Santos de paú e objectos pertencentes a Candomblé que passão a ser dirigidos a Secretaria de Polícia. Ficando porem depositados em Juizo, á Caixa com os objectos d'Ouro acima declarados, eo testamento de Domingos Sudré reconhecido pelo Tab[am] Lopes da Costa. E por nada mais haver mandou o Subdelegado lavrar o presente auto, que vai pelo mesmo Subdelegado assignado, comigo Escrivão José Joaquim de Meirelles, que o fiz, e escrevi e o assignei, _____ testamunhos José Thomas Muniz

---

1. *chocalhos*
2. *envernizada*
3. *arrombaram*

Barretto, José Paulino de Campos Lima, [Franciscano?] Alvez da Palma, José Joaquim de Meirelles.
Está Conforme

O Esc^am José Joaquim de Meirelles

Declaro que o Original está asfignado pelo Subdelegado, e pelos testem^os.

Meirelles

Item I. Correspondence from Antonio Fernandes Leal, Subdelegate of the Freguesia of Brotas, to the Chief of Police

February 3 1887
Arquivo Público do Estado da Bahia
Maço 6252

Candomblé House; Seclusion of three Crioulas

Bahia and Subdelegacy of the 1st District of the Freguesia of Brotas February 3 1887

Most Excellent Sir

I report to your Excellency that I, having read yesterday at 8 o'clock in the morning an epigraph in the *20 of August* newspaper[1] = Letter = immediately I directed myself to Quintas das Beatas to the house of Domingas Maria do Rosario, lover of Peregrino Sermita[2] Bittencourt, employed in the Monte Socorro Bank of this City, which house[3] is used exclusively for Candomblé.

There, I found shut up in a room, three young crioulas from 17 to 20 years old, seminude and with their heads shaved, whom I ordered conducted to the Station so as to interrogate them. They declared to me to be called: Roza Lima de Oliveira, Maria do Carmo, and Joanna Valeria da Purificação; that they found themselves detained by Domingas since the 20th day of the past month, that she obligated them to do all the domestic service, washing and starching and that as soon as they finished their tasks, they were again secluded in the room so as to make the Saint;[4] that they didn't run away because they would go crazy if they did; that she obligated them to shave their heads by order of the Saint and ultimately she had them in a rigorous submission, and had told them that they would be there for six months to a year in order to make the Saint.

On the occasion that I was interrogating one of these who makes the Saint entered into the reception room the individuals = Evaristo de Santa Anna Gomes and Peregrino, who came carrying books for Evaristo to prove to me how I had committed an abuse in taking possession of the makers of the Saint; they became so importune and bothersome that I had them removed from my presence, before they obliged me to order their imprisonment for disobedience, and for more, as they manifested by their comportment.

The makers of the Saint, I sent to their houses, ordering them not to return to the house of such maliciously sly people, who in this way make a lovely fount for their expenses, thereby feeding the repugnant vice of their long, lazy lives. May God Guard Your Excellency

---

1. *20 of August* is the name of the newspaper.
2. Or *Sernita*.
3. The house of Domingas Maria do Rosario, that is.
4. To be initated in Candomblé.

Most Excellent Sir Doctor Chief of Police
The Subdelegate
Antonio Fernandes Leal

Item I (Portuguese). Correspondencia de Antonio Fernandes Leal, Subdelegado da Freguezia de Brotas, ao Chefe de Policia

3 Fevereiro 1887
Aquivo Público do Estado da Bahia
Maço 6252

Casa de Candomblé; Recolhimento de tres Crioulas

Bahia e Subdelegacia do 1º districtio da Freguesia de Brotas 3 de Fevereiro de 1887

Ex^m S^r

Communico a V. Ex^{cia} que tendo eu, hontem as 8 horas da manhã lido uma epigraphe do jornal vinte de Agosto = Carta = incontinente dirijime ás Quintas das Beatas á casa de Domingas Maria do Rosario, amasia de Peregrino Sermita[1] Bittencourt, empregado na Caixa Monte Socorro d'esta Cidade, casa esta, que só serve de Candomblé.

Alli, encontrei fechados em um quarto, tres raparigas crioulas de idade 17 a 20 annos, seminuas e com as cabeças rapadas,[2] as quaes mandei condusir á Estação á fim de interrogal-as. Declararão-me chamar se: Roza Lima de Oliveira, Maria do Carmo, e Joanna Valeria da Purificação; que se achavão detidas por Domingas desde o dia 20 do mez findo, que essa lhes obrigava á fazerem todo o serviço domestico, lavando e gomando e que logo que terminavão suas tarefas, erão de novo recolhidas no tal quarto a fim de faserem Santo; que ellas não fugissem p^r que ficarião doudas se o fisessem; que obrigou lhes a rapar[3] a cabeça por ordem do Santo e finalmente as tinha n'uma submissão rigoroza, e lhes tinha dito que alli estarião por seis mezes a um anno á fim de fazerem Santo.

Na occasião d'estar eu interrogando a uma d'essas que fas Santo, entrou me na sala d'audiencia os individuos = Evaristo de Santa Anna Gomes e Peregrino, que vinha carregado de livros a fim de Evaristo provar-me como tinha eu feito uma arbitrariedade apoderando-me das factoras de Santo; tornarão-se tão importunos e inconvenientes, que os fiz retirar de minha presença, antes que me obrigassem mandal-os recolher por desobedientes, e por mais, conforme manifestarão pelos seos comportaments.

As factoras de Santo, as mandei para suas casas ordenando-lhes; que mais não voltassem á casa de similhantes espertos, que fazem d'esse meio uma bella fonte

---

1. Or *Sernita.*
2. *raspadas*
3. *raspar*

para suas despezas, alimentando assim o vicio torpe ____[4] suas ociozas vidas de tantos annos. Deos Guarde a V. Ex^{cia}

Exmo Sr D^{or} Chefe de Policia

O Subdelegado
Antonio Fernandes Leal

---

4. *das* or *nas*

Notes

Introduction

1. The Recôncavo is the immediate area surrounding the Bay of All Saints; in the colonial period and nineteenth century it was largely dedicated to the cultivation of export crops (specifically sugar, tobacco, manioc, and, later, cotton) and to some subsistence farming.

2. "African American," in this sense, refers to the peoples and cultures of African descent throughout the western hemisphere. The term will have that meaning throughout the text unless specified otherwise.

3. E. Bradford Burns, *A History of Brazil*, 2nd ed. (New York: Columbia University Press, 1980), 17.

4. Emilia Viotti da Costa, *The Brazilian Empire* (Chicago: University of Chicago, 1985), 199. The Tordesillas treaty was an agreement signed in 1494 which divided much of the New World between the Spanish and Portuguese empires.

5. Salvador was the capital of colonial Brazil from 1549 to 1763, when the seat of government was moved to Rio de Janeiro.

6. Burns, *A History of Brazil*, 278. Emilia Viotti da Costa estimates that "shortly after independence" the country had a total population of 3,960,866. Of this number, she estimates that 2,813,351 were free and 1,147,515 were enslaved. *The Brazilian Empire*, 128.

7. João Jose Reis, *Slave Rebellion in Brazil: The Muslim Uprising of 1835 in Bahia* (Baltimore: Johns Hopkins University Press, 1993), 6. Reis notes further that whites represented 28.2 percent of the city's populace in 1835.

8. Ibid., 22–23. These were terms used by Bahian elites to describe the mass of free people in Salvador and Recôncavo towns: "artisans, street vendors, washerwomen, day laborers, vagabonds, prostitutes" (22). Most of these people had African ancestors.

9. For further discussion of the dichotomy in Brazilian cultural ideology between "house" as private, protected space, and "street" as public, potentially dangerous, and chaotic space, see Roberto Da Matta, *A casa & a rua* (Rio de Janeiro: Editora Guanabara Koogan, 1991), and Sandra Lauderdale Graham, *House and Street: The Domestic World of Servants and Masters in Nineteenth-Century Rio de Janeiro* (Austin: University of Texas Press, 1992).

10. On *candomblé* iconography, see Carybé, *Os deuses africanos no candomblé da Bahia* (Salvador: Editora Bigraf, 1993). On ritual and practice see Roger Bastide, *O candomblé da Bahia (rito nàgô)* (São Paulo: Companhia Editora Nacional, 1978); Maneula Carneiro da Cunha, *Candomblés da Bahia* (Rio de Janeiro: Civilização Brasileira, 1991); and the series *Escritos sobre a religião dos orixás*, edited by Carlos Eugenio M. de Moura (various publishers, 1981–1994). On cosmology, mythology, and connections to Africa see Juana Elbein dos Santos, *Os nàgô e a morte* (Petrópolis: Vozes, 1975), and Pierre Verger, *Orixás: Deuses iorubas na África e no novo mundo*

(Salvador and São Paulo: Corrupio/Circulo do Livro, 1981). For a short introduction to Candomblé in English, see Chapter 3 of Joseph Murphy, *Working the Spirit: Ceremonies of the African Diaspora* (Boston: Beacon Press, 1994).

11. This text briefly addresses some aspects of the interaction between Africans and Indians in nineteenth-century Bahia—especially relating to pharmacopoeic and ritual knowledge-sharing and to the development of traditions honoring the native spirits as "owners of the land" within Afro-Brazilian *candomblés*. However, the early-twentieth-century development of specifically denominated Candomblés-de-Caboclo (a form of Candomblé that conspicuously incorporates and specifically cultivates Brazilian Amerindian spirits) is outside the scope of this study. For more detailed treatment of the Candomblé-de-Caboclo within the Jeje-Nagô and Congo-Angola Candomblé traditions, see Jocélio Teles de Santos, *O dono da terra: O caboclo nos candomblés da Bahia* (Salvador: SarahLetras, 1995).

1. Slavery, *Africanos Libertos*, and the Question of Black Presence in Nineteenth-Century Brazil

1. Emília Viotti da Costa, *The Brazilian Empire: Myths and Histories* (Chicago: University of Chicago Press, 1985), 126.

2. The donatory captaincies were fifteen land grants about fifty leagues wide with uncharted inland boundaries (supposedly reaching to the Tordesillas line) given by King João III of Portugal to landlords, mostly minor nobility and merchants, who were responsible for colonizing the areas at their own expense. These captaincies were the basis of the earliest land organization in Brazil.

3. Stuart Schwartz, *Sugar Plantations in the Formation of Brazilian Society: Bahia, 1550–1835* (Cambridge, England: Cambridge University Press, 1985).

4. *Engenho* means either "sugar mill" or "sugar plantation," depending on the context.

5. The Dutch, who occupied areas of northeastern Brazil in the first half of the seventeenth century, were largely responsible for spreading the sugar industry to the West Indies after they were finally expelled from Brazil.

6. J. E. Inikori, ed., *Forced Migration: The Impact of the Export Slave Trade on African Societies* (New York: Africana Publishing, 1982), 19–20. Inikori's calculation is an intermediate figure between Philip Curtin's more conservative figure of 11 million and other estimates which run as high as 60 million. Inikori's estimate does not include the number of people who died at various stages of the process before reaching the American ports.

7. Philip Curtin, *The Atlantic Slave Trade: A Census* (Madison: University of Wisconsin Press, 1969). Curtin estimates that 3.7 million Africans were enslaved in Brazil during the period of the Atlantic slave trade.

8. Schwartz, *Sugar Plantations*, 346–53. In fact, Schwartz indicates that the ratio of men to women was sometimes as high as three to one in the Recôncavo. João José Reis, however, found that the slave population in rural areas of Bahia between 1813 and 1827 showed a proportion of 158 men to 100 women. Reis, *Slave Rebellion in Brazil*, 7.

9. Robert Conrad, "Nineteenth-Century Brazilian Slavery," in *Slavery and Race Relations in Latin America*, ed. Robert Brent Toplin (Westport, Conn.: Greenwood Press, 1974), 160–62.

10. Henry Koster, *Travels in Brazil*, vol. II (London: Longman, Hurst, Rees, Orm and Brown, 1817), 141.

11. Katia M. de Queirós Mattoso, *Bahia, século XIX: uma provincia no imperio* (Rio de Janeiro: Nova Fronteira, 1992), 162. The general exception was for skilled jobs such as *mestre de açúcar*. These were almost uniformly held by men.

12. Conrad, "Nineteenth-Century Brazilian Slavery," 160–62; Costa, *The Brazilian Empire*, 132.

13. See Robert Conrad, *World of Sorrow: The African Slave Trade to Brazil* (Baton Rouge: Louisiana State University Press, 1986), 7–15.

14. James Lockhart and Stuart B. Schwartz, *Early Latin America: A History of Colonial Spanish America and Brazil* (Cambridge, England: Cambridge University Press, 1983), 218–19.

15. Conrad, "Nineteenth-Century Brazilian Slavery," 160–62.

16. Dale Thurston Graden, "From Slavery to Freedom in Bahia, Brazil, 1791–1900" (Ph.D. diss., University of Connecticut, 1991), 98.

17. Manuela Carneiro da Cunha, *Negros, estrangeiros: os escravos libertos e sua volta à Africa* (São Paulo: Brasiliense, 1985).

18. The definitive work on the Malê Revolt is João José Reis, *Slave Rebellion in Brazil: The Muslim Uprising of 1835 in Bahia* (Baltimore: Johns Hopkins University Press, 1993).

19. Reis, *Slave Rebellion in Brazil*, 192; da Cunha, *Negros, estrangeiros*, 74.

20. Muniz Sodré, *O Terreiro e a Cidade: a forma social negro-brasileira* (Petrópolis: Vozes, 1988), 65.

21. Da Cunha, *Negros, estrangeiros*, 82; Viotti da Costa, *The Brazilian Empire*, 55. Of course, in their efforts to restrict meanings of nationhood and citizenship, the Brazilians had the powerful precedent of North American revolutionary history and the U.S. Constitution, upon which Brazilian framers drew heavily.

2. Salvador

1. Salvador was an especially important distribution point for the resale of slaves destined for the mines of the interior and the coffee estates of the south.

2. Ana de Lourdes Ribeiro da Costa, "'Ekabó!': trabalho escravo, condições de moradia e reordenamento urbano em Salvador no século XIX" (master's thesis, Universidade Federal da Bahia, 1989), 26.

3. A stock market.

4. Katia de Queirós Mattoso, *Bahia, século XIX: uma provincia no império* (Rio de Janeiro: Nova Fronteira, 1992), 436.

5. Mary C. Karasch, *Slave Life in Rio de Janeiro, 1808–1850* (Princeton: Princeton University Press, 1987), 362. See also Fayette Wimberly, "The African Liberto and the Bahian Lower Class: Social Integration in Nineteenth-Century Bahia, Brazil, 1870–1900" (Ph.D. diss., University of California at Berkeley, 1988), 180.

6. In "'Ekabó!'" Ribeiro described the *cães de costa* as a particularly offensive-looking dog that was common to Salvador.

7. James Wetherell, *Stray Notes from Bahia: Being an Extract from Letters during Residence of Fifteen Years* (Liverpool: Webb and Hunt, 1860).

8. João José Reis, *Slave Rebellion in Brazil: The Muslim Uprising of 1835 in Bahia* (Baltimore: Johns Hopkins University Press, 1993), 6; Anna Amélia Vieira Nascimento, *Dez freguisias da cidade do Salvador: aspectos sociais e urbanos do século XIX* (Salvador: Fundação Cultural do Estado da Bahia, 1986), 65.

9. Mattoso quoted in Reis, *Rebelião escrava no Brasil: a história do levante dos malês (1835)* (São Paulo: Brasiliense, 1986), 21.

10. *De ganho* is a term indicating earning.

11. Reis, *Slave Rebellion in Brazil,* 12.

12. Maria Dundas Graham, *Journal of a Voyage to Brazil, and Residence There during Part of the Years 1821, 1822, 1823* (1824; reprint, New York: Praeger, 1969), 126.

13. Wetherell, *Stray Notes,* 16–17.

14. Reis, *Slave Rebellion in Brazil,* 3.

15. Ibid.

16. Robert Avé-Lallemant, *Viagem pelo norte do Brasil* (Rio de Janeiro: Instituto Nacional do Livro, 1961), 20.

17. Stuart Schwartz, *Sugar Plantations in the Formation of Brazilian Society: Bahia, 1550–1835* (Cambridge, England: Cambridge University Press, 1985), 563 note 60; B. J. Barickman, "The Slave Economy of Nineteenth-Century Bahia: Export Agriculture and Local Market in the Recôncavo, 1780–1860" (Ph.D. diss., University of Illinois at Urbana-Champaign, 1991), 38–39.

18. Figures cited in Ribeiro da Costa, "'Ekabó!,'" 39–40.

19. Reis, *Slave Rebellion in Brazil,* 6; Paulo Cesar Souza, *A Sabinada: a revolta separatista da Bahia (1837)* (São Paulo: Brasiliense, 1987), 10; Nascimento, *Dez freguesias,* 65; Mattoso, *Bahia, século XIX,* 110. Mattoso estimates that from 1810 to 1870 Bahia's population grew from 50,000 to 100,000 inhabitants.

20. Reis, *Slave Rebellion in Brazil,* 6.

21. Barickman, "The Slave Economy," 38–39.

22. Costa, "'Ekabó!,'" 42. "Caboclo" is a term denominating Indians or people of mixed white and Indian ancestry.

23. Herbert Klein, "Nineteenth-Century Brazil," in *Neither Slave nor Free: The Freedmen of African Descent in the Slave Societies of the New World,* ed. D. W. Cohen and Jack Greene (Baltimore: Johns Hopkins University Press, 1972), 316.

24. João José Reis, "Slave Rebellion in Brazil" (Ph.D. diss., University of Minnesota, 1982), 8.

25. Katia Mattoso, cited in João Reis, *Slave Rebellion in Brazil,* 8; Stuart Schwartz, *Sugar Plantations,* 250. Of the colonial period, Schwartz writes, "The plantation regime did not create the rankings, but its internal structure with ownership by Europeans, coerced labor provided by Indians and then African or black slaves, and artisan or managerial roles filled by poorer whites, freed blacks and persons of color, reinforced the social hierarchy and reaffirmed the gradations in a practical and demonstrable way" (251).

26. João Reis, "Nas malhas do poder escravista: a invasão do candomblé do Accú na Bahia, 1829," *Religião e Sociedade* 13, no. 3 (1986): 119.

27. Henry Koster, *Travels in Brazil* (London: Longman, Hurst, Rees, Orm and Brown, 1817), 216–17.

28. Ibid., 217.

29. Reis, *Slave Rebellion in Brazil,* 5.

30. Maria Inês C. de Oliveira, *O liberto: seu mundo e os outros* (São Paulo: Corrupio, 1988).

31. Katia Mattoso, *Bahia: a cidade de Salvador e seu mercado no século dezenove* (São Paulo: HUCITEC, 1978), 161–69.

32. F. W. O. Morton, "The Conservative Revolution of Independence" (Ph.D. diss., Oxford University, 1974), 46–58.

33. Reis, *Slave Rebellion in Brazil,* 10.

34. On women as heavy manual laborers see Mattoso, *Bahia, a cidade do Salvador.* On women as watercarriers see Luis Viana Filho, *O negro na Bahia,* 3rd ed. (Rio de Janeiro: Nova Fronteira, 1988), photo portfolio.

35. Costa, "'Ekabó!,'" 62–63; Reis, *Slave Rebellion in Brazil,* 161.

36. Costa, "'Ekabó!,'" 58–60.

37. Ibid., 219, 272.

3. The *Bolsa de Mandinga* and *Calundu*

1. John Mbiti, one of the foremost scholars of African religion and philosophy, has suggested that the unity within diversity among the religious experiences and beliefs of traditional African peoples is sufficiently great to make the use of the singular term "African religion" more appropriate than the plural "African religions." Mbiti, *African Religions and Philosophy,* 2nd ed. (Oxford, England: Heinemann International, 1990), xiii.

2. Mbiti, *African Religions,* 5. See also Geoffrey Parrinder, *African Traditional Religion* (1954; reprint, Westport, Conn.: Greenwood Press, 1970); Noel Q. King, *African Cosmos: An Introduction to Religion in Africa* (Belmont, Calif.: Wadsworth Publishing, 1986); Mary C. Karasch, "Commentary," in *Roots and Branches: Current Directions in Slave Studies,* ed. Michael Craton (Toronto: Pergamon Press, 1979), 140; Muniz Sodré, "A sombra do retrato," in *Escravos brasileiros do século XIX na fotografia de Christiano, Jr.,* orgs. Paulo Cesar de Azevedo and Mauricio Lissovsky (São Paulo: Ex Libris, 1988); and Monica Schuler, "Afro-American Slave Culture," in *Roots and Branches: Current Directions in Slave Studies,* ed. Michael Craton (Toronto: Pergamon Press, 1979), 121.

3. Sodré, "A sombra do retrato."

4. Charles H. Long, *Significations: Signs, Symbols, and Images in the Interpretation of Religion* (Philadelphia: Fortress, 1986), 7.

5. Jonathan Z. Smith, *To Take Place: Toward Theory in Ritual* (Chicago: University of Chicago, 1987), 27.

6. In Brazil, illiteracy was a general phenomenon throughout the entire society in the colonial and imperial period. Until the end of the nineteenth century, not more than 15 percent of the population was literate. One of the outstanding characteristics of Muslim slaves and freedpeople was that many (the spiritual leaders most particularly) had some level of literacy in Arabic.

7. João José Reis and Eduardo Silva, *Negociação e conflito: A resistência negra no Brasil escravista* (São Paulo: Companhia das Letras, 1989), 15.

8. Lawrence Sullivan, *Icanchu's Drum: An Orientation to Meaning in South American Religions* (New York: Macmillan, 1988), 4.

9. Charles Long developed the idea of African American religion as one of "mashing out a meaning" of humanity and of blackness in the context of the New World experience of slavery and oppression. Charles H. Long, oral presentation at the conference "A Consultation on Black Studies" at the University of California at Santa Barbara, April 1993.

10. William Peitz, "The Problem of the Fetish, I," *Res: Anthropology and Aesthetics* 9 (Spring 1985): 5–17; William Peitz, "The Problem of the Fetish, II," *Res: Anthropology and Aesthetics* 13 (Spring 1987): 23–45; and William Peitz, "The Problem of the Fetish, IIIa," *Res: Anthropology and Aesthetics* 16 (Autumn 1988): 105–23.

11. Roger Bastide, *The African Religions of Brazil: Toward a Sociology of the*

Interpenetration of Civilizations (Baltimore: Johns Hopkins University Press, 1978), 135.

12. Ibid.

13. Laura de Mello e Souza, *O diabo e a terra de Santa Cruz: Feitiçaria e religiosidade popular no Brasil colonial* (São Paulo: Companhia das Letras, 1994), Chapter 1.

14. Ibid., 70.

15. The well-known aphorism of André João Antonil dates from this period: "Brazil is the black's hell, the white's purgatory, and the paradise of mulatos and mulatas." Antonil, *Cultura e opulência do Brasil por suas drogas e minas* (1711), cited in Souza, *O diabo e a terra de Santa Cruz*, 70.

16. Ibid.

17. Ibid., 210.

18. Ibid., 210–11.

19. Bastide suggests that in Uruguay and Argentina, as well as in other countries of Latin America, the former presence of Muslim slaves may be deduced from the existence and meaning of the term "mandinga" in those places. Roger Bastide, *African Civilisations in the New World* (New York: Harper and Row, 1971), 105. See also Bastide, *African Religions of Brazil*, 150–51.

20. See Souza, *O diabo e a terra de Santa Cruz*, 210–26; Reis, *Slave Rebellion in Brazil*, 171; and May 11 and 12, 1853, Capitães Mores, maço 6230, Arquivo Público do Estado da Bahia, Salvador (hereafter APEB).

21. The writing may have been Arabic. May 11, 1853, Capitães Mores, maço 6230, APEB. My thanks to Alexandra Brown for bringing this document to my attention.

22. Arquivo Nacional da Torre do Tombo (hereafter ANTT), Inquisição de Lisboa, Processo no. 9972. Cited in Souza, *O diabo e a terra de Santa Cruz*, 217.

23. According to historian Luiz Mott, cited in Souza, the *pedra d'ara* was a section of marble with an internal orifice into which were deposited relics of martyred saints and over which priests consecrated the host and wine. Souza, *O diabo e a terra de Santa Cruz*, 214.

24. Ibid., 218.

25. Ibid.

26. Ibid., 218–19. It is interesting to consider possible connections between the lightning stone, the June fires of the feast of St. John, and the Yoruba/Fon deity of fire, storm, and justice, Xangô/Heviosso.

27. Henry Koster, *Travels in Brazil* (London: Longman, Hurst, Rees, Orm and Brown, 1817), 94–95.

28. Souza, *O diabo e a terra de Santa Cruz*, 206.

29. Ibid.

30. Sonia Maria Giacomini, *Mulher e escrava: uma introdução ao estudo da mulher negra no Brasil* (Petrópolis: Vozes, 1988), Chapter 5: "A senhora e a escrava."

31. Processo no. 631 from the Lisbon Inquisition, ANTT. Cited in Souza, *O diabo e a terra de Santa Cruz*, 206–207. Marcelina was stripped of her clothes and another slave was made to beat her as the master asked her how often she had had sex with her lover, a fellow slave, who was also present and was "beaten at the same time and on the same occasion."

32. Parrinder, *African Traditional Religion*, 15–17, 113.

33. Pietz, "The Problem of the Fetish, I," 14.

34. Pietz, "The Problem of the Fetish, IIIa." See also Willem Bosman, *A New and Accurate Description of the Coast of Guinea* (1705; reprint, London: Cass, 1967).
35. Pietz, "The Problem of the Fetish, I," 5–6.
36. Pietz, "The Problem of the Fetish, II," 23; "The Problem of the Fetish, I," 7.
37. Pietz, "The Problem of the Fetish, II," 23, 36.
38. Pietz, "The Problem of the Fetish, I," 7.
39. Ibid., 10.
40. Ibid., 16.
41. Ibid.
42. Ibid., 17.
43. Michael Taussig, *The Devil and Commodity Fetishism in South America* (Chapel Hill: University of North Carolina Press, 1980). The "Tio" (Uncle) of the Bolivian highland mines is a devil configuration who is propitiated and venerated by those who appeal to him for safety and success in their work. Similarly, in the Cauca valley of Colombia, the devil is seen as the force behind productivity in the canefields. In both canefields and mines, rituals are performed to effect the good will of a gluttonous and extraordinarily ambivalent spirit, who is associated simultaneously with the force of life (productivity) and the forces of death and destruction.
44. Reis, *Slave Rebellion in Brazil,* 171.
45. João José Reis, "Magia jeje na Bahia: a invasão do calundu do Pasto de Cachoeira, 1785," *Revista Brasileira de Historia* 8, no. 16 (1988): 57–58.
46. Nuno Marques Pereira, *Compêndio narrativo do peregrino da América* (1728); quoted and translated in Bastide, *African Religions of Brazil,* 137. Marques Pereira's book was published in the eighteenth century, although the events described took place in the seventeenth century.
47. Marques Pereira, cited in Luiz da Camara Cascudo, *Dicionário do folclore brasileiro,* 5th ed. (São Paulo: Edições Melhoramentos, 1980), 182.
48. Souza, *O diabo e a terra de Santa Cruz,* 267, 352.
49. Processo no. 252, maço 26, Lisbon Inquisition, ANTT, cited in Souza, *O diabo e a terra de Santa Cruz,* 267.
50. Processo no. 252, maço 26, Lisbon Inquisition, ANTT, cited in Souza, *O diabo e a terra de Santa Cruz,* 267. Contemporary Candomblé adherents often refer to the *orixás* as "winds."
51. Processo no. 252, maço 26, Lisbon Inquisition, ANTT, cited in Souza, *O diabo e a terra de Santa Cruz,* 353.
52. Reis, "Magia jeje," 57–81.
53. "Jeje," the comprehensive term by which people from Aja-Fon linguistic and cultural groups were known in Bahia, would have been an appropriate general designation for all six of the Africans except for the one who belonged to the Tapa ethnic group. Africans from old Dahomey were one of the most important of the Jeje sub-groups in Bahia.
54. Reis speculates that this iron instrument was possibly an *agogo* (a double-sided bell), or a *gan* (a simple single bell). Both are widely used in Afro-Brazilian ceremonies. Reis, "Magia jeje," 70.
55. "Wax balls of earth set with beans, with rice." Reis, "Magia jeje," 73.
56. In this case it appears that the owner of the house was a "Mina" ex-slave named José Pereira, who rented it to another African, João do Espírito Santo, who

in turn sublet a room to Sebastião de Guerra. Although the documents do not specify, it is possible that the other African couples were subletting their rooms as well. As Reis writes, this was a common arrangement among Africans—both freed and slave—who lived in the urban areas of Salvador and Recôncavo towns. Reis, "Magia jeje," 67.

4. "Dis Continuity," Context, and Documentation

1. Raimundo Nina Rodrigues, *O animismo fetichista dos negros bahianos* (Rio de Janeiro: Civilização Brasileira, 1935), 28.

2. Julio Braga, *Na gamela do feitiço: repressão e resistencia nos candomblés da Bahia* (Salvador: EDUFBA, 1995). See especially Chapter 2: "Martiniano e a Resistência Religiosa."

3. See Yeda Pessoa de Castro's pamphlet "A presença cultural negro-africana no Brasil: mito e realidade" (Salvador: Centro de Estudos Afro-Orientais [CEAO]of the Universidade Federal da Bahia, 1981); Yeda Pessoa de Castro, "Africa descoberta: uma historia recontada," *Revista de Antropologia* 23 (1980): 135–40; Vivaldo da Costa Lima, *A familia-do-santo nos candomblés jeje-nagos da Bahia* (Salvador: UFBa, 1977); Renato da Silveira, "Pragmatismo e milagres de fé no extremo ocidente," in *Escravidão e invenção de liberdade: estudos sobre o negro no Brasil*, ed. João José Reis (São Paulo: Brasiliense, 1988); Beatriz Góis Dantas, "Repensando a pureza nagô," *Religião e Sociedade* 8 (1982): 15–20; João José Reis, "Magia jeje na Bahia: a invasão do calundo do Pasto de Cachoeira, 1785," *Revista Brasileira de Historia* 8, no. 16 (1988): 57–81; and João Reis, "Nas malhas do poder escravista: a invasão do candomblé do Accú na Bahia, 1829," *Religião e Sociedade* 13, no. 3 (1986): 108–27. Valdina Oliveira Pinto also provided key information in personal conversations in March 1997.

4. Renato da Silveira, "Pragmatismo e milagres de fé no extremo occidente," in *Escravidão e invenção da liberdade,* ed. João José Reis (São Paulo: Brasiliense, 1988).

5. Reis, "Magia jeje," 59; Katia de Queirós Mattoso, *To Be a Slave in Brazil, 1550–1888* (New Brunswick, N.J.: Rutgers University Press, 1986), 91.

6. Roger Bastide, *The African Religions of Brazil: Toward a Sociology of the Interpenetration of Civilizations* (Baltimore: Johns Hopkins University Press, 1978), 47.

7. Ibid., 52.

8. The role of *libertos* as healers and spiritual leaders in Candomblé is examined in detail in Chapter 6.

9. One of the central elements in many historical and present-day forms of Afro-Brazilian religion, as I am coming to understand it, is the experience of the human body as the locus of deeply divergent identities and as the primary space in which those contested qualities of self take each other's measure and attempt a resolution, or at least a continuance, in the direction of greater human identification with Spirit. The experience of enslavement and of race- and color-based oppression is apprehended at a very corporeal level—in terms of the work people do, the physical spaces they are allowed to inhabit, the significance imputed to their physical features, etc. But within the ritual space of Afro-Brazilian religion, the experience of an alternative ontological identity of connection to a more internal/

eternal Self (which is also Deity) happens, in its most profound moments, within the body as well.

10. Personal conversations with George Houston Bass, professor of Theater and Afro-American Studies, Brown University, Providence, Rhode Island, March–April 1990.

11. Bastide, *The African Religions of Brazil*, 19.

12. Personal conversation with Charles Long, May 1997.

13. Reis, "Magia jeje"; reference to the 1807 Madre de Deus *candomblé* comes from June 19, 1807, Capitães Mores, maço 417–1, APEB.

14. For Nuno Marques Pereira's observations see Luís da Câmara Cascudo, *Dicionário do folclore brasileiro*, 5th ed. (São Paulo: Edições Melhoramentos, 1979), 182. For Luzia Pinta's *calundu* see Laura de Mello e Souza, *O diabo e a terra de Santa Cruz: feitiçaria e religiosidade popular no Brasil colonial* (São Paulo: Companhia das Letras, 1994), 267, 352–57. For the 1785 calundu in Cachoeira see Reis, "Magia jeje." The statement from Francisco Dosû was recorded, July 4, 1807, Capitães Mores, maço 417–1, APEB.

15. See, for example, July 24, 1831, Capitães Mores, maço 2681, Judiciário: Juizes de Paz da 1ª Vara, 1830–1831, APEB, which refers to "santos," drums, and other instruments that were confiscated and destroyed by police. I thank João Reis for bringing this document to my attention. See also November 4, 1855, Capitães Mores, maço 6231, Policia: Subdelegados 1854–1858, APEB, which reports that "rattles and tambourines" were apprehended by police from the homes of Africans in the Sé *freguesia*.

16. For Luzia Pinta see Souza, *O Diabo*, 267 and 352. For the *candomblé* at Quintas de Barra see April 13, 1858, Capitães Mores, maço 2994–1: Policia, Delegados 1842–1866, APEB. My thanks to Alexandra Brown and João Reis for bringing this document to my attention.

17. Castro, "Africa descoberta."

18. Roger Bastide, *O candomblé da Bahia (rito nagô)* (São Paulo: Companhia Editora Nacional/MEC, 1978), 15; Artur Ramos, *Introdução a antropologia brasileira* (Rio de Janeiro: Casa do Estudante do Brasil, 1943), 359.

19. Edison Carneiro, *Candomblés da Bahia*, 8th ed. (1948; reprint, Rio de Janeiro: Civilização Brasileira, 1991), 21.

20. Castro, "A presença cultural negro-africana," 4.

21. Yeda Pessoa de Castro and Guillherme A. de Souza Santos, "Culturas africanas nas Américas: um esboço de pesquisa conjunta da localização dos emprés-timos" (paper presented at FESTAC [World Black and African Festival of Arts and Culture], Lagos, Nigeria, 1977). Cited in Mary C. Karasch, *Slave Life in Rio de Janeiro, 1808–1850* (Princeton: Princeton University Press, 1987), 286 note 98.

22. June 19, 1807, Capitães Mores, maço 417–1, APEB. Verger notes that in Africa, Bantu religious traditions appear to be centered around rituals "for the ancestors of a limited family group, rather than the worship of gods linked to forces of nature." He suggests that while it is possible that other forms may exist, it appears that in Bahia, the Bantu form borrowed heavily from West African, especially Yoruba, orientations. Pierre Verger, "The Orixás of Bahia," in *Os deuses africanos no candomblé da Bahia*, ed. Carybé (Salvador: Bigraf, 1993), 235–63.

23. See, for example, Reis "Magia jeje"; July 4, 1807, Capitães Mores, maço 417–1, APEB; and Reis, "Nas malhas do poder escravista," 108–27.

24. Reis, "Magia jeje"; July 4, 1807, Capitães Mores, maço 417–1, APEB.

25. Both the testimony of Francisca, Dosû's Jeje companion, and Dosû's own testimony are found in July 4, 1807, Capitães Mores, maço 417–1, APEB. Chapter 6 includes a discussion of Dosû's work as an African spiritual leader/healer.

26. Castro, "Africa descoberta," 138; Lima, *A familia-de-santo*, 69, 72.

27. Castro, "Africa descoberta," 138.

28. Peter Wood, *Black Majority: Negroes in Colonial South Carolina from 1670 through the Stono Rebellion* (New York: Knopf, 1974), 169; Manoel Querino, *Costumes africanos no Brasil* (Rio de Janeiro: Civilização Brasileira, 1938), 40.

29. João José Reis, *Slave Rebellion in Brazil: The Muslim Uprising of 1835 in Bahia* (Baltimore: Johns Hopkins University Press, 1993), 146.

30. Raimundo Nina Rodrigues, *Os africanos no Brasil*, 7th ed. (Brasilia: Editora Universidade de Brasilia, 1988), 109. *Os africanos no Brasil* was originally published in 1933 from a 1906 manuscript.

31. Rodrigues, *O animismo*, 63.

32. Ibid., see especially Chapters 2 and 4.

33. The founding and early organization of Casa Branca and its precursor, the Barroquinha *terreiro*, is described in more detail as part of the profiles of Chapter 6.

34. Reis, *Slave Rebellion in Brazil*, 146. Reis writes that "the Nagô strength in the Malê community was reflected in its priestly class, primarily Nagô elders" (146).

35. Paulo Fernando de Moraes Farias, "Enquanto isso, do outro lado do mar . . . : os arokin e a identidade iorubá," *Afro-Asia* 17 (1996): 142–43.

36. Reis, *Slave Rebellion in Brazil*, 124.

37. The *orixá funfun* are the *orixás* within the Yoruba pantheon related to water, peace, and calm, and to the lighter colors of the spectrum, particularly white.

38. Reis, *Slave Rebellion in Brazil*, 124–25. Furthermore, the translator's note (1916) of Spix and Martius, *Atraves da Bahia* remarked that on Fridays throughout the year, large numbers of the faithful came to the church to leave offerings of money, wax, and oil. It is not clear whether the reference to the Friday pilgrimages was from the period of Spix and Martius's visit (1817–1820) or from the translator's own epoch; nonetheless it suggests possible further connection between Oxalá, Bonfim, and Islam. Johan B. von Spix and Karl von Martius, *Através da Bahia* (Salvador: Imprensa Oficial do Estado, 1916).

39. Farias, "Enquanto isso," 143.

40. July 4, 1807, Capitães Mores, maço 417–1, APEB.

41. Luis Claudio Dias do Nascimento and Cristiana Isidoro, *Boa Morte em Cachoeira* (Cachoeira, Bahia: Centro de Estudos, Pesquisa e Ação Sócio-Cultural de Cachoeira, 1988). I have drawn this generalization from my own observations of this procession as well.

42. July 27, 1862, Capitães Mores, maço 6234, Policia: Delegados 1861–1862, APEB.

43. Rodrigues, *O animismo*, 168.

44. Pierre Verger, *Fluxo e refluxo do tráfico de escravos entre o golfo de Benin e a Bahia de Todos os Santos dos séculos XVIII e XIX* (Salvador: Corrupio, 1987), 9–11. For a slightly different conceptualization of the cycles see Luis Viana Filho, *O negro na Bahia*, 3rd ed. (Rio de Janeiro: Editora Nova Fronteira, 1988). See especially the first section, "Imigração."

45. This conjunction of historical events helps to explain many of the similarities between Candomblé in Bahia and Santeria/Lucumí in Cuba—both of which developed with major influences from Yoruba traditions.

46. Verger notes, however, that during the height of the Benin cycle, as many as a third of the slaves entering Bahia were of Angolan or central African origin. See Pierre Verger, *Bahia and the West Coast Trade* (Ibadan: Ibadan University Press, 1964).

47. January 20, 1809, Capitães Mores, maço 417–1, APEB.

48. Reis, "Magia jeje." See Chapter 3 for further discussion of a mixed-ethnicity, predominantly Jeje *calundu* in late-eighteenth-century Cachoeira.

49. The 1829 reference is to a letter from the Juiz de Paz of Brotas to the President of the Province of Bahia, August 28, 1829, Capitães Mores, maço 2688, APEB. João Reis has analyzed the raid on this *candomblé* in the essay "Nas malhas do poder escravista." The 1809 *quilombo* is mentioned in two sources—one an interview with an imprisoned Jeje slave and the other an interview five months later with an imprisoned Nagô slave. July 4, 1807 and December 6, 1807, Capitães Mores, maço 417–1, APEB.

50. August 28, 1829, Capitães Mores, maço 2688, APEB. The Juiz de Paz reported that although more African men were originally present, only three were captured because the others escaped.

51. June 5, 1843, Capitães Mores, maço 6235, APEB. My thanks to João Reis for bringing this document to my attention.

52. June 26, 1874, Capitães Mores, maço 5827, APEB.

53. Rodrigues, *O animismo*, 171.

54. For the 1826 *quilombo* see Rodrigues, *Os africanos no Brasil*, 48. For the 1843 Cabula funereal gathering see the *Correio Mercantil* of October 24, 1843; thanks to João Reis for bringing this newspaper article to my attention. For the Easter 1862 *candomblé* see April 23, 1862, Capitães Mores, maço 5754, APEB.

55. Verger, *Fluxo e refluxo*, 349.

56. Reis, *Slave Rebellion in Brazil*, 155.

57. Verger, "The Orixás of Bahia," 240, 253–54.

58. Ibid., 240.

59. Ibid., 248.

60. See Rodrigues, *O animismo* on Gantois at end of nineteenth century. Renato da Silveira has prepared an excellent study of the origins of the Barroquinha *candomblé* community in which he cites the participation of Yorubas from several different kingdoms (especially Oyo and Ketu) as evidence of such a pan-ethnic synthesis within the Candomblé tradition—and within the Barroquinha organization itself. See Silveira, "Narrativa histórica e antropológica sobre a fundação do candomblé da Barroquinha, o mais antigo terreiro keto da Bahia" (unpublished paper, n.d.).

61. Fayette Wimberly, "The Expansion of Afro-Bahian Religious Practices in Nineteenth-Century Cachoeira," in *Afro-Brazilian Culture and Politics: Bahia, 1790s to 1990s*, ed. Hendrik Kraay (Armonk, N.Y.: M. E. Sharpe, 1998), 82–83.

62. Silveira, "Narrativa Histórica." Wimberly notes that the Cachoeira branch of Boa Morte included substantial participation from Jeje members. Wimberly, "Expansion of Afro-Bahian Religious Practices," 85.

63. João Reis, "The Politics of Identity and Difference among Slaves and Freedmen in Nineteenth Century Bahia" (paper presented at the conference "The World the Diaspora Makes," Ann Arbor, Mich., 1992), 15. Cited in Silveira, "Narrativa histórica."

64. April 13, 1858, Capitães Mores, maço 2994–1: Policia, Delegados 1842–1866, APEB.

65. Richard Price, *Maroon Societies: Rebel Slave Communities in the Americas*, 2nd ed. (Baltimore: Johns Hopkins University Press, 1979), 27.

66. Verger, "The Orixás of Bahia," 248.

67. Bastide, *The African Religions of Brazil*, 66.

68. Ibid. Bastide describes Exú as "god of vengeance." This designation can perhaps be understood in terms of Exú's association with dialectics, dialogue, and order—what goes around, comes around.

69. On *candomblé* participants as "insubordinate" and "vagrants," see especially October 21, 1855, in which a local block inspector complains in great detail about being disrespected by *crioulos* who were going toward a *candomblé* house. Capitães Mores, maço 6231, Policia: Subdelegados 1854–1858, APEB.

70. Bastide, *The African Religions of Brazil*, 66.

71. June 8, 1854, Capitães Mores, maço 6298, APEB.

72. See Rodrigues, *O animismo,* 147 for another description of an offering to Exú.

73. Michael Taussig, *The Devil and Commodity Fetishism in South America* (Chapel Hill: University of North Carolina Press, 1980), 169.

74. Sheila Walker, "African Gods in the Americas: The Black Religious Continuum," *The Black Scholar* (November–December 1980): 33.

75. See Jocélio Teles dos Santos, *O dono da terr: ocaboclo nos candomblés da Bahia* (Salvador: Editora SarahLetras, 1995).

76. See Juana Elbein dos Santos and Deoscoredes M. dos Santos, "Ancestor Worship in Bahia: The Egun-Cult," *Journal de la Societe des Americanistes* 58 (1969): 79–108.

77. These were common among the documents from the police correspondence in the APEB. For especially detailed instances, see April 24, 1854, Capitães Mores, maço 6230, APEB and April 13, 1858, Capitães Mores, maço 2994–1: Policia, Delegados 1842–1866, APEB.

78. See, for example, November 4, 1855, Capitães Mores, maço 6231, Policia: Subdelegados 1854–1858, APEB.

79. See, for example, February 25, 1857, Capitães Mores, maço 6480, APEB and July 24, 1862, Capitães Mores, maço 6234, Policia: Delegados 1861–1862, APEB.

80. See, for example, November 15, 1865, Capitães Mores, maço 5786, APEB and February 14, 1874, Capitães Mores, maço 5822, APEB.

81. A series of articles published in 1896 in the *Revista Brasileira.* These were translated into French in 1900 and even later into Portuguese; they became the basis of the classic work *O animismo.*

82. Beatriz Góis Dantas, "Repensando a pureza nagô," *Religião e Sociedade* 8 (1982): 15–20. See also Beatriz Góis Dantas, *Vovô nagô e papai branco: usos e abusos de África no Brasil* (Rio de Janeiro: Graal, 1988).

83. Rodrigues, *Os africanos no Brasil,* 215–16.

84. Of course, the increasing influence of *crioulos,* especially after the end of the slave trade, might be viewed as another "wave" of blacks.

5. The Nineteenth-Century Development of Candomblé

1. Xangô, Zangu, and Tambor de Mina are among other terms with specifically religious connotations. They have been used to refer to Afro-Brazilian religion in Recife, São Paulo, and Maranhão, respectively.

2. In the records I consulted, I found no evidence of a *branco* being imprisoned as a result of participation in Candomblé, even though whites were sometimes present during ceremonies.

3. Anyone who is familiar with present-day Candomblé will be aware that the leadership and resource base of initiates in the religion is now heavily female. In Chapter 7 I explore the idea of Candomblé as "women's space" and suggest some possible explanations for the change in the leadership base from the nineteenth century to the twentieth century.

4. One of the leaders whose status was unknown was a female slave and therefore not white. She was probably African or *crioula.*

5. Report of Police Rounds by Domingos José Freire de Carvalho, Commandante Geral, June 1, 1859, Capitães Mores, maço 3024, Corpo de Policia, 1850–1869. Jocélio Teles kindly brought this document to my attention. See also Pierre Verger, *Fluxo e refluxo do tráfico de escravos entre o golfo de Benin e a Bahia de Todos os Santos dos séculos XVIII e XIX* (Salvador: Corrupio, 1987), 532, and Ana de Lourdes Ribeiro da Costa, "'Ekabó!': trabalho escravo, condições de moradia e reordenamento urbano em Salvador no Século XIX" (master's thesis, Universidade Federal da Bahia, 1989), 127.

6. Subdelegate of Sé to Chief of Police, November 30, 1847, Capitães Mores, maço 6229, Policia, Delegados, APEB. It is interesting to note that while the client base of the shoemaker/priest was mixed, the meetings held in his home were all African. Or at least they were identified that way by the neighbor who denounced him.

7. This incident occurred in 1835. Cited in Verger, *Fluxo e refluxo,* 349.

8. Other sources indicate that *candomblés*—as well as a related but distinct cult of ancestors, the Eguns—were also present on the island of Itaparica in the nineteenth century. See Juana Elbein dos Santos and Deoscóredes dos Santos, "Ancestor Worship in Bahia: The Egun Cult," *Journal de la Societé des Americanistes* 58 (1969): 79–108.

9. Katia de Queirós Mattoso, *Testamentos de escravos libertos na Bahia no século XIX* (São Paulo, HUCITEC, 1979), 32. Costa suggests that São Pedro, Santo Antonio, and Sé were the *freguesias* most heavily populated by *libertos*—in that order; "'Ekabó!,'" 197. And Vieira Nascimento lists Santo Antonio, Sé, and São Pedro—again in descending order; Ana Amélia Vieira Nascimento, *Dez freguisias da cidade de Salvador: Aspectos sociais e urbanos do século XIX* (Salvador: Fundação Cultural do Estado da Bahia, 1986), 99.

10. A *figa* is an amulet of a closed fist with thumb between the index and middle fingers that represents protection from negative influences and harm. It has become one of the most common elements of popular Bahian iconography.

6. Healing and Cultivating *Axé*

1. *Axé* is the Yoruba term for spiritual energy, or life force—but the concept of a generative and transformative energy present in varying degrees and qualities in all beings is widely held in traditional African societies. Because of the dominance of Yoruba language and cultural traditions in Brazilian Candomblé I have used the term *axé* rather than corresponding Fon or Bantu terms. However, the principle is the same.

2. Kofi Asare Opoku, *West African Traditional Religion* (Accra, Ghana and Jurong, Singapore: FEP International, 1978), 149.

3. I. A. d'Almeida to the Subdelegate of Cachoeira, February 17, 1874, Capitães Mores, maço 5822, Policia: Registro de Correspondencia Expedida para Subdelegados, APEB.

4. Raimundo Nina Rodrigues, *O animismo fetichista dos negros bahianos* (Rio de Janeiro: Civilização Brasileira, 1935), 186. See also Wimberly's discussion of Anacleto Urbana da Natividade, an overseer and Yoruba *candomblé* leader in São Félix who saved the lives of many people during a cholera epidemic in the mid-1850s. Local white landowners were among his grateful clients, and one family in particular gave him land on which to maintain his *terreiro*. Fayette Wimberly, "The Expansion of Afro-Bahian Religious Practices in Nineteenth-Century Cachoeira," in *Afro-Brazilian Culture and Politics: Bahia, 1790s to 1990s*, ed. Hendrik Kraay (Armonk, N.Y.: M. E. Sharpe, 1998), 82–83.

5. Mary C. Karasch, *Slave Life in Rio de Janeiro, 1808–1850* (Princeton: Princeton University Press, 1987), 74–75.

6. Dwight Hopkins, oral presentation at the symposium "Religions of People of Color: Identity, Culture, and Freedom," Iliff School of Theology, Denver, Colorado, March 1997. See also Hopkins, *Down, Up, and Over: Slave Religion and Black Theology* (Minneapolis: Fortress Press, 1999), Chapter 3.

7. The cultivation of alternative identities for non-black participants in Candomblé was also an important element in the religion's role as an alternative orientation to human relations in nineteenth-century (and twentieth-century) Bahia.

8. Hopkins, *Down, Up, and Over*.

9. Captain José Roiz de Gomes to a fellow Capitão Mor, January 20, 1809, Capitães Mores, maço 417–1, APEB.

10. Luis dos Santos Vilhena, *A Bahia no século XVIII*, 3 vols. (Salvador: Editora Itapuã, 1969), vol. 2, 479–80. This manuscript consists of letters written in the late eighteenth century and was originally published in 1802.

11. Conde de Ponte to Visconde de Anadia, Salvador, April 7, 1807, in *Anais da Biblioteca Nacional do Rio de Janeiro* 37 (1918): 450–51; quoted in João José Reis, *Slave Rebellion in Brazil: The Muslim Uprising of 1835 in Bahia* (Baltimore: Johns Hopkins University Press, 1993), 42.

12. Reis, *Slave Rebellion in Brazil*, 42.

13. Ibid.

14. Report on the black prisoners in custody at the São Francisco Jail, July 4, 1807, Capitães Mores, maço 417–1, APEB.

15. Katia de Queirós Mattoso, *Bahia, século XIX XIX: uma provincia no império* (Rio de Janeiro, Nova Fronteira, 1992), 161.

16. In Brazil, the rates of *alforria* varied greatly according to time and place. Also, in general, manumission was more common during periods of economic distress.

17. Rodrigues, *O animismo*, 111.

18. E. Bolaji Idowo, *African Traditional Religion* (Maryknoll, N.Y.: Orbis, 1975), 201, 203.

19. Suzanne Preston Blier, *African Vodun: Art, Psychology, and Power* (Chicago: University of Chicago Press), 107, 213.

20. Roger Bastide, *O candomblé da Bahia (rito nagô)* (São Paulo: Companhia Editora Nacional/MEC, 1978), 214–15; Melville J. Herskovitz, *Dahomey: An Ancient West African Kingdom*, vol. 2 (New York: Augustin, 1938), 272.

21. From the *freguesia* of Santo Antonio alem do Carmo to the Chief of Police, maço 6470, Policia: Assuntos, 1823–1846, APEB.

22. Because the language of this letter is not precise, it is not clear whether Sunsão in fact was (that is, manifested) "Santa Barbara of the *terreiro*" or if the statements about the divinity were meant to be separate from the discussion of Sunsão immediately preceding them. In either case the distinct sense is that Santa Barbara/ Xangô was an active and protective force in the life of the community.

23. Rodrigues, *O animismo*, 173.

24. Ibid., 45; Roger Bastide, *African Religions of Brazil: Toward a Sociology of the Interpenetration of Civilizations* (Baltimore: Johns Hopkins University Press, 1978), 66.

25. Rodrigues, *O animismo*, 45.

26. *Correio Mercantil*, July 12, 1849; letter from a police authority to the President of the Province, July 9, 1849, Capitães Mores, maço 3113, Policia Assuntos, APEB. I gratefully acknowledge João Reis and Jocélio Teles, respectively, for bringing these documents to my attention.

27. Secretary of Police, Andre Corsino Pinto da Gama to President of the Province, February 21, 1853, Capitães Mores, maço 3116, Policia Assuntos, APEB.

28. Basing her calculations on two surveys taken to determine electoral eligibility among the *freguesia*'s inhabitants (one in 1848 and the other in 1868), Nascimento suggests that the majority of the population in Brotas consisted of poor people of color. See Ana Amélia Vieira Nascimento, *Dez freguisias da cidade de Salvador: aspectos sociais e urbanos do século XIX* (Salvador: Fundação Cultural do Estado da Bahia, 1986), 89. Mattoso, however, using the 1872 census, found that Brotas was one of two predominately white *freguesias* in Bahia, the other being Conceição da Praia. These two districts had white populations of 50.9 percent and 62 percent, respectively. Mattoso, *Bahia, século XIX*, 123–24. I have chosen to use Vieira Nascimento's figures because they represent data collected closer to the date of the document I am discussing.

29. Ana de Lourdes Ribeiro da Costa, "'Ekabó!': trabalho escravo, condições de moradia e reordenamento urbano em Salvador no século XIX" (master's thesis, Universidade Federal da Bahia, 1989), 151.

30. Nascimento, *Dez freguisias*, 89.

31. Opoku, *West African Traditional Religion*, 149.

32. Ibid.

33. There are several other cases in the documentation of healer-sorcerers

apparently being apprised of the imminent arrival of police and either hiding or preparing themselves to meet the authorities on their own terms. Two of those cases are discussed later in this chapter.

34. The APEB documents, not surprisingly, do not make extensive reference to police violence in raids on *candomblés*. However, travelers' accounts, such as that of Maria Graham, include descriptions of violent police behavior which are corroborated by reports of the destruction of objects during raids and some complaints of police thievery and harassment. Also, there are notices from the post-1835 period of police indiscriminately assaulting dark-skinned blacks in several *freguesias* after orders were issued to keep Africans under strict surveillance.

35. Costa, "'Ekabó!,'" 133–40; Nascimento, *Dez freguisias*, 85.

36. *O oculo magico*, October 11 and 13, 1866. Cited in Costa, "'Ekabó!,'" 134.

37. José Eleuterio Rocha to the Chief of Police, April 24, 1854, Capitães Mores, maço 6230, APEB.

38. Blier, *African Vodun*, 87.

39. Bastide, *African Religions of Brazil*, 231.

40. Blier, *African Vodun*, 213.

41. See especially Fernando Ortiz, *Los Negros Brujos* (1906; reprint, Miami: Ediciones Universal, 1973), 66–67; Rodrigues, *O animismo*, 83, 147.

42. See Chapter 7 for more discussion of African food as ritual food in *candomblé*.

43. Rodrigues describes such a scene of "feeding the saint" in Chapter 4 of *O animismo*, 141–47.

44. Ortiz, *Los negros brujos*, 79.

45. Capitães Mores, maço 2688, APEB.

46. Antonio Gonçalves, Subdelegate of Victoria to Chief of Police, June 5, 1843, Capitães Mores, maço 6235, APEB. My thanks to João Reis for bringing this document to my attention.

47. A reverse case occurred in the 1785 Cachoeira *calundu* where one witness identified a black man as a *crioulo* when in fact he was African born. See João José Reis, "Magia jeje na Bahia: a invasão do calundo do Pasto de Cachoeira, 1785," *Revista Brasileira de Historia* 8, no. 16 (1988): 67. Also, in the 1807 report of blacks in the São Francisco jail, two women—Anastácia and Jeronima—were identified as both *preta* and *crioula*. The term "preta/preto" was generally used to denote Africans and not Brazilian-born blacks. APEB, maço 417–1.

48. Rodrigues, *O animismo*, 186.

49. The tensions are highlighted even more strikingly with the realization that most of the rank and file of Salvador's nineteenth-century police force were mulattos.

50. Maria Inês Cortes de Oliveira, *O liberto, o seu mundo e os outros* (São Paulo, Salvador: Corrupio, 1988), 69.

51. Literally, *dadores de ventura*, "givers of luck." This term has the implication not only of someone who "tells" fortunes, but who is also able to *change* fortune, to "give luck."

52. Two letters from J. A. A. F. Henriques to the Subdelegate of São Pedro, July 25 and 26, 1862, Capitães Mores, maço 5754, Policia: Registro de Correspondencia Expedida com Subdelegados 1862–1863, APEB. Also, Pompílio Manuel de Castro to the Chief of Police, July 27, 1862, which includes Report of Search and Items

Found, July 25, 1862, Capitães Mores, maço 6234, Policia: Delegados 1861–1862, APEB. My thanks to Alexandra Brown for bringing the two documents from maço 6234 to my attention.

53. Oliveira, *O liberto*. Oliveira also indicates that men and women who left testaments often had problems of succession—they were single, widowed, married without children, or people with "natural" (extra-matrimonial) offspring (9).

54. João José Reis and Eduardo Silva, *Negociação e conflito: a resistencia negra no Brasil escravista* (São Paulo: Companhia das Letras, 1989), 15.

55. Antonio Fernandes Leal to Chief of Police, February 3, 1887, Capitães Mores, maço 6252, APEB.

56. Antonio Joaquim Rodrigues Pinto, Acting Subdelegate of Sé to Chief of Police, January 29, 1876, Capitães Mores, maço 6244, APEB.

57. Rodrigues, *O animismo*, 78–85. The details of the process of "making the saint" in Candomblé are considered secret, privileged information. Although contemporary versions of initiatory procedures have been described by a number of observers, within the community of Candomblé devotees this is generally deemed inappropriate.

58. Vivaldo da Costa Lima, "O conceito de 'nação' nos candomblés da Bahia," *Afro-Asia* 12 (June 1976): 77; Valdina Pinto, personal conversation, March 1997.

59. Edison Carneiro, *Candomblés da Bahia*, 8th ed. (Rio de Janeiro: Civilização Brasileira, 1991), 56.

60. Juana Elbein dos Santos, *Os nagô e a morte: pàde, asèsè e o culto égun na Bahia* (Petrópolis: Vozes, 1975), 28–29.

61. Renato da Silveira, "Narrativa histórica e antropológica sobre a fundação do candomblé da Barroquinha, o mais antigo terreiro keto da Bahia," (unpublished paper. n.d.), 11–12.

62. Carneiro, *Candomblés da Bahia*, 56.

63. Deoscóredes dos Santos, *Historia de um terreiro nagô* (1962; reprint, São Paulo: Max Limonad, 1988), 9.

64. Pierre Verger, *Orixás: deuses iorubás na Africa e no novo mundo* (Salvador: Corrupio, 1981), 28.

65. Vivaldo da Costa Lima, *A familia-de-santo nos candomblés jeje-nagos da Bahia* (Salvador: UFBa, 1977), 198; Vivaldo de Costa Lima, "Nações-de-Candomble," in *Encontro de nações-de-candomblé* (Salvador: Ianamá and CEAO [Centro de Estudos Afro-Orientais da UFBa], 1984), 23–24: and Lima, "O conceito da 'nação,'" 80.

66. Silveira "Narrativa histórica," 30. The statement comes from Ketu oral tradition in Bahia, but Silveira recognizes that thorough studies of Bantu tradition in *candomblé* must be conducted before this can be said with any certainty.

67. Ibid., 12.

68. Lima, "O conceito da 'nação,'" 80–81.

69. Silveira, "Narrativa histórica," 32.

70. Ibid., 33.

71. Ibid., 30.

72. Oxumarê is a Yoruba deity associated with the rainbow and the idea of continuity. It is often depicted as a serpent with its tail in its mouth, forming a circle; it corresponds to the *vodun* Dã. Lima, "O conceito de 'nação,'" 83.

73. Ibid., 82–83.

7. Networks of Support, Spaces of Resistance

1. James Wetherell, *Stray Notes from Bahia: Being Extracts from Letters, etc., during a Residence of Fifteen Years* (London: Webb and Hunt, 1860), 5, 54; Mary C. Karasch, *Slave Life in Rio de Janeiro, 1808–1850* (Princeton: Princeton University Press, 1987), 2.

2. Wetherell, *Stray Notes from Bahia*, 31.

3. Maria Inês Cortês de Oliveira, *O liberto: o seu mundo e os outros* (São Paulo: Corrupio, 1988), 55.

4. Ibid., 95–96.

5. For a fuller discussion of color- and class-based tensions among Afro-Bahians in the late nineteenth and early twentieth centuries, see Kim D. Butler, *Freedoms Given, Freedoms Won: Afro-Brazilians in Post-Abolition São Paulo and Salvador* (New Brunswick, N.J.: Rutgers University Press, 1998); see especially Chapters 2 and 5. Butler notes that notwithstanding the effects of such tensions and divisions among Afro-Bahians, Candomblé played a significant role as a base of "pan-African identity and solidarity" among people of African descent in Salvador.

6. By "silent" I mean those spaces of black experience for which documentation in the dominant material sources is scant. I do, however, recognize the problematic nature of privileging written sources with the idea of "speech" while relegating to "silence" the oral, corporeal, and ritual traditions of subjugated peoples.

7. I am grateful to Charles Long for continuing to emphasize to me the importance of holding in tandem the relationships between "orientation," "awareness," and "movement/lived experience." Personal conversation, May 1997.

8. *Capoeira* is an Afro-Brazilian martial art developed during slavery as both a form of protection and as a collective entertainment.

9. Muniz Sodré, *A verdade seduzida: por um conceito de cultura no Brasil* (Rio de Janeiro: Francisco Alvez, 1988), 125.

10. This chapter focuses particularly on the capital city, although I also make comparative reference to Recôncavo communities at various points.

11. João José Reis, *Slave Rebellion in Brazil: The Muslim Uprising of 1835 in Bahia* (Baltimore: Johns Hopkins University Press, 1993), 183. Reis reports that the records of the Malê rebellion trial indicate only ten children mentioned for over 300 adults associated with the investigation. Furthermore, he cites Oliveira's testamentary research indicating that of 259 freedpeople, 70 percent had no children and of those who did have children most had just one. Oliveira suggests that birth control and the relatively advanced age at which most manumitted Africans were able to purchase their freedom were factors that help account for the low birthrate among freedpeople. See also Robert Edgar Conrad, *World of Sorrow: The African Slave Trade to Brazil* (Baton Rouge: Louisiana State University Press, 1986), 7–15; and Sonia Maria Giacomini, *Mulher e escrava: uma introdução ao estudo da mulher negra no Brasil* (Petrópolis: Vozes, 1988), Chapter 1.

12. Giacomini, *Mulher e escrava*, Chapter 1; Conrad, *World of Sorrow*, 6–20.

13. Katia de Queirós Mattoso, *Bahia, século XIX: uma província no império* (Rio de Janeiro, Nova Fronteira, 1992), 161, 166, and 209.

14. Giacomini, *Mulher e escrava*, 44.

15. Ibid., 39–41.

16. Karasch, *Slave Life in Rio de Janeiro*, 291.

17. Katia de Queirós Mattoso, *Bahia, século XIX: uma provincia no império* (Rio de Janeiro: Nova Fronteira, 1992), 161.

18. Louis Agassiz and Elizabeth Cary Agassiz, *A Journey in Brazil* (Boston: Houghton, Mifflin, 1889), 129–30. *A Journey in Brazil* is a description of the Agassiz's visit to Brazil in 1865.

19. See Mattoso on legal marriage among blacks as a way of "conquering a recognized space" in the larger society. Mattoso, *Bahia, século XIX*, 194.

20. Katia de Queirós Mattoso, *To Be a Slave in Brazil, 1550–1888* (New Brunswick, N.J.: Rutgers University Press, 1986), 86–87.

21. Ibid.

22. Mattoso, *Bahia, século XIX*, 86–87.

23. Vivaldo da Costa Lima, "O conceito de 'nação' nos candomblés da Bahia," *Afro-Asia* 12 (June 1976): 77; Deoscóredes dos Santos, *História de um terreiro nagô* (1962. Reprint, São Paulo: Max Limonad, 1988), 9; see also Butler, *Freedoms Given, Freedoms Won*, 54–55. The *terreiro* of Axé Opô Afonjá was founded in 1910 by Mãe Aninha and others, who for various reasons were disaffected with the leadership and community at Casa Branca.

24. Lima, "O conceito de 'nação,'" 77.

25. See glossary for definitions of italicized terms.

26. Henry Koster, *Travels in Brazil*, ed. C. Harvey Gardiner (1817; reprint, Carbondale: Southern Illinois University Press, 1966), 182.

27. Reis, *Slave Rebellion in Brazil*, 186.

28. Ibid., 184–86.

29. Wetherell, *Stray Notes from Bahia*, 29–30 and 84. See also Viana Filho, *O Negro na Bahia*, 3rd ed. (Rio de Janeiro: Editora Nova Fronteira, 1988), photographic folio between pages 128 and 129. Free *crioulos* and *pardos* had more offspring than slaves and African *libertos* did; in fact the majority of black children born in Brazil had Brazilian-born parents.

30. Oliveira, *O liberto*, 69–70. On lullabies as sources of African values see Yeda Pessoa e Castro, "No canto do acalanto," pamphlet no. 12 in occasional papers series *Ensaios/Pesquisas*, Centro de Estudos Afro-Orientais, Universidade Federal da Bahia, 1990.

31. Oliveira, *O liberto*, 69; Raimundo Nina Rodrigues, *O animismo fetichista dos negros bahianos* (Rio de Janeiro: Civilização Brasileira, 1935), 168–71.

32. Lima, "O Conceito de 'Nação,'" 69.

33. Rodrigues, *O animismo*, 73.

34. Ibid., 131–33.

35. Ruth Landes, *The City of Women* (1947; reprint, Albuquerque: University of New Mexico, 1994), 215. Seu Martiniano's reference to "Dr. Nina" is Raimundo Nina Rodrigues, the forensic psychologist who initiated the academic study of *candomblé* and for whom Seu Martiniano served as an important informant in the late nineteenth and early twentieth centuries.

36. Landes, *City of Women*, 215–16.

37. Rodrigues, *O animismo*, 61–62.

38. Ibid., 61. Recall, for example, the description of the altar room of the *preta velha* in Chapter 6.

39. Fayette Wimberly, "The Expansion of Afro-Bahian Religious Practices in

Nineteenth-Century Cachoeira," in *Afro-Brazilian Culture and Politics: Bahia, 1790s to 1990s*, ed. Hendrik Kraay (Armonk, N.Y.: M. E. Sharpe, 1998), 82.

40. Roger Bastide, *The African Religions of Brazil: Toward a Sociology of the Interpenetration of Civilizations* (Baltimore: Johns Hopkins University Press, 1978), 118, 127.

41. Ana de Lourdes Ribeiro da Costa, "'Ekabó!': trabalho escravo, condições de moradia e reordenamento urbano em Salvador no século XIX" (master's thesis, Universidade Federal da Bahia, 1989), 96–97; Cunha, *Negros, estrangeiros: Os escravos libertos e sua volta à África* (São Paulo: Brasiliense, 1985), 78–80.

42. Reis, *Slave Rebellion in Brazil*, 165.

43. Karasch, *Slave Life in Rio*, 299–300.

44. Raimundo Nina Rodrigues, *Os africanos no Brasil*, 7th ed. (Brasilia: Editora Universidade de Brasilia, 1988), 102.

45. Reis, *Slave Rebellion in Brazil*, 161; Cecilia Moreira Soares, "As ganhadeiras: mulher e resistencia negra em Salvador no século XIX," *Afro-Asia* 17 (1996): 64–65; Maximiliano Habsburgo, *Bahia 1860: esboços de viagem* (Rio de Janeiro: Tempo Brasileiro, 1982), 125.

46. Soares, "As ganhadeiras," 64–65.

47. Jean Baptiste Debret, *Viagem pitoresca e historica ao Brasil*, vol. 1 (1839; reprint, São Paulo: Livraria Martins, n.d.), 143–44, 222, vol. 1, plates 9 and 33.

48. Capitães Mores, maços 5754 and 6234, APEB; Wimberly, "The Expansion of Afro-Bahian Religious Practices," 86.

49. *O Alabama*, November 8, 1864, 3–4, cited in Dale Graden, "So Much Superstition among These People!: Candomblé and the Dilemmas of Afro-Bahian Intellectuals, 1864–1871," in *Afro-Brazilian Culture and Politics*, ed. Hendrik Kraay (Armonk, N.Y.: M. E. Sharpe, 1998), 68–69. The *O Alabama* article indicates the pan-black character of the *terreiro*. In addition to the women cited, there are seven men mentioned: six drummers (*alabês*) and a "man at the door who guides the ceremony." Of the five who were identified by color or ethnicity, two were *crioulos*, one was an African, and the other was a *pardo*. One of the *crioulos* is further identified as a slave and the *pardo* is identified as "a guard in the 4th Battalion."

50. Personal conversation, 1994, Salvador Bahia.

51. Reis, *Slave Rebellion in Brazil*, 161; Costa, "'Ekabó!,'" 62–63. Costa notes that in 1855, over 80 percent of female slaves did domestic work. While some of these women and girls may have also been involved in street vending on a part-time basis, their major responsibilities were household-related chores.

52. Katia Mattoso is one of the principal proponents of the "greater independence" argument for African women in Brazil. See *Bahia, século XIX*, 163. For Giacomini's response, see *Mulher e escrava*. Although I tend to agree more with Giacomini's assessment than with Mattoso's about the "independence" of black women in slave-era Brazil, I do agree with Mattoso that African women experienced a widened sense of pan-ethnic black identity in Brazil. This was an identity they were centrally involved in creating—in *candomblés*, in *cantos*, and in other spaces.

53. Soares, "As ganhadeiras," 60.

54. I have suggested in Chapter 3 that some aspects of *feitiçaria* in the Portuguese empire were related to attempts by black women to protect themselves from the sexual exploitation of masters and the corresponding ire of mistresses. Oliveira additionally remarks that freed status did not exempt black women from being

sexually exploited and that part of the motivation among them for establishing a constant relationship with a male (whether legalized or not) was to minimize undesired attentions from other men. See Oliveira, *O liberto,* 68. See also Katia Mattoso, *Bahia, século XIX,* 194.

55. Giacomini, *Mulher e escrava,* 65 and 70.

56. Ibid., 52–55.

57. APEB, Francisco Eziquiel Moreira, Subdelegado of Conceição da Praia to the Chief of Police, March 10, 1847, Capitães Mores, maço 6229, APEB. On the disturbing regularity of slave suicides in Brazil, see Katia de Queirós Mattoso, *To Be a Slave in Brazil, 1550–1888* (New Brunswick, N.J.: Rutgers University Press, 1986), 135. See also Karasch, *Slave Life in Rio,* 316–20. For a recollection of Margaret Garner's story see Levi Coffin, *Reminiscences of Levi Coffin* (1876; reprint, New York: Arno, 1968), 558–60 and 562–63. For a powerful fictional treatment of the same event, see Toni Morrison, *Beloved* (New York: Knopf, 1987).

58. Reis, *Slave Rebellion in Brazil,* 174; Renato da Silveira, "Narrativa histórica e antropológica sobre a fundação do Candomblé da Barroquinha, o mais antigo terreiro keto da Bahia" (unpublished paper, n.d.), 23.

59. The *pano da costa* was a heavy, striped cloth imported to Brazil that was popular among blacks. It was a central element in the clothing of nineteenth-century Afro-Bahian women and is a basic element in the ritual clothing of women in *candomblé.* Rodrigues and Wetherell suggest that the cloth was of African origin. Robert Conrad says that it was manufactured in Manchester, England, and shipped to Africa from Brazilian ports to be exchanged for slaves. The cloth was decidedly not to European tastes, according to Conrad, and it continued to be used in the slave traffic even after the 1807 abolition agreements. The *pano da costa* and other elements of nineteenth-century black women's clothing related to *candomblé* are discussed later in this chapter.

60. "Circumstantiated Report of the Blacks Found in the Vila de São Francisco Jail," July 4, 1807, Capitães Mores, maço 417–1, APEB.

61. Katia de Queirós Mattoso, *Bahia: a cidade de Salvador e seu mercado no século XIX* (São Paulo, HUCITEC, 1978), 219; Mieko Nishida, "From Ethnicity to Race and Gender: Transformations of Black Lay Sodalities in Salvador, Brazil," *Journal of Social History* 32, no. 2 (Winter 1998).

62. Karasch has noted the existence in Rio of an *irmandade* of black metalworkers dedicated to São Jorge. São Jorge was associated with Ogum, the Yoruba *orixá* of iron and metalwork. Karasch, *Slave Life in Rio,* 85.

63. Mattoso, *Bahia, século XIX,* 402.

64. Bastide, *The African Religions of Brazil,* 54. This observation is corroborated in studies of Cuba and Venezuela where *cabildos* or *cofradias* are recognized as having been important to the maintenance of African religious traditions in those countries. See, for example, Miguel Acosta Saignes on Venezuela, "Las cofradías coloniales y el folklore," *Cultura Universitaria* XLVII, no. 47 (ene–feb 1955); and Fernando Ortiz on Cuba, *Ensayos etnograficos* (Havana: Editorial Sciencias Sociais, n.d.).

65. Bastide, *The African Religions of Brazil,* 54.

66. Silveira, "Narrativa histórica," 7.

67. Dillard Poole, "The Struggle for Self-Affirmation and Self-Determination: Africans and People of African Descent in Salvador da Bahia, 1800–1850" (Ph.D.

diss., Indiana University, 1991), 213–14; Patricia Mulvey, "The Black Lay Brotherhoods in Colonial Brazil: A History" (Ph.D. diss., City University of New York, 1976), 88. Nossa Senhora do Rosario was the most popular patron of black confraternities in the colonial era in Brazil, as well as in Portugal and Portuguese-controlled areas of Africa. In Salvador, the Rosario *irmandade* was founded by blacks from Angola, who—beginning in the mid-eighteenth century—undertook a major expansion project, constructing the church in which the *irmandade* is presently housed. According to historian Carlos Ott, because most of the members were slaves and freedpeople who worked during the day for masters and their own sustenance, work on the sanctuary was carried out at night—by moonlight—over many years, as members sang African and Christian songs among themselves. See Silveira, "Narrativa histórica," and Carlos Ott, "A irmandade de N.S. do Rosário dos pretos do Pelourinho," *Afro-Asia*, no 6–7 (1968): 119–26.

68. Poole, "The Struggle for Self-Affirmation," 212–14. São Benedito was a popular saint among blacks in colonial and imperial Brazil. He was recognized as black or African.

69. Mattoso, *To Be a Slave in Brazil*, 128–29.

70. Poole, "The Struggle for Self-Affirmation,"186–90.

71. Nishida, "From Ethnicity to Race and Gender," 332.

72. Silveira, "Narrativa histórica," 12.

73. Ibid.

74. Mattoso, *Bahia: A Cidade do Salvador e o Seu Mercado*, 219.

75. João José Reis, "'Death to the Cemetery': Funerary Reforms and Rebellion in Bahia, 1836," *History Workshop Journal* 34 (1992): 35 and 38.

76. Oliveira, *O liberto*, 83–85. João Reis has written about the great popular protests that arose, especially in 1836, in the wake of early attempts to end the practice of allowing burials in churches. See Reis, "Death to the Cemetery," and *A morte é uma festa: ritos fúnebres e revolta popular no Brasil do século XIX* (Sao Paulo: Companhia das Letras, 1991).

77. Mattoso, *Bahia, século XIX*, 416.

78. See Chapter 6 for a discussion of Barroquinha/Casa Branca as one of the earliest recognized, continually functioning *candomblés* in Bahia.

79. Mulvey, "The Black Lay Brotherhoods," 130–31. An exception to the growing multi-ethnic character of Afro-Bahian lay associations was the Sociedade Protetora dos Desvalidos, which was organized in the nineteenth century as a mutual aid society of black *crioulos*. The Desvalidos constitutionally limited the participation of women. See Nishida, "From Ethnicity to Race and Gender," 339–41.

80. Wetherell, *Stray Notes from Bahia*, 24; Pierre Verger, *Fluxo e refluxo do tráfico de escravos entre o golfo de Benin e a Bahia de Todos os Santos dos séculos XVIII e XIX* (Salvador: Corrupio, 1987), 507. Verger further notes that "white metal rings" were found in the houses of some of suspected participants in the Malê Revolt (343).

81. Debret, *Viagem*, vol. 1, 149.

82. Ibid., 187 and plate 22. Debret further noted that hair length was a factor in owner preference of house slaves. Women with longer hair (usually mulattas) were chosen as household servants over Africans and *crioulas* with shorter hair. See ibid., 128–29 and plate 6.

83. Ibid., 232–33 and plate 36.

84. Wetherell, *Stray Notes from Bahia*, 126.

85. Ibid., 69.

86. See, for example, August 28, 1929, Capitães Mores, maço 2688, APEB; April 13, 1858, Capitães Mores, maço 2994–1, Policia: Delegados 1842–1866, APEB; July 27, 1862, Capitães Mores, maço 6234, Policia: Delegados 1861–1862, APEB.

87. Wetherell, *Stray Notes from Bahia,* 69 and 114.

88. Verger, *Fluxo e refluxo,* 349; April 13, 1858, Capitães Mores, maço 2994–1: Policia, Delegados 1842–1866, APEB; July 5, 1879, Capitães Mores, maço 6244, APEB. *Colares* are beaded necklaces corresponding in color to one or more *orixás* that are worn as a means of aligning the bearer's energy with that of the deity, as well as for protection and identification of status as an initiate.

89. Rodrigues, *Os africanos,* 118–19; Verger, *Fluxo e refluxo,* 308.

90. See also the photographic folio between pages 128 and 129 of Viana Filho, *O negro na Bahia* for pictures of black Bahian women in typical dress in the late nineteenth and early twentieth centuries.

91. Habsburgo, *Bahia 1860,* 82.

92. Wetherell, *Stray Notes from Bahia,* 72–73.

93. Rodrigues, *Os africanos,* 118–19.

94. Agassiz and Agassiz, *A Journey in Brazil,* 82–84.

95. José Francisco da Silva Lima, "A Bahia de ha 66 anos," *Revista do Instituto Geographico e Historico da Bahia* 34 (1908): 95.

96. Wetherell, *Stray Notes from Bahia,* 33.

97. José Pinheiro Lisboa to the Subdelegate of Sé and to the Chief of Police, August or September 1843, Capitães Mores maço 6471, Policia: Assuntos Diversos 1842–1843, APEB.

98. Wetherell, *Stray Notes from Bahia,* 6.

99. Johan B. von Spix and Karl von Martius, *Atraves da Bahia* (Salvador: Imprensa Official do Estado, 1916), 90.

100. Debret, *Viagem,* 252.

101. Muniz Sodré, *O terreiro e a cidade: a forma social negro-brasileira* (Petrópolis: Vozes, 1988), 123.

102. Sterling Stuckey, "Christian Conversion and the Challenge of Dance," in *Choreographing History,* ed. Susan Leigh Foster (Bloomington: Indiana University Press, 1995), 57.

103. Karasch, *Slave Life in Rio,* 247–49.

104. Stuckey, "Christian Conversion," 57.

105. Further discussion of the role of the circle dance in Candomblé and in the creation of Afro-Brazilian identity follows in Chapter 8.

106. Ubaldino José da Cruz to the Vice-President of the Province, Joaquim Marcellino de Brito, Capitães Mores, maço 2684, Juiz de Paz, APEB. My thanks to João Reis for bringing this document to my attention.

107. Prefeitura Municipal do Salvador, *Repertorio de fontes sobre a escravidão exis-tentes no arquivo municipal de Salvador: as posturas (1631/1889)* (Salvador: Fundação Gregório de Mattos, Prefeitura Municipal do Salvador, 1988), 75.

108. The edict of 1831 is mentioned in *Repertorio de fontes,* 47. References to the prohibitions of 1827, 1829, 1854, 1871, and 1885 are found in APEB, maços 2684, 2688, 6230, 5814, and 6249 respectively. Neither the published list of edicts nor my examination of the public archives is exhaustive—there were very likely more

prohibitions of *batuques* and other drum-and-dance gatherings in Bahia during the nineteenth century.

109. Stuart Schwartz, *Sugar Plantations in the Formation of Brazilian Society: Bahia, 1550–1835* (Cambridge, England: Cambridge University Press, 1985), 484.

110. January 20, 1809, Capitães Mores, maço 417–1, APEB.

111. Ibid.

112. Reis, *Slave Rebellion in Brazil,* 44–45.

113. Silveira, "Narrativa histórica," 15–16. Recall as well that Arcos was among the first white honorary members of the Martírios *irmandade.*

114. October 5, 1835, Capitães Mores, maço 2684, APEB.

115. Raimundo Nina Rodrigues, *O animismo: fetichista dos negros bahianos* (Rio de Janeiro: Civilização Brasileira, 1935), 70–71.

116. Graden, "So Much Superstition," 58–59.

117. The relationship of Bahian elites (both white and Afro-Brazilian) to Candomblé is a fascinating and multi-textured story, which, unfortunately cannot be told here in the richness it deserves.

118. J. A. A. F. Henriques to the Subdelegate of Rua do Paço, May 1, 1862, Capitães Mores, maço 5457, Policia: Registro de Correspondencia com Subdelegados 1862–1863, APEB. Subsequently, Henriques served as provincial president from November 1871 to June 1872.

119. Acting Alternate Subdelegate of Victoria to the Chief of Police, March 22, 1866, Capitães Mores, maço 6202, Policia: Delegados 1866, APEB. Alexandra Brown kindly shared this document with me.

120. Felippa Laura Maria da Conceição to Chief of Police, November 14, 1874, Capitães Mores, maço 6497, Policia: Assuntos Diversos 1873–1874, APEB.

121. Thomas Lindley, *Narrativa de uma viagem ao Brasil,* trans. Thomas Newlands Neto (São Paulo: Nacional, 1969), 163–64.

122. Daily Report from the director of the House of Corrections to Chief of Police, November 21 and 22, 1849, Capitães Mores, maço 6473, APEB. A further detail on Eliza Maria mentioned that she had been "imprisoned in this jail since the year 1847 and in other prisons since 1843, as she is completing her sentence." One can only imagine the conditions under which she may have conceived the child while imprisoned. No information was available about the baby's health.

123. Verger suggested that the two principal jails in nineteenth-century Salvador, the Aljube and the House of Correction, were segregated along the lines of legal status—the Aljube exclusively for slaves and the House of Correction for free and freed people. See Verger, *Fluxo e refluxo,* 535. I have not found this distinction to hold in all cases, although it was probably true in a general sense. (For example, in November 1849, a group of fourteen people arrested in a *batuque,* including eleven *libertos,* one free *crioula,* and two female slaves, were all imprisoned in the Aljube. See Antonio Peixoto de Miranda Veras to the Chief of Police, November 3, 1849, Capitães Mores, maço 6473, Assuntos Diversos 1848–1853, APEB.) In any case, some of the group of twenty-one from Silveira's house were probably held in the House of Correction because the majority of them were free or freedpeople.

124. A. C. d'Assis to Subdelegate of Rua do Paço, December 6, 1869, Capitães Mores, maço 5807, Policia: Registro de Correspondencia Expedida para Subdelegados 1869–1870, APEB.

125. Joaquim Antonio Moutinho to the Chief of Police, March 22, 1855, Capitães

Mores, maço 6231, Policia: Subdelegados 1854–1858, APEB; also in same maço, Aguedo Feliciano Castilho to Joaquim Antonio Moutinho, March 16, 1855.

126. José Maria de Mattos, General Report, November 2, 1846, Capitães Mores, maço 6254, Policia: Correspondencia Recebida 1840–1851, APEB. "First line" or *tropa paga* (paid troop) was the designation for full-time soldiers for whom the army was their livelihood. Even for full-time soldiers the pay was very low and living conditions poor. Most of the rank and file who joined did so because they could not avoid doing otherwise. In contrast, officers—who were disproportionately white and in better economic and/or social situations than rank-and-file troops—joined for the prestige and social mobility. See F. W. O. Morton, "The Military and Society in Bahia, 1800–1821," *Journal of Latin American Studies* 7, no. 2 (1985): 250–58, and Mattoso, *Bahia, século XIX,* 224–25.

127. See, for example, J. A. A. F. Henriques to eighteen Subdelegates of the City, April 24, 1862, and J. A. A. F. Henriques to João d'Azevedo Piapitinga, May 3, 1862, both in Capitães Mores, maço 5754, Policia: Registro de Correspondencia Expedida com Subdelegados 1862–1863, APEB.

128. J. A. A. F. Henriques to the Subdelegate of the Second District of Santo Antonio, April 19, 1862, Capitães Mores, maço 5754, Policia: Registro de Correspondencia Expedida com Subdelegados 1862–1863, APEB.

129. João de Azevedo Piapitinga to João Antonio de Araújo Freitas Henriques, April 21, 1862, Capitães Mores, maço 6234, Policia: Delegados 1861–1862, APEB. My thanks to Alexandra Brown and João Reis for bringing this document to my attention.

130. J. A. A. F. Henriques to the Subdelegate of the Second District of Santo Antonio, April 23 1862, Capitães Mores, maço 5754, Policia: Registro de Correspondencia Expedida com Subdelegados 1862–1863, APEB.

131. Although I was not able to locate Piapitinga's April 26th missive, the subdelegate's response was clearly indicated in Henriques' subsequent letter.

132. J. A. A. F. Henriques to João d'Azevedo Piapitinga, May 3, 1862, Capitães Mores, maço 5754, Policia: Registro de Correspondencia Expedida com Subdelegados 1862–1863, APEB.

133. See Joaquim Antonio Moutinho to Francisco Liberato de Mattos, Capitães Mores, maço 6231, Policia: Subdelegados 1854–1858, APEB. This letter, indicating that religious objects were found and reporting the arrest of several African freedpeople and slaves, was submitted to the Chief of Police by the Subdelegate of Sé.

134. João de Azevedo Piapitinga to Francisco Liberato de Mattos, November 5, 1855, Capitães Mores, maço 6231, Policia: Subdelegados 1854–1858, APEB. I am grateful to João Reis for sharing this document with me.

135. Francisco de Moura Rosa to the Subdelegate of the Second District of Santo Antonio; also in same maço, Inspector Rosa to the Chief of Police, November 8, 1855; and João de Azevedo Piapitinga to the Chief of Police, November 12, 1855. Capitães Mores, maço 6231, Policia: Subdelegados 1854–1858, APEB.

136. Aguedo Feliciano Castilho to Joaquim Antonio Moutinho, October 8, 1855, Capitães Mores, maço 6231, Policia: Subdelegados 1854–1858, APEB. The facts that Oliveira identified himself as an "authority" and that this identity was not challenged by the inspector—combined with a reference in the documentation to several properties that he owned, the designation *cidadão,* and the fact that while

the Africans were identified by race/ethnicity he was not—suggests that Oliveira was probably white or a very light-skinned *pardo.*

137. Antonio Gomes de Abreu Guimarães to the President of the Province of Bahia, August 28, 1829, Capitães Mores, maço 2688, APEB. This document published in João Reis, "Nas malhas do poder escravista: a invasão do candomblé do Accú na Bahia, 1829," *Religião e Sociedade* 13, no. 3 (1986): 108–27.

138. Aguedo Feliciano Castilho to Joaquim Antonio Moutinho, October 8, 1855, Capitães Mores, maço 6231, Policia: Subdelegados 1854–1858, APEB.

139. It is perhaps even more correct to make the distinction at the level of organized, violent rebellion because other forms of organized slave resistance, such as *quilombos,* were notably multi-ethnic, even including marginalized whites in some instances.

140. Rodrigues offers an example of the tenacity of African specificity simultaneous with a larger African identity in his discussion of members of the Tapa "nation" in Salvador in the 1890s who spoke their own language among themselves, but who, like other African-born blacks, many *crioulos,* and even some *pardos,* spoke Yoruba as a kind of lingua franca. See Rodrigues, *Os africanos no Brasil,* 109.

8. Candomblé as *Feitiço*

1. Charles H. Long, "Perspectives for a Study of African-American Religion in the United States," in *African-American Religion: Interpretive Essays in History and Culture,* ed. Timothy Fulop and Albert J. Raboteau (New York: Routledge, 1997), 27.

2. Julio Braga, *Na gamela do feitiço: repressão e resistencia nos candomblés da Bahia* (Salvador: EDUFBA, 1995), 45.

3. Personal conversation, 1994.

4. Charles H. Long, "African-American Religion in the United States of America," in *The Charles H. Long Reader* (Princeton: Charles H. Long Imagination of Matter Project, Moses Mesoamerica Archive, Princeton University, 1995; xerox), 505–506. The phrase "what is the case" is a reference to Wittgenstein—"the world is what is the case." On black religiosity in the United States as a "conjure" orientation, see Theophus Smith, *Conjuring Culture: Biblical Formations of Black America* (New York: Oxford University Press, 1994).

5. João José Reis, *Slave Rebellion in Brazil: The Muslim Uprising of 1835 in Bahia* (Baltimore: Johns Hopkins University Press, 1993), 142. Reis emphasizes that *crioulo* slaves were not necessarily passively accepting of their oppression, rather that the means they used to confront the diminishments of slavery were different, perhaps more dissimulative.

6. Muniz Sodré, *O terreiro e a cidade: a forma social negro-brasileira* (Petrópolis: Vozes, 1988), 19.

7. Dwight Hopkins, *Down, Up, and Over: Slave Religion and Black Theology* (Minneapolis: Fortress, 1999), Chapter 3.

8. Where space is at a premium, a group of related *orixás* may share the same room or house. In other circumstances, when access to the natural environment is available, a well, a waterfall, a tree, or some other natural element may be consecrated to a deity and considered its residence.

9. Sodré, *O terreiro e a cidade,* 61.

10. Carolyn M. Jones and Julia M. Hardy, "From Colonialism to Community:

Religion and Culture in Charles H. Long's *Significations*," *Callaloo* (Spring 1988): 582–96. This article is an interview with Charles H. Long.

11. Personal conversation, November 1994, Salvador, Bahia.

12. Ashis Nandy, *The Intimate Enemy: Loss and Recovery of Self under Colonialism* (Delhi: Oxford University Press, 1983), 111.

13. Reis, for example, writes that because the slave class in Bahia was largely foreign born, "its culture could not be directly traced to the slave experience in the New World." He further suggests that slaves in Bahia did not develop "a 'slave consciousness' as such . . . a consciousness immediately derived from the position of slaves in the social relations of production." See "Slave Resistance," *Luso-Brazilian Review* 25, no. 1 (1988): 132.

14. Roger Bastide, *African Civilisations in the New World* (New York: Harper and Row, 1971), 89–90.

15. Indeed, even within the space of work, adjustments (movements) were made to orient the body toward an alternative identity. The cadenced movements and insistence on collectivity in work of African *cantos*, for example, indicated efforts to insert some measure of control and self-defined identity into the labor required of slaves.

16. Sheila S. Walker, "African Gods in the Americas: The Black Religious Continuum," *The Black Scholar* (November–December 1980): 30–31.

17. Pierre Verger, *Orixás: deuses iorubás na Africa e no novo mundo* (Salvador: Corrupio, 1981), 33.

18. Ibid.

19. Raimundo Nina Rodrigues, *O animismo: Fetichista dos negros bahianos* (Rio de Janeiro: Civilização Brasileira, 1935), 101.

20. Karen McCarthy Brown, *Mama Lola: A Vodou Priestess in Brooklyn* (Berkeley: University of California Press, 1991), 252–53.

Coda

1. Caio Prado Jr., *História econômica do Brasil* (São Paulo: Brasiliense, 1983), 192–93.

2. Conversation with Ubiratan Castro, Universidade Federal da Bahia, October 1994. See also, for example, the study of Miguel Santana, a mulatto who owned a company of stevedores in the early decades of the twentieth century and who held important posts in several of the city's most prestigious Candomblé *terreiros*. José Guilherme da Cunha Castro, ed., *Miguel Santana* (Salvador: EDUFBA, 1996).

3. Thomas Skidmore, *Black into White: Race and Nationality in Brazilian Thought* (New York: Oxford University Press, 1974), 13.

4. Skidmore, *Black into White*, 19.

5. Julio Braga, *Na gamela do feitiço: repressão e resistencia nos candomblés da Bahia* (Salvador: EDUFBA, 1995), 20.

6. Ibid.

7. Paul Gilroy, *The Black Atlantic: Modernity and Double Consciousness* (Cambridge, Mass.: Harvard University Press, 1993), 39.

Bibliography

Abiodun, Rowland. "Understanding Yoruba Art and Aesthetics: The Concept of Àse." *African Arts* 27 (July 1994): 68–78.

Abiodun, Rowland, and Ulli Beier. *A Young Man Can Have the Embroidered Gown of an Elder—But He Can't Have the Rags of an Elder: Conversations on Yoruba Culture.* Bayreuth: Iwalewa-Haus, 1991.

Agassiz, Elizabeth Cary, and Louis Agassiz. *A Journey in Brazil.* Boston: Houghton Mifflin, 1889.

Apter, Emily, and William Pietz. *Fetishism as Cultural Discourse.* Ithaca: Cornell University Press, 1993.

Aufderheide, Patricia. "Upright Citizens in Criminal Records: Investigations in Cachoeira and Geremoabo, Brazil, 1780–1836." *The Americas* 38, no. 2 (1981): 173–84.

Avé-Lallemant, Robert. *Viagem pelo norte do Brasil, no ano de 1859.* 2 vols. Rio de Janeiro: Instituto Nacional do Livro, 1961.

Azevedo, Paulo Cesar de, and Mauricio Lissovsky, orgs. *Escravos brasileiros do século XIX na fotografia de Christiano, Jr.* São Paulo: Ex Libris, 1988.

Barickman, B. J. "The Slave Economy of Nineteenth-Century Bahia: Export Agriculture and Local Market in the Recôncavo, 1780–1860." Ph.D. diss., University of Illinois, Urbana-Champaign, 1991.

Bastide, Roger. *African Civilisations in the New World.* New York: Harper and Row, 1971.

———. *The African Religions of Brazil: Toward a Sociology of the Interpenetration of Civilizations.* Baltimore: Johns Hopkins University Press, 1978.

———. *O candomblé da Bahia (rito nagô).* São Paulo: Companhia Editora Nacional/MEC, 1978.

Beattie, Petter M. "The House, the Street, and the Barracks: Reform and Honorable Masculine Social Space in Brazil, 1864–1945." *Hispanic American Historical Review* 76, no. 3 (1996): 439–73.

Berlin, Ira, and Philip Morgan, eds. *Cultivation and Culture: Labor and the Shaping of Slave Life in the Americas.* Charlottesville: University Press of Virginia, 1993.

Blier, Suzanne Preston. *African Vodun: Art, Psychology, and Power.* Chicago: University of Chicago Press, 1995.

Bosman, Willem. *A New and Accurate Description of the Coast of Guinea.* 1705. Reprint, London: Cass, 1967.

Braga, Julio. *O jogo de búzios: um estudo da adivinhação no candomblé.* São Paulo: Brasiliense, 1988.

———. *Na gamela do feitiço: repressão e resistencia nos candomblés da Bahia.* Salvador: EDUFBA, 1995.

Brandon, George. *Santeria from Africa to the New World: The Dead Sell Memories.* Bloomington: Indiana University Press, 1993.

Brown, Karen McCarthy. *Mama Lola: A Vodou Priestess in Brooklyn.* Berkeley: University of California Press, 1991.

Burns, E. Bradford. *A History of Brazil.* 2nd ed. New York: Columbia University Press, 1980.

———. *Latin America: A Concise Interpretive History.* 5th ed. Englewood Cliffs, N.J.: Prentice Hall, 1990.

Butler, Kim. *Freedoms Given, Freedoms Won: Afro-Brazilians in Post-Abolition São Paulo and Salvador.* New Brunswick, N.J.: Rutgers University Press, 1998.

Carneiro, Edison. *Candomblés da Bahia.* 8th ed. 1948. Reprint, Rio de Janeiro: Civilização Brasileira, 1991.

———. *Negros bantus.* Rio de Janeiro: Civilização Brasileira, 1937.

Carvalho, José Jorge de. "A força da nostalgia: a concepção de tempo histórico dos cultos afro-brasileiros tradicionais." *Religião e Sociedade* 14, no. 2 (1987): 36–61.

Carybé. *Os deuses africanos no candomblé da Bahia/African Gods in the Candomblé of Bahia.* 2nd ed. Salvador: Bigraf, 1993.

Cascudo, Luíz da Camâra. *Dicionario do folclore brasileiro.* 5th ed. São Paulo: Edições Melhoramentos, 1980.

Castro, José Guilherme da Cunha. *Miguel Santana.* Salvador: EDUFBA, 1996.

Castro, Yeda Pessoa de. "Africa descoberta: uma história recontada." *Revista de Antropologia* 23 (1980): 135–40.

———. "A presença cultural negro-africana no Brasil: mito e realidade." Salvador: Centro de Estudos Afro-Orientais, 1981.

Conrad, Robert. *Children of God's Fire: A Documentary History of Black Slavery in Brazil.* Princeton: Princeton University Press, 1983.

———. *The Destruction of Brazilian Slavery, 1850–1888.* Berkeley: University of California Press, 1972.

———. "Nineteenth-Century Brazilian Slavery." In *Slavery and Race Relations in Latin America,* edited by Robert Brent Toplin. Westport, Conn.: Greenwood Press, 1974.

———. *World of Sorrow: The African Slave Trade to Brazil.* Baton Rouge: Louisiana State University Press, 1986.

Costa, Ana de Lourdes Ribeira da. "'Ekabó!': trabalho escravo, condições de moradia e reordenamento urbano em Salvador no século XIX." Master's thesis, Universidade Federal da Bahia, 1989.

Costa, Emília Viotti da. *The Brazilian Empire: Myths and Histories.* Chicago: University of Chicago Press, 1985.

Cunha, Manuela Carneiro da. *Negros, estrangeiros: os escravos libertos e sua volta à África.* São Paulo: Brasiliense, 1985.

Curtin, Philip D. *The Atlantic Slave Trade: A Census.* Madison: University of Wisconsin Press, 1969.

Daniel, Yvonne Payne. "Embodied Knowledge within Sacred Choreographies of the Orishas." Paper presented at the annual meeting of the American Association of Anthropology, Chicago, Ill., November 1991.

Dantas, Beatriz Góiz. "Repensando a pureza nagô." *Religião e Sociedade* 8 (1982): 15–20.

———. *Vovó nagô e papai branco: usos e abusos da Africa no Brasil.* Rio de Janeiro: Graal, 1988.

Debret, Jean Baptiste. *Viagem pitoresca e histórica ao Brasil.* 2 vols. 4th ed. São Paulo: Livraria Martins, n.d.

Dzidzienyo, Anani. "The African Connection and the Afro-Brazilian Condition." In *Race, Class, and Power in Brazil,* edited by Pierre-Michel Fontaine. Los Angeles: CAAS, 1985, 135–53.

Encontro de nações-de-candomblé. Salvador: Ianamá and CEAO/UFBa, 1984.

Expilly, Charles. *Mulheres e costumes do Brasil.* São Paulo: Companhia Editora Nacional, 1935.

Farias, Paulo Fernando de Moraes. "Enquanto isso, do outro lado do mar . . . : os aròkin e a identidade iorubá." *Afro-Asia* 17 (1996): 139–55.

Flexor, Maria Helena Ochi. *Abreviaturas: manuscritos dos séculos XVI ao XIX.* São Paulo: Edições Arquivo do Estado de São Paulo, 1991.

Fontaine, Pierre-Michel, ed. *Race, Class, and Power in Brazil.* Los Angeles: CAAS, 1985.

Frantz, Nadine Pence. "Material Culture, Understanding, and Meaning: Writing and Picturing." *Journal of the American Academy of Religion* 66 (Winter 1998): 791–815.

Freyre, Gilberto. *The Masters and the Slaves.* New York: Knopf, 1956.

Fry, Peter, Sergio Carrara, and Ana Luiza Martins-Costa. "Negros e brancos no carnaval da velha republica." In *Escravidão e inveção da liberdade: estudos sobre o negro no Brasil,* edited by João José Reis. São Paulo: Brasiliense, 1988.

Fulop, Timothy, and Albert J. Raboteau. *African-American Religion: Interpretive Essays in History and Culture.* New York: Routledge, 1997.

Giacomini, Sonia Maria. *Mulher e escrava: uma introdução ao estudo da mulher negra no Brasil.* Petrópolis: Vozes, 1988.

Gilroy, Paul. *The Black Atlantic: Modernity and Double Consciousness.* Cambridge, Mass.: Harvard University Press, 1993.

Gleason, Judith. *Oya: In Praise of the Goddess.* Boston: Shambhala, 1987.

Glissant, Edouard. *Caribbean Discourse: Selected Essays.* Charlottesville: University Press of Virginia, 1992.

Graden, Dale Thurston. "From Slavery to Freedom in Bahia, Brazil, 1791–1900." Ph.D. diss., University of Connecticut, 1991.

———. "'So Much Superstition among These People!': Candomblé and the Dilemmas of Afro-Bahian Intellectuals, 1864–1871." In *Afro-Brazilian Culture and Politics: Bahia, 1790s to 1990s,* edited by Hendrik Kraay. Armonk, N.Y.: M. E. Sharpe, 1998.

Graham, Maria Dundas. *Journal of a Voyage to Brazil, and Residence There during Part of the Years 1821, 1822, 1823.* 1824. Reprint, New York: Praeger, 1969.

Graham, Sandra Lauderdale. "Documenting Slavery." *Luso-Brazilian Review* 21, no. 2 (1984): 95–99.

———. *House and Street: The Domestic World of Servants and Masters in Nineteenth-Century Rio de Janeiro.* Austin: University of Texas, 1992.

Habsburgo, Maximiliano. *Bahia 1860: esboços de viagem.* Rio de Janeiro: Tempo Brasileiro, 1982.

Herskovitz, Melville J. *Dahomey: An Ancient West African Kingdom.* 2 vols. New York: J. J. Augustin, 1938.

Holloway, Thomas. "'A Healthy Terror': Police Repression of Capoeira in Nineteenth-Century Rio de Janeiro." *Hispanic American Historical Review* 69 (November 1989): 637–76.

Hopkins, Dwight. *Down, Up, and Over: Slave Religion and Black Theology*. Minneapolis: Fortress, 1999.

Idowu, E. Bolaji. *African Traditional Religion: A Definition*. Maryknoll, N.Y.: Orbis, 1975.

Inikori, J. E. *Forced Migration: The Impact of the Export Slave Trade on African Societies*. New York: Africana Publishing, 1982.

Jones, Carolyn M., and Julia M. Hardy. "From Colonialism to Community: Religion and Culture in Charles H. Long's *Significations*." *Callaloo* (Spring 1988): 582–96.

Karasch, Mary C. "Commentary." In *Roots and Branches: Current Directions in Slave Studies*, edited by Michael Craton. Toronto: Pergamon Press, 1979.

———. *Slave Life in Rio de Janeiro, 1808–1850*. Princeton: Princeton University Press, 1987.

Kassoy, Boris, and Maria Luzia Tucci Carneiro. *O olhar europeu: o negro na iconografia brasileira do século XIX*. São Paulo: EDUSP, 1994.

Kidder, Daniel. *Sketches of Residence and Travels in Brazil*. 2 vols. Philadelphia: Sorin and Ball 1845.

King, Noel Q. *African Cosmos: An Introduction to Religion in Africa*. Belmont, Calif.: Wadsworth Publishing, 1986.

Klein, Herbert. "Nineteenth-Century Brazil." In *Neither Slave nor Free: The Freedmen of African Descent in the Slave Societies of the New World*, edited by D. W. Cohen and Jack Greene. Baltimore: Johns Hopkins University Press, 1972.

Koster, Henry. *Travels in Brazil*. London: Longman, Hurst, Rees, Orm and Brown, 1817.

———. *Travels in Brazil*. Edited by C. Harvey Gardiner. 1817. Reprint, Carbondale: Southern Illinois University Press, 1966.

Kraay, Hendrik. "'O abrigo da farda': o exército brasileiro e os escravos fugidos, 1800–1881." *Afro-Asia* 17 (1996): 29–56.

Kraay, Hendrik, ed. *Afro-Brazilian Culture and Politics: Bahia, 1790s to 1990s*. Armonk, N.Y.: M. E. Sharpe, 1998.

Landes, Ruth. *The City of Women*. 1947. Reprint, Albuquerque: University of New Mexico, 1994.

Lima, José Francisco da Silva. "A bahia de ha 66 anos." *Revista do Instituto Geographico e Historico da Bahia* 34 (1908): 93–117.

Lima, Vivaldo da Costa. "O conceito de 'nação' nos candomblés da Bahia." *Afro-Asia* 12 (June 1976): 65–87.

———. *A familia-de-santo nos candomblés jeje-nagôs da Bahia*. Salvador: UFBa, 1977.

Lockhart, James, and Stuart B. Schwartz. *Early Latin America: A History of Colonial Spanish America and Brazil*. Cambridge, England: Cambridge University Press, 1983.

Lody, Raul. *Coleção culto afro-brasileiro: um documento do candomblé na cidade do Salvador*. Salvador: Fundação Cultural do Estado da Bahia, 1985.

———. *O povo do santo: religião, historia e cultura dos orixás, voduns, inquices e caboclos*. Rio de Janeiro: Pallas, 1995.

Long, Charles H. *The Charles H. Long Reader*. Princeton: The Charles H. Long

Imagination of Matter Project, Moses Mesoamerica Archive, Princeton University, 1995. Xerox.

———. "Perspectives for the Study of African-American Religion in the United States." In *African-American Religion: Interpretive Essays in History and Culture*, edited by Timothy Fulop and Albert Raboteau. New York: Routledge, 1997.

———. *Significations: Signs, Symbols, and Images in the Interpretation of Religion*. Philadelphia: Fortress, 1986.

Lopes, Nei. *Bantos, malês e identidade negra*. Rio de Janeiro: Forense Universitaria, 1988.

Maggie, Yvonne. *Medo do feitiço: relações entre magia e poder no Brasil*. Rio de Janeiro: Arquivo Nacional, 1992.

Marks, Morton. "Uncovering Ritual Structures in Afro-American Music." In *Religious Movements in Contemporary America*, edited by Irving I. Zaretsky and Mark P. Leone. Princeton: Princeton University Press, 1974.

Matta, Roberto da. *Carnivals, Rogues and Heroes: An Interpretation of the Brazilian Dilemma*. Translated by John Drury. Notre Dame, Ind.: University of Notre Dame Press, 1991.

———. *A Casa & A Rua*. Rio de Janeiro: Editora Guanabara Koogan, 1991.

Mattoso, Katia de Queirós. *Bahia: a cidade de Salvador e seu mercado no século XIX*. São Paulo: HUCITEC, 1978.

———. *Bahia, século XIX: uma provincia no império*. Rio de Janeiro: Nova Fronteira, 1992.

———. *Familia e sociedade na Bahia do século XIX*. São Paulo: Corrupio, 1988.

———. *Testamentos de escravos libertos na Bahia no século XIX*. São Paulo, HUCITEC, 1979.

———. *To Be a Slave in Brazil, 1550–1888*. New Brunswick, N.J.: Rutgers University Press, 1986.

Mbiti, John. *African Religions and Philosophy*. 2nd ed. Oxford, England: Heinemann International, 1990.

Megenny, William W. "Sudanic/Bantu/Portuguese Syncretism in Selected Chants from Brazilian Umbanda and Candomblé." *Anthropos: International Review of Ethnology and Linguistics* 84, nos. 4–6 (1989): 363–83.

Mintz, Sidney W., and Richard Price. *The Birth of African-American Culture: An Anthropological Perspective*. Boston: Beacon Press, 1992.

Morton, F. W. O. "The Conservative Revolution of Independence." Ph.D. diss., Oxford University, 1974.

———. "The Military and Society in Bahia, 1800–1821." *Journal of Latin American Studies* 7, no. 2 (1985): 249–69.

Moura, Carlos Eugênio Marcondes de, ed. *Bandeira de Alaira: outros escritos sobre a religião dos orixás*. São Paulo: Nobel, 1982.

———. *Meu sinal está no seu corpo: escritos sobre a religião dos orixás*. São Paulo: Edicon/EDUSP, 1989.

Mulvey, Patricia Ann. "Black Brothers and Sisters: Membership in the Black Lay Brotherhoods of Colonial Brazil." *Luso-Brazilian Review* 17 (Winter 1980): 253–79.

———. "The Black Lay Brotherhoods of Colonial Brazil: A History." Ph.D. diss., City University of New York, 1976.

Nandy, Ashis. *The Intimate Enemy: Loss and Recovery of Self under Colonialism.* Delhi: Oxford University Press, 1983.

Nascimento, Ana Amélia Vieira. *Dez freguesias da cidade de Salvador: aspectos sociais e urbanos do século XIX.* Salvador: Fundação Cultural do Estado da Bahia, 1986.

Nascimento, Luis Claudio Dias do, and Cristiana Isidoro. *Boa Morte em Cachoeira.* Cachoeira, Bahia: Centro de Estudos, Pesquisa e Ação Sócio-Cultural de Cachoeira, 1988.

Nishida, Mieko. "From Ethnicity to Race and Gender: Transformations of Black Lay Sodalities in Salvador, Brazil." *Journal of Social History* 32 (Winter 1998): 329–48.

———. "Manumission and Ethnicity in Urban Slavery: Salvador, Bahia, 1808–1888." *Hispanic American Historical Review* 73 (1993): 361–91.

Oliveira, Maria Inês Cortês de. *O liberto: oseu mundo e os outros, Salvador, 1790–1890.* São Paulo: Corrupio, 1988.

Omari, Mikelle Smith. "Cultural Confluence in Candomblé Nagô: A Socio-Historical Study of Art and Aesthetics in an Afro-Brazilian Religion." Ph.D. diss., University of California at Los Angeles, 1984.

Opoku, Kofi Asara. *West African Traditional Religion.* Accra: FEP International Private Limited, 1978.

Ortiz, Fernando. *Ensayos etnograficos.* Havana: Editorial Sciencias Sociais, n.d.

———. *Los Negros Brujos.* 1906. Reprint, Miami: Ediciones Universal, 1973.

Parrinder, Geoffrey. *African Traditional Religion.* Westport, Conn.: Greenwood Press, 1970.

Pietz, William. "Fetishism and Materialism." In *Fetishism as Cultural Discourse,* edited by Emily Apter and William Pietz. Ithaca: Cornell University Press, 1993.

———. "The Problem of the Fetish, I." *Res: Anthropology and Aesthetics* 9 (Spring 1985): 5–17.

———. "The Problem of the Fetish, II: The Origin of the Fetish." *Res: Anthropology and Aesthetics* 13 (Spring 1987): 23–45.

———. "The Problem of the Fetish, IIIa: Bosman's Guinea and the Enlightenment Theory of Fetishism." *Res: Anthropology and Aesthetics.* 16 (Autumn 1988): 106–23.

Poole, Dillard. "The Struggle for Self-Affirmation and Self-Determination: Africans and People of African Descent in Salvador da Bahia, 1800–1850." Ph.D. diss., Indiana University, Bloomington, Indiana, 1991.

Price, Richard. *Maroon Societies: Rebel Slave Communities in the Americas.* 2nd ed. Baltimore: Johns Hopkins University Press, 1979.

Querino, Manoel. *Costumes Africanos no Brasil.* Rio de Janeiro: Civilização Brasileira, 1938.

Ramos, Artur. *Introdução à antropologia brasileira.* Rio de Janeiro: Casa do Estudante do Brasil, 1943.

Rego, Waldeloir. *Capoeira angola: ensaio sócio-etnográfico.* Salvador: Editora Itapuã, 1968.

Reis, João José. "'Death to the Cemetery': Funerary Reform and Rebellion in Bahia, 1836." *History Workshop Journal* 34 (1992): 33–46.

———. "Magia jeje na bahia: a invasão do calundo do Pasto de Cachoeira, 1785." *Revista Brasileira de Historia* 8, no. 16 (1988): 57–81.

———. "Nas malhas do poder escravista: a invasão do candomblé do Accú na Bahia, 1829." *Religião e Sociedade* 13, no. 3 (1986): 108–27.

———. *Rebelião escrava no Brasil: a história do levante dos malês.* São Paulo: Brasiliense, 1986.

———. "Resistencia escrava em Ilhéus." *Anais do Arquivo Publico do Estado da Bahia* 44 (1979): 285–97.

———. "Slave Rebellion in Brazil." Ph.D. diss., University of Minnesota, 1982.

———. *Slave Rebellion in Brazil: The Muslim Uprising of 1835 in Bahia.* Baltimore: Johns Hopkins University Press, 1993.

———. "Slave Resistance in Brazil: Bahia, 1807–1835." *Luso-Brazilian Review* 25, no. 1 (1988): 111–44.

Reis, João José, ed. *Escravidão e invenção da liberdade: estudos sobre o negro no Brasil.* São Paulo: Brasiliense, 1988.

Reis, João José, and Eduardo Silva, orgs. *Negociação e confilto: a resistencia negra no Brasil escravista.* São Paulo: Companhia das Letras, 1989.

Rodrigues, Raimundo Nina. *Os Africanos no Brasil.* 7th ed. Brasilia: Editora Universidade de Brasília, 1988.

———. *O animismo fetichista dos Negros bahianos.* Rio de Janeiro: Civilização Brasileira, 1935.

Rugendas, João Mauricio. *Viagem pitoresca através do Brasil.* 4th ed. São Paulo: Livraria Martins Editora, 1949.

Russell-Wood, A. J. R. *The Black Man in Slavery and Freedom in Colonial Brazil.* New York: St. Martin's Press, 1982.

Saignes, Miguel Acosta. "Las cofradías coloniales y el folklore." *Cultura Universitaria* XLVII, no. 47 (ene–feb 1955).

Santos, Deoscóredes Maximiliano dos. *Historia de um Terreiro Nagô.* 1962. Reprint, São Paulo: Max Limonad, 1988.

Santos, Jocélio Teles dos. *O dono da terra: o caboclo nos candomblés da Bahia.* Salvador: Editora SarahLetras, 1995.

Santos, Juana Elbein dos. *Os nàgô e a morte: pàdè, asèsè e o culto égun na Bahia.* Petrópolis: Vozes, 1975.

Santos, Juana Elbein dos, and M. Deoscóredes. "Ancestor Worship in Bahia: The Egun-Cult." *Journal de la Societé des Americanistes* 58 (1969): 79–108.

Scarry, Elaine. *The Body in Pain: The Making and Unmaking of the World.* New York: Oxford University Press, 1985.

Schuler, Monica. "Afro-American Slave Culture." In *Roots and Branches: Current Directions in Slave Studies,* edited by Michael Craton. Toronto: Pergamon Press, 1989.

Schwartz, Stuart. *Sugar Plantations in the Formation of Brazilian Society: Bahia, 1550–1835.* Cambridge, England: Cambridge University Press, 1985.

Silva, Marilena Rosa Nogueira da. *Negro na rua: a nova face da escravidão.* São Paulo: HUCITEC, 1988.

Silveira, Renato da. "Narrativa histórica e antropológica sobre a fundação do candomblé da Barroquinha, o mais antigo terreiro keto da Bahia." Unpublished paper, n.d.

———. "Pragmatismo e milagres de fé no extremo ocidente." In *Escravidão e invenção da liberdade,* edited by João José Reis. São Paulo: Brasiliense, 1988.

Skidmore, Thomas. *Black into White: Race and Nationality in Brazilian Thought.* New York: Oxford University Press, 1974.

Smith, Jonathan. *To Take Place: Toward Theory in Ritual.* Chicago: University of Chicago Press, 1987.

Smith, Theophus. *Conjuring Culture: Biblical Formations of Black America.* New York: Oxford University Press, 1994.

Soares, Cecília Moreira. "As ganhadeiras: mulher e resistência negra em Salvador no século XIX." *Afro-Asia* 17 (1996): 57–71.

Sodré, Muniz. "A sombra do retrato." In *Escravos brasileiros do século XIX na fotografia de Christiano, Jr.,* edited by Paulo Cesar de Azevedo and Mauricio Lissovsky. São Paulo: Ex Libris, 1988.

———. *O terreiro e a cidade: a forma social negro-brasileira.* Petrópolis: Vozes, 1988.

———. *A verdade seduzida: por um conceito de cultura no Brasil.* Rio de Janeiro: Francisco Alvez Editora, 1988.

Souza, Laura de Mello e. *O diabo e a terra de Santa Cruz: feitiçaria e religiosidade popular no Brasil colonial.* São Paulo: Companhia das Letras, 1994.

Spix, Johan B. von, and Karl von Martius. *Através da Bahia.* Salvador: Imprensa Oficial do Estado, 1916.

Stuckey, Sterling. "Christian Conversion and the Challenge of Dance." In *Choreographing History,* edited by Susan Leigh Foster. Bloomington: Indiana University Press, 1995.

Sullivan, Lawrence. *Icanchu's Drum: An Orientation to Meaning in South American Religions.* New York: Macmillan, 1988.

Taussig, Michael. *The Devil and Commodity Fetishism in South America.* Chapel Hill: University of North Carolina Press, 1980.

———. "Maleficium: State Fetishism." In *Fetishism as Cultural Discourse,* edited by Emily Apter and William Pietz. Ithaca: Cornell University Press, 1993.

Toplin, Robert Brent. *Slavery and Race Relations in Latin America.* Westport, Conn.: Greenwood Press, 1974.

Verger, Pierre. *Bahia and the West Coast Trade.* Ibadan: Ibadan University Press, 1964.

———. *Fluxo e refluxo do tráfico de escravos entre o golfo de Benin e a Bahia de Todos os Santos dos séculos XVIII e XIX.* Salvador: Corrupio, 1987.

———. *Notícias da Bahia, 1850.* Salvador: Corrupio, 1981.

———. *Orixás: deuses iorubás na Africa e no novo mundo.* Salvador: Corrupio, 1981.

———. "The Orixás of Bahia." In *Os deuses africanos no candomblé da Bahia,* edited by Carybé. Salvador: Bigraf, 1993.

———. *Trade Relations between the Bight of Benin and Bahia from the 17th to the 19th Centuries.* Ibadan, Nigeria: Ibadan University Press, 1976.

Vianna Filho, Luis. *O negro na Bahia.* 3rd ed. Rio de Janeiro: Nova Fronteira, 1988.

Vilhena, Luís dos Santos. *A Bahia no século XVIII.* 3 vols. 1921. Reprint, Salvador: Editora Itapuã, 1969.

Voeks, Robert. "Sacred Leaves of Brazilian Candomblé." *Geographical Review* 80 (April 1990): 118–31.

———. *Sacred Leaves of Candomblé: African Magic, Medicine, and Religion in Brazil.* Austin: University of Texas Press, 1997.

Walker, Sheila. "African Gods in the Americas: The Black Religious Continuum." *The Black Scholar* (November–December 1980): 25–36.

———. "A Choreography of the Universe: The Afro-Brazilian Candomblé as a Microcosm of Yoruba Spiritual Geography." *Anthropology and Humanism Quarterly* 16 (June 1991): 42–50.

————. "'The Feast of Good Death': An Afro-Catholic Emancipation Celebration in Brazil." *SAGE: A Scholarly Journal on Black Women* 3, no. 2 (1986): 27–31.

Wetherell, James. *Stray Notes from Bahia: Being Extracts from Letters, etc., during a Residence of Fifteen Years.* London: Webb and Hunt, 1860.

Wimberly, Fayette. "The African Liberto and the Bahian Lower Class: Social Integration in Nineteenth-Century Bahia, Brazil, 1870–1900." Ph.D. diss., University of California at Berkeley, 1988.

————. "The Expansion of Afro-Bahian Religious Practices in Nineteenth-Century Cachoeira." In *Afro-Brazilian Culture and Politics: Bahia, 1790s to 1990s,* edited by Hendrik Kraay. Armonk, N.Y.: M. E. Sharpe, 1998.

Wood, Peter. *Black Majority: Negroes in Colonial South Carolina from 1670 through the Stono Rebellion.* New York: Knopf, 1974.

Index

Rachel E. Harding is Associate Director of the Gandhi Hamer King Center for the Study of Religion and Democratic Renewal at the Iliff School of Theology. She earned a Ph.D. in Latin American History from the University of Colorado in 1997. Her essay, "'What Part of the River You're In': African American Women in Devotion to Òsun" is forthcoming in *Osun across the Waters: A Yoruba Goddess in Africa and the Americas* (Indiana University Press, 2000). Harding is also a poet and has published work in *Callaloo, Chelsea, Feminist Studies, The International Review of African American Art, Hambone,* and in several anthologies.